Good Housekeeping

THE COOK'S YEAR

Good Housekeeping

THE COOK'S YEAR

OVER 300 RECIPES TO MAKE THE MOST OF SEASONAL PRODUCE

COLLINS & BROWN

First published in Great Britain in 2003
by Collins & Brown Limited
The Chrysalis Building
Bramley Road
London W10 6SP

An imprint of **Chrysalis** Books Group plc

Published in association with The National Magazine
Company Limited.
Good Housekeeping is a trademark of The National Magazine
Company Limited.

The Good Housekeeping website address is
www.goodhousekeeping.co.uk

1 2 3 4 5 6 7 8 9 0

British Library Cataloguing-in-Publication Data:
A catalogue record for this book is available from the
British Library.

ISBN 1 84340 107 X

Designer: Nigel Soper
Editor: Barbara Dixon
Editorial Assistant: Serena Webb
Indexer: Isobel Mclean
Project Editor: Gillian Haslam

Reproduction by Classic Scan, Singapore
Printed and bound in China by Imago
This book was typeset using Futura and Joanna

NOTES

- Both metric and imperial measures are given for the recipes. Follow either set of measures, not a mixture of both, as they are not interchangeable.
- Level spoon measures are:
  1 tsp = 5ml spoon; 1 tbsp = 15ml spoon.
- Ovens must be preheated to the specified temperature.
- Large eggs should be used except where otherwise specified. Free-range eggs are recommended.
- The use of golden granulated, caster and icing sugar is recommended.
- Some of the desserts contain raw or lightly cooked eggs. The young, elderly, pregnant women and anyone with an immune-deficiency disease should avoid these, because of the possible risk of salmonella.

CONTENTS

INTRODUCTION

WHO DECIDED we needed to have every type of fruit and vegetable available throughout the year? Supermarkets may argue their customers want this sort of choice, but is that really true? Consider that strawberries may be available all year round, but for around 10 months they will have lost much of their delicious flavour.

Because so much produce is stocked in our shops continuously, it is easy for most of us to forget the times of year when various foods are at their best. Travel to Italy, for example, and the situation is completely different. Ask for mushrooms in the summer and you will be told, "no it's not the season, the thing to eat in the summer is tomatoes." Go to the market and you'll see stalls piled high with a huge variety. Choose from big fat raggedy beef tomatoes, charming plum tomatoes on the vine, regular plum tomatoes, deep red sweet cherry tomatoes and baby plum tomatoes. Cut into any of them and they'll taste amazing – you only need a drizzle of olive oil and a sprinkling of fragrant basil to complete the ultimate salad. Italian consumers are demanding – they wouldn't dream of buying a tomato unless it was bursting with flavour; its having a perfect uniform shape is not high on their priority list. Perhaps we should be more like that?

Use this book as a guide to help you seek out the best value and ultimate tasting produce around, so you can plan optimum eating month by month. Why not visit your local farmers' market to refamiliarize yourself with the seasonality of meat and fish as well as fruit and vegetables? You'll soon discover that you can't beat buying local and seasonal produce for freshness and taste. Happy cooking!

Felicity

FELICITY BARNUM-BOBB

JANUARY

*A quiet month, after the excesses of
the festive season, when spicy foods warm us
as the weather gets colder*

S OME COOKS THINK OF JANUARY AS a cold, dark month, but they're wrong. If you know what to buy, the post-Christmas slow period is one of the best months of the year for shopping and cooking. And the best if you're a citrus-lover, since oranges simply don't get any better than navels from southern Spain. Clementines and satsumas follow close behind, and sometimes – if you're lucky – surpass their larger relations in sweetness and flavour. Kumquats are more of an acquired taste for some people, but if you like them, this is the best month to buy; for an unusual approach to using them, see the recipe for Glazed Carrots and Kumquats on page 23. Any fruit from the southern hemisphere is likely to be good, since the depth of our winter is the height of their summer. Apples from New Zealand and South Africa should be in top condition, as well as more obvious exotics such as lychees and bananas. Fresh cranberries will also be hanging around after the Christmas festivities, and you should look out for dried fruits such as dates and prunes: picked and dried in the autumn, they are now at their most tender.

Vegetables

While foreign produce dominates the fruit shelves, natives dominate the vegetables. Root vegetables began their season in the autumn, but they are at their best now and should be taken full advantage of for baking, roasting, mashing, soups and braising. Parsnips, turnips, sweet potatoes, swede, celeriac, Jerusalem artichokes – these are highly versatile foods that can be used as

Left: Shepherd's Pie (see page 18)

GAME
Hare
Partridge
Pheasant
Snipe
Wild duck
Wild geese
Woodcock

Jerusalem
   artichokes
Leeks
Parsnips
Potatoes
Spinach
Swede
Turnips

FISH
Brill
Cod
Haddock
Hake
Halibut
Herring
Mussels
Oysters
Plaice
Sole
Whiting

FRUIT
Apples
Bananas
Clementines
Cranberries
Kiwi fruit
Kumquats
Lemons
Limes
Lychees
Oranges
Satsumas

VEGETABLES
Broccoli
Brussels sprouts
Cabbages
Carrots
Kale

BEST BUY
Cabbages

alternatives to potatoes in many dishes, just in case you tire of the ubiquitous spud. They take particularly well to a small but lively addition of something sharp, such as citrus or vinegar, or piquant, such as spices or chilli. Celeriac, with its indescribable taste (a little sweet, a little nutty, a little like celery) is the least known of all these, and deserves to have a wider following.

The other great veggie stars of the month are cabbages, and their close relation the Brussels sprout. They may vary in size from quite small to positively gargantuan, and they're not just one of the best choices of the month but among the cheapest. Try the Brussels Sprouts in Lemon Dressing on page 24 with its zingy dressing of gremolata. Tightly packed white and red cabbage are top choices for coleslaw or other salads, but the frilly, deep green Savoy is generally regarded as best of all for flavour when the cabbage is going to be boiled, steamed, braised (best of all), or used for making a stuffed cabbage dish of any type. Savoy has a somewhat shorter shelf life than white and red cabbage, both of which can be stored without refrigeration for a week or more and not come to any grief. Their keeping quality makes them good standby items when there are no other veg in the house.

Meat and Fish

On the protein front, January may see some good prices for red meat – and at the beginning of the month, if your butcher has unsold meat or poultry from Christmas, this may be a time to stock the freezer. Game is well into its season and birds may be getting on a bit. Shellfish is not at its best apart from mussels and oysters, both of which should be tiptop. But the real stars, the other reason January is such a good time to be cooking, are the flat and round fish. The species around the British Isles are at their best when the water is cold, and January is a great time for just about all of them. The long-running depletion of fish stocks – and recent regulations to stop over-fishing – have made some of the better-known fish

an expensive rarity. All the more reason, therefore, to make the acquaintance of hake, whiting, gurnard, ling, huss, grey mullet and witch sole. All are cheaper than the better known species, and some are just as good: in fish-loving Spain, for instance, hake and whiting are highly prized. Whatever type of fish you buy, look at the buying tips in the box below. And whatever you buy, whether animal or vegetable, don't write off January as a cook's dry season.

BUYING FISH

Fish is no longer living by the time it reaches the fishmonger's slab, obviously, but it should look as if it's still wriggling. The skin should be bright, shiny, and taut; the eyes should be clear, bright and protuberant rather than sinking in with a dull, dark appearance. And the smell of the fish, paradoxically, should not be 'fishy' but a faint, fresh scent that reminds you of the seaside. The best way to judge is by getting your nose right down to the fish you're thinking of buying – or ask the fishmonger to hold it up for you if it's behind glass. If you're buying fillets, the smell is even easier to judge. The flesh should look bright and firm; if very dull, it may have been filleted too far in advance.

TWICE-BAKED GOAT'S CHEESE SOUFFLES

PREPARATION TIME: 20 minutes

COOKING TIME: 1 hour 50 minutes,
plus 45 minutes cooling

PER SERVING: 400cals, 36g fat, 10g carbohydrate

SERVES 8

FOR THE TOMATO FILLING

3tbsp olive oil

2 level tbsp tomato purée

2 garlic cloves, crushed

400g can chopped plum tomatoes

Large sprig fresh or ¼ level tsp dried thyme

FOR THE SOUFFLÉ

50g (2oz) butter, plus extra to grease

50g (2oz) plain flour

300ml (½ pint) milk

4 large eggs, separated

225g (8oz) soft, creamy goat's cheese

2 level tsp coarsely ground black pepper

284ml carton double cream

Fresh herbs to garnish

1 Preheat the oven to 180°C (160°C fan oven) mark 4. To make the filling, heat the oil in a small pan and add the tomato purée and garlic. Cook, stirring, for 1 minute. Add the tomatoes and thyme and season with some salt and coarsely ground black pepper. Bring to the boil, then simmer gently, stirring from time to time, for 45 minutes or until the sauce is very thick. Put to one side to cool.

2 Base-line and lightly butter eight 150ml (¼ pint) ramekin dishes.

3 Melt the butter in a medium-sized pan and stir in the flour. Mix to a smooth paste. Blend in the milk and stir continuously until the mixture boils and is smooth. Cool a little, then beat in the egg yolks and cheese. Season well. Whisk the egg whites in a clean grease-free bowl to soft peaks and fold into the cheese mixture.

4 Fill each ramekin two-thirds full and put 2 level tsp tomato filling in the centre of each. Cover with the remaining soufflé mixture. Put the remaining tomato filling to one side.

5 Put the ramekins in a roasting tin and add enough hot water to come halfway up the side of the dishes. Cook for 20 minutes or until firm to the touch. Remove from the roasting tin and allow to cool.

6 Run a round-bladed knife around the edge of the soufflés and carefully turn out into individual ovenproof dishes.

7 Add the coarsely ground black pepper to the cream and spoon 2–3tbsp on top of each soufflé. Cook at 200°C (180°C fan oven) mark 6 for 20–25 minutes or until golden.

8 Meanwhile, reheat the remaining tomato filling and spoon a little on top of each soufflé and garnish with a sprig of herbs. Serve immediately.

MUSSELS IN A CREAMY CURRY BROTH

PREPARATION TIME: 25 minutes

COOKING TIME: 8 minutes

PER SERVING: 300cals, 24g fat, 3g carbohydrate

SERVES 8

8tbsp olive oil

4 shallots, peeled and finely chopped

1 level tsp curry powder

1.4kg (3lb) mussels (see Cook's Tip)

450ml (¾ pint) dry white wine

200g (7oz) crème fraîche

Freshly chopped flat-leafed parsley to garnish (optional)

(Illustrated)

1 Heat the oil in a large pan, add the shallots and curry powder and cook for 5 minutes or until the shallots are softened.

2 Add the mussels, wine and 225ml (8fl oz) of water, cover and bring slowly to the boil. Bubble for a few seconds until the mussels open.

3 Remove from the heat, discard any mussels that haven't opened and stir in the crème fraîche. If you like, sprinkle with the parsley, then season with salt and freshly ground black pepper to taste.

COOK'S TIP To prepare the mussels, rinse them under cold running water to remove grit and sand, then, using a small stiff brush, scrub the shells to remove any barnacles. Pull off the hairy 'beards' and tap any open mussels with the back of a knife. If any remain open, throw them away. Give the mussels a final rinse before using.

TURKEY, HAM AND SPINACH BROTH

PREPARATION TIME: 20 minutes,
plus overnight soaking
COOKING TIME: 1 hour 15 minutes
PER SERVING: 290cals, 9g fat, 31g carbohydrate

SERVES 6

125g (4oz) green or yellow split peas, soaked overnight in
　　double their volume of cold water
25g (1oz) butter
225g (8oz) onion, chopped
1 level tbsp ground coriander
40g (1½oz) pearl barley
2 litres (3½ pints) ham or turkey stock
1 bay leaf, 1 stick celery, 1 fresh thyme sprig, tied together
225g (8oz) potatoes, peeled and cut into chunks
400g (14oz) carrots, peeled and cut into chunks
150g (5oz) each cooked turkey and ham, cut into chunks
150g (5oz) baby spinach leaves, washed and dried
Fresh coriander sprigs to garnish
50g (2oz) Parmesan cheese, finely grated (optional)

1　Drain the split peas and put in a pan with cold water to cover. Bring to the boil and simmer for 10 minutes. Drain the peas and discard the liquid. Meanwhile, melt the butter in a pan, add the onion and cook for 10 minutes or until soft but not coloured. Add the ground coriander and cook for 30 seconds.

2　Add the split peas, pearl barley and stock. Add the bay leaf bundle to the pan. Bring to the boil and simmer for 40 minutes or until the peas and barley are tender. Add the potatoes and cook for 5 minutes then add the carrots and cook for 5–10 minutes. Season well with salt and freshly ground black pepper.

3　Add the turkey, ham and spinach and bring back to the boil. Simmer for 2–3 minutes. Garnish with coriander and freshly ground black pepper and serve with grated Parmesan, if you like.

TO PREPARE AHEAD Complete the recipe to the end of step 2 up to two days ahead. Cool, cover and chill.
TO USE Complete the recipe.
TO FREEZE Complete the recipe, omitting the spinach. Cool, pack and freeze.
TO USE Thaw overnight at cool room temperature. Reheat, then add the spinach. Simmer for 2–3 minutes. Garnish and serve.

CHEDDAR AND STILTON RAREBITS

PREPARATION TIME: 15 minutes
COOKING TIME: 10–15 minutes, plus cooling
PER RAREBIT: 110cals, 8g fat, 7g carbohydrate

MAKES ABOUT 16

1 small thin French stick (see Cook's Tip), sliced into
　　rounds about 5mm–1cm (¼–½in) thick
50g (2oz) butter, melted
75g (3oz) Stilton cheese
2 large egg yolks
25g (1oz) walnuts, roughly chopped
75g (3oz) Cheddar cheese, coarsely grated
1 level tsp English mustard powder
A good pinch of mild chilli powder
Fresh oregano sprigs to garnish

1　Preheat the oven to 200°C (180°C fan oven) mark 6. Brush both sides of the bread rounds with the melted butter and bake for 10–12 minutes. Transfer to a wire rack to cool. Preheat the grill.

2　With a fork, mash the Stilton with one egg yolk and stir in the walnuts. Season with salt and freshly ground black pepper and spread over half of the toasts, right to the edges. Mix the Cheddar with the remaining egg yolk, the mustard powder and chilli and spread on the remaining toasts.

3　Arrange on a grill pan and grill for a few minutes until hot and bubbling. Cool slightly and serve warm, garnished with oregano.

TO FREEZE Complete the recipe to the end of step 2. Put toasts in a single layer on a baking sheet, freeze, pack between layers of greaseproof paper or clingfilm; put back in the freezer.
TO USE Put on baking sheets straight from the freezer and cook at 200°C (180°C fan oven) mark 6 for 10–12 minutes or until the cheese bubbles.
COOK'S TIP Serve these as a nibble with drinks. You can also use good-quality sliced bread. Spread the cheese over the whole slice, cook and cut into squares.

COUSCOUS AND HADDOCK SALAD

PREPARATION TIME: 15 minutes

COOKING TIME: 10 minutes, plus cooling

PER SERVING: 550cals, 18g fat, 66g carbohydrate

SERVES 2

175g (6oz) couscous

125g (4oz) cooked, flaked smoked haddock

50g (2oz) cooked peas

A pinch of curry powder

2 spring onions, sliced

1 small egg, hardboiled and chopped

2tbsp olive oil

2tsp lemon juice

1 Cook the couscous according to the packet instructions.

2 Mix the couscous with the haddock, peas, curry powder, spring onions and chopped egg.

3 Toss with the olive oil and lemon juice and season with plenty of salt and freshly ground black pepper.

(*Illustrated*)

SEEDED CARROT SALAD

PREPARATION TIME: 15 minutes,
plus 30 minutes marinating
PER SERVING: 180cals, 16g fat, 8g carbohydrate

SERVES 8

700g (1½lb) carrots, peeled, then shredded in a food
processor
50g (2oz) sunflower seeds, toasted
2 level tbsp sesame seeds
1 level tbsp poppy seeds
4tbsp freshly chopped flat-leafed parsley
6tbsp light olive oil
1tbsp sesame oil
2tbsp white wine vinegar
1tbsp runny honey

1 Put the carrots, seeds and parsley in a large bowl and toss everything
together to mix well.
2 Put the olive and sesame oils, white wine vinegar and honey in a screw-
top jar, season well with salt and freshly ground black pepper and shake
well to mix everything together.
3 Pour the dressing over the salad and toss well. Leave at room temperature
for 30 minutes to allow the flavours to develop.

CHICKEN IN A POT

PREPARATION TIME: 20 minutes
COOKING TIME: 1 hour 40 minutes
PER SERVING: 470cals, 34g fat, 10g carbohydrate

SERVES 6

2 tbsp vegetable oil
1 large onion, cut into wedges
2 rindless streaky bacon rashers, chopped
1.4–1.6kg (3–3½lb) whole chicken
6 medium carrots, peeled
2 small turnips, cut into wedges
1 garlic clove, peeled and crushed
1 bouquet garni (1 bay leaf, a few parsley and thyme
sprigs tied with string)
600ml (1 pint) hot chicken stock
100ml (3½fl oz) dry white wine
12 button mushrooms
3tbsp freshly chopped flat-leafed parsley

1 Preheat oven to 200°C (180°C fan oven) mark 6. Heat the oil in a
flameproof casserole, then add the onion and bacon and fry for 5
minutes until golden. Remove and put to one side.
2 Add the chicken and brown all over for 10 minutes. Remove and put to
one side. Add the carrots, turnips and garlic and fry for 5 minutes.
3 Return the bacon and onion to the pan, then put the chicken back in.
Add the bouquet garni, stock and wine; then season with salt and freshly
ground pepper. Bring to the boil, then cover and cook in the oven
for 30 minutes.
4 Remove from the oven and add mushrooms. Baste, then re-cover and
cook for 50 minutes.
5 Stir in the parsley, then carve the chicken and serve with the vegetables
and cooking liquid.

(Illustrated)

SHEPHERD'S PIE

PREPARATION TIME: 45 minutes
COOKING TIME: 1 hour 40 minutes
PER SERVING: 760cals, 44g fat, 48g carbohydrate

SERVES 6

FOR THE MINCE
2tbsp vegetable oil
2 medium onions, chopped
2 medium carrots, peeled and chopped
2 garlic cloves, chopped
1 celery stick, chopped
900g (2lb) minced lamb
400g (14oz) large flat mushrooms, roughly chopped
2 level tbsp plain flour
150ml (¼ pint) red wine
400g can chopped tomatoes

FOR THE MASH
1.4kg (3lb) floury potatoes, peeled and
   cut into large chunks
150g (5oz) butter
150ml (¼ pint) milk, warmed
4 level tbsp freshly chopped chives
75g (3oz) grated Cheddar cheese

1 Heat the oil in a pan, then add the onions, carrots, garlic and celery. Cook for 10 minutes or until soft. Add the lamb and separate using a fork. Cook over a high heat for 10 minutes or until the mince is brown and there's a little liquid left. Add the mushrooms and cook for 1–2 minutes.

2 Add the flour and cook for 1 minute, then add the wine and tomatoes. Season with salt and freshly ground black pepper, bring to the boil, cover and simmer for 50 minutes or until tender. Uncover and cook for a further 5–10 minutes if necessary to bubble away excess liquid.

3 Meanwhile, prepare the mash. Put the potatoes in a pan of cold salted water. Bring to the boil, cover and simmer for 20–30 minutes or until soft. Drain, put back in the pan and heat for 1 minute to dry off. Mash well, then beat in the butter, milk and chives. Season well.

4 Divide the mince mixture between six individual ovenproof dishes and top with the mash. Roughen the surface with a fork and sprinkle with the cheese. Grill for 3 minutes or until the tops are golden. Alternatively, brown in the oven at 190°C (170°C fan oven) mark 5 for 20–25 minutes.

(Illustrated on page 8)

STEAK WITH CHIPS

PREPARATION TIME: 15 minutes,
plus 30 minutes soaking
COOKING TIME: 20 minutes
PER SERVING: 380cals, 14g fat, 26g carbohydrate

SERVES 2

350g (12oz) large floury potatoes, such as Maris Piper,
   peeled and cut into chips
Groundnut oil for frying
2 sirloin or rump steaks – about 175g (6oz) each
Mustard and tomato ketchup to serve

1 Soak the potato chips in cold water for 30 minutes, then drain and dry well. Heat the oil to 170°C (350°F) or until one chip rises to the surface as soon as it's dropped in the pan. Quarter fill the frying basket with chips and cook for 5 minutes or until the chips just begin to colour. Drain and set aside. Repeat with the remaining chips.

2 Season the steaks with plenty of freshly ground black pepper and cook for 2 minutes on each side for rare, 3 minutes each side for medium rare and 5 minutes for well done. Gentle finger prodding is a good method of testing steak – if it feels soft like your cheek, it's rare, if it's firmer like the tip of your nose, its medium, and if it's more firm like your forehead, it's well done.

3 Meanwhile, increase the heat of the oil for the chips to 190°C (375°F), then return the precooked chips in batches to the fryer and cook for 5 minutes or until golden brown and crisp. Drain well on kitchen paper and season with salt and freshly ground black pepper. Serve the steaks with the chips, mustard and tomato ketchup.

PAN-FRIED CHICKEN WITH RED WINE SAUCE

PREPARATION TIME: 5 minutes
COOKING TIME: 25–30 minutes
PER SERVING WITH SKIN: 610cals, 42g fat,
10g carbohydrate
PER SERVING WITHOUT SKIN: 470cals, 24g fat,
10g carbohydrate

SERVES 6

25g (1oz) butter
1tbsp oil
6 chicken breasts – around 150g (5oz) each
175g (6oz) rindless streaky bacon, chopped
225g (8oz) button mushrooms
225g (8oz) button onions
6tbsp brandy
350ml (12fl oz) red wine
750ml (1¼ pints) chicken stock
4 level tbsp redcurrant jelly

1 Preheat the oven to 150°C (130°C fan oven) mark 2. Melt the butter and oil in a pan. Add the chicken breasts and cook in batches, skin-side down, over a high heat for 3 minutes on each side or until golden. Remove from the pan and put in the oven to finish cooking while you make the sauce.
2 Add the bacon, mushrooms and onions to the frying pan. Cook for 4–5 minutes or until golden. Remove and set aside. Add the brandy, wine, stock and redcurrant jelly. Bring to the boil and bubble furiously for 15–20 minutes or until the sauce is syrupy.
3 Return the chicken, bacon, mushrooms and onions to the pan. Bring to the boil, season with salt and freshly ground black pepper and serve.

LEEK, MUSHROOM AND ARTICHOKE CROÛTE

PREPARATION TIME: 30 minutes,
plus cooling and chilling overnight
COOKING TIME: 30–35 minutes
PER SERVING: 270cals, 19g fat, 22g carbohydrate

SERVES 8

3tbsp olive oil
2 garlic cloves, crushed
125g (4oz) shiitake mushrooms, sliced
1tbsp balsamic vinegar
50g (2oz) whole cooked chestnuts, roughly chopped
Young fresh thyme sprigs
400g can artichoke hearts, drained and quartered
350g (12oz) leeks, washed and sliced
375g sheet ready-rolled puff pastry
1 egg, lightly beaten, to glaze
Cranberry sauce and a little extra-virgin olive oil to serve

1 Heat 2tbsp of the olive oil in a large pan and fry the garlic for 1 minute. Add the mushrooms and cook over a low heat for 3 minutes to soften. Add the balsamic vinegar, chestnuts, ½tsp of thyme leaves – stripped off the sprigs – and the artichokes, then cook for 1 minute.
2 Heat the remaining 1tbsp of oil in a large clean pan, add the leeks and cook for 4 minutes to soften slightly. Turn into a bowl and cool for 5 minutes.
3 Unroll the pastry and sprinkle the surface with the remaining thyme sprigs. Roll the leaves slightly into the pastry. Flip the pastry over so that the herbs are on the underside and roll the pastry out lightly to a 38x25.5cm (15x10in) rectangle. Using a sharp knife, cut the pastry in half vertically to create two long thin rectangles.
4 Spoon half the mushroom mixture down the centre of each piece of pastry, top with the leeks and season with salt and freshly ground black pepper. Brush the pastry edges with water and fold each side of the pastry up over the filling to seal.
5 Cut both rolls in half and put on to a greased baking sheet. Cover and chill overnight or freeze for up to one month.
6 Preheat the oven to 200°C (180°C fan oven) mark 6. Brush the pastry with egg to glaze. Cook for 20 minutes (25 minutes from frozen) until the pastry is golden. Slice each croûte into six and serve three slices per person, topped with a dollop of cranberry sauce and a light drizzle of olive oil.

GAME AND HERB PIES

PREPARATION TIME: 40 minutes,

plus 10 minutes chilling

COOKING TIME: 1 hour

PER SERVING: 1,000cals, 77g fat, 50g carbohydrate

SERVES 8

900g (2lb) puff pastry

Flour to dust

1 egg, beaten

FOR THE FILLING

700g (1½lb) boneless mixed game, such as rabbit and
   pheasant, cut into bite-sized pieces

1 level tbsp crushed, dried green peppercorns

25g (1oz) plain flour

2 tbsp oil

75g (3oz) butter

175g (6oz) rindless, smoked, streaky bacon, in one piece
   if possible, roughly chopped

225g (8oz) shallots or button onions, blanched in boiling
   water and peeled

4 garlic cloves, crushed

600ml (1 pint) dry white wine

1 tsp dried or 1 level tbsp freshly chopped thyme

450ml (¾ pint) double cream

225g (8oz) brown-cap mushrooms, large ones halved or
   sliced

700g (1½lb) washed and prepared spinach

2 level tbsp each freshly chopped basil, parsley, mint and
   tarragon or 1 tsp dried tarragon

Fresh herb sprigs, dried green peppercorns and garlic to
   garnish (see Cook's Tips)

1 Roll out the pastry on a lightly floured worksurface to 3mm (⅛in) thick and use to line eight 7.5cm (3in) base-measurement brioche moulds (see Cook's Tips). Prick the bases well and chill for 10 minutes.

2 Preheat the oven to 200°C (180°C fan oven) mark 6. Line the pastry bases with greaseproof paper and fill with baking beans. Cook for 20 minutes, then remove the paper and beans, brush lightly with the beaten egg to seal and return to the oven for a further 5–10 minutes or until light golden.

3 Meanwhile, make the filling. Season the game with the crushed peppercorns and roll it in the flour. Heat the oil with 50g (2oz) of the butter in a large flameproof casserole. Add the game and bacon in batches and fry for 1–2 minutes or until golden. Remove from the pan and put to one side.

4 Add the shallots or onions to the pan with the garlic and fry for about 3–4 minutes or until golden brown. Pour in the wine and dried thyme, if using, bring to the boil, then bubble for about 10 minutes or until reduced to a syrupy consistency.

5 Return the game and bacon to the pan and season with salt and freshly ground black pepper. Bring to the boil, then add the cream and fresh thyme, if using, and simmer for a further 8–10 minutes or until the liquid is reduced by half. Cover and simmer gently for 20 minutes or until very tender.

6 Heat the remaining butter in a wide-based pan and fry the mushrooms over a high heat until golden, then put to one side. In the same pan, cook the spinach, with just the water that clings to its leaves, for 2–3 minutes, until just wilted and all the excess liquid has evaporated. Drain, squeeze out all the liquid, then roughly chop and season well.

7 Reduce the oven to 180°C (160°C fan oven) mark 4. Divide the spinach between the baked pastry cases. Add the chopped fresh herbs and fried mushrooms to the game mixture and spoon into the cases. Cover loosely with foil and cook for 10–15 minutes until piping hot to the centre. Serve the pies garnished with deep-fried herb sprigs, green peppercorns and garlic slices (see Cook's Tips).

COOK'S TIPS To make one large pie, use a 23cm (9in) base diameter, 5cm (2in) high fluted flan tin. Bake the pastry case as in step 1 for 40 minutes.

● To garnish the pie, fry washed and dried sprigs of herbs and slices of garlic in hot oil for 2–3 seconds. Drain on absorbent kitchen paper. Fry extra crushed green peppercorns in a little oil. These can be made ahead and stored in an airtight container. Sprinkle over the pies to serve.

(Illustrated)

SMOKED COD AND SWEETCORN CHOWDER

PREPARATION TIME: 15 minutes

COOKING TIME: 30 minutes

PER SERVING: 530cals, 30g fat, 32g carbohydrate

SERVES 6

130g pack Cubetti di Pancetta

50g (2oz) butter

3 leeks – about 450g (1lb) – trimmed and thinly sliced

25g (1oz) plain flour

568ml carton milk

700g (1½lb) undyed smoked cod loin or haddock, skinned and cut into 2cm (¾in) cubes

326g can sweetcorn in water, drained

450g (1lb) small new potatoes, sliced

142ml carton double cream

½ level tsp paprika

2tbsp freshly chopped flat-leafed parsley

1 Fry the pancetta in a large pan, until the fat runs out. Add the butter to the pan to melt, then add the leeks and cook until softened.

2 Stir in the flour and cook for a few seconds, then pour in the milk and 300ml (½ pint) of water.

3 Add the smoked cod or haddock to the pan with the sweetcorn and potatoes. Bring to the boil and simmer for 10–15 minutes, until the potatoes are cooked.

4 Stir in the cream, season with salt and freshly ground black pepper and the paprika and cook for 2–3 minutes to warm through. Ladle into wide shallow bowls and sprinkle each with a little chopped parsley.

TO FREEZE Complete the recipe to the end of step 3. Add the cream and paprika and cool quickly. Pack and freeze.

TO USE Thaw overnight in the fridge. Put in a pan, cover and bring to the boil, then simmer on a low heat for 15–20 minutes or until bubbling.

(Illustrated)

GLAZED CARROTS AND KUMQUATS

PREPARATION TIME: 10 minutes
COOKING TIME: 10 minutes
PER SERVING: 100cals, 6g fat, 12g carbohydrate

SERVES 6

700g (1½lb) carrots, peeled and cut into long thin batons
175g (6oz) small kumquats, halved and pips removed
40g (1½oz) butter

1 Cook the carrots in boiling salted water until tender, but still retaining their bite – about 10 minutes. After 5 minutes, add the kumquats to the pan and continue to cook.
2 Drain, then toss in the butter and plenty of freshly ground black pepper.

BUBBLE AND SQUEAK CAKES

PREPARATION TIME: 15 minutes
COOKING TIME: 45 minutes
PER SERVING: 260cals, 20g fat, 18g carbohydrate

SERVES 6

550g (1¼lb) potatoes
125g (4oz) butter
175g (6oz) each trimmed leeks and green cabbage, washed and finely shredded
Flour to dust
1tbsp oil

1 Cook the potatoes in a large pan of boiling salted water until tender, then drain and mash.
2 Melt 50g (2oz) of the butter in a large non-stick frying pan, add the leeks and cabbage and fry for 5 minutes, stirring, or until soft and beginning to colour. Combine the leeks and cabbage with the potatoes and season well with salt and freshly ground black pepper. When cool enough to handle, mould into 12 cakes and dust with flour.
3 Heat the oil and the remaining butter in a non-stick frying pan and cook the cakes for 4 minutes on each side or until they are golden, crisp and hot through.

BRUSSELS SPROUTS IN LEMON DRESSING

PREPARATION TIME: 10 minutes

COOKING TIME: 10 minutes

PER SERVING: 260cals, 24g fat, 6g carbohydrate

SERVES 6

900g (2lb) Brussels sprouts

150ml (¼ pint) olive oil

Finely grated zest and juice of 1 lemon

1½ level tbsp Dijon mustard

3 level tbsp freshly chopped parsley

Gremolata to garnish (see below)

1 Cook the sprouts in boiling salted water for 7–10 minutes until tender but still retaining their bite.

2 Meanwhile, whisk the oil with the lemon zest, 1 tbsp of lemon juice, mustard and parsley and season with salt and freshly ground black pepper.

3 Drain the sprouts well and toss in the dressing. Serve immediately, garnished with the Gremolata scattered on top.

GREMOLATA

PREPARATION TIME: 3 minutes

PER SERVING: 5cals, trace fat, trace carbohydrate

2 level tbsp grated lemon zest

1 garlic clove, finely chopped

2 level tbsp freshly chopped flat-leafed parsley

Mix all the ingredients together and use as a garnish.

SPICY RED CABBAGE

PREPARATION TIME: 30 minutes

COOKING TIME: 1 hour 10 minutes

PER SERVING: 130cals, 8g fat, 14g carbohydrate

SERVES 8

75g (3oz) butter

2 red onions, finely chopped

1 trimmed leek – around 175g (6oz) – well washed and finely sliced

1 small red cabbage – around 1.1kg (2½lb) – finely shredded

2 red apples, cored and sliced

Juice of 1 lemon

2 tbsp red wine vinegar

2 level tbsp light muscovado sugar

1 cinnamon stick, broken

4 cloves

2 star anise

1 Heat the butter in a large pan, add the onions and cook until soft. Add the leeks and cook for a further 5 minutes.

2 Add the cabbage, apples, lemon juice, vinegar, sugar and spices. Season well with salt and freshly ground black pepper, cover and cook, stirring from time to time, over a low heat for 1 hour or until the cabbage is just soft.

POTATO AND HORSERADISH GRATIN

PREPARATION TIME: 20 minutes
COOKING TIME: 1 hour 25 minutes
PER SERVING: 310cals, 12g fat, 40g carbohydrate

SERVES 6

1kg (2¼lb) floury potatoes, cut into 5mm (¼in) slices
1 medium onion, chopped
1 litre (1¾ pints) milk
75g (3oz) bacon rashers, cut into narrow strips
25g (1oz) butter
2 level tbsp hot horseradish sauce

1 Preheat the oven to 190°C (170°C fan oven) mark 5. Put the potatoes and onion in a pan with 750ml (1¼ pints) of the milk, bring to the boil, simmer for 10 minutes and drain.

2 Dry-fry the bacon until crisp and brown.

3 Use a little of the butter to grease a 1.6 litre (2¾ pint) shallow ovenproof dish. Put half the potato mixture in the dish, sprinkle the bacon over, then add the remaining potato. Mix the horseradish sauce with the remaining milk and season with salt and freshly ground black pepper. Pour the milk over the potatoes and dot the rest of the butter on top.

4 Put the dish on a baking tray and cook for 1–1¼ hours or until the potatoes are soft.

SWISS-STYLE POTATOES

PREPARATION TIME: 20 minutes,
plus 10 minutes cooling
COOKING TIME: 40 minutes
PER SERVING: 380cals, 20g fat, 40g carbohydrate

SERVES 6

6 medium-sized waxy potatoes, such as Desirée – around
    1.4kg (3lb) – unpeeled and scrubbed
75g (3oz) butter, melted plus extra to grease
6 slices Emmenthal cheese
6 sprigs fresh flat-leafed parsley to garnish

1 Preheat the oven to 220°C (200°C fan oven) mark 7. Grease two large baking trays.

2 Put the potatoes into a large pan of cold salted water and cover. Bring to the boil and cook for 5–8 minutes, then drain, transfer to a bowl and leave to cool for 10 minutes.

3 Peel the potatoes, then rub each one lengthways along a coarse grater to give long strands.

4 Make three mounds of potato on each baking tray. Drizzle the melted butter over each mound, season generously with salt and freshly ground black pepper and roast for 30 minutes or until golden.

5 Remove the rösti from the oven and put one slice of cheese on top of each. Put back in the oven and continue to cook for 10 minutes or until golden and bubbling. Garnish each rösti with a sprig of parsley and serve immediately.

GINGER PARFAIT

PREPARATION TIME: 20 minutes
FREEZING TIME: 6 hours
PER SLICE: 420cals, 32g fat, 32g carbohydrate

SERVES 10

150g (5oz) gingernut biscuits

15g (½oz) unsalted butter, melted

2 large eggs

175g (6oz) golden icing sugar

1 level tbsp ground ginger

568ml carton double cream

1 Put the biscuits in a food processor and whiz for 10 seconds to make crumbs.

2 Use some of the melted butter to grease a 900g (2lb) loaf tin. Line the tin with clingfilm, then brush the clingfilm with the rest of the butter. Spoon about 3tbsp of the biscuit crumbs into the loaf tin and tip the tin around to give it an even coating of crumbs. Put in the freezer.

3 Put the eggs, icing sugar and ginger in a bowl and whisk together for 5–10 minutes until the mixture is thick and mousse-like and leaves a ribbon trail.

4 Whisk the cream until soft peaks form, then fold into the egg mixture. Put 3tbsp of the biscuit crumbs to one side, then fold in the remainder. Pour the mixture into the prepared loaf tin and sprinkle with the remaining biscuit crumbs. Cover with clingfilm, then freeze for 6 hours.

5 To serve, dip the tin into hot water for 10 seconds, then unwrap and turn out on to a board. Cut into 2cm (¾in) slices and serve.

(Illustrated)

COFFEE AND CHOCOLATE ICE CREAM

PREPARATION TIME: 1 hour, plus 1 hour chilling
COOKING TIME: 20 minutes
FREEZING TIME: About 4 hours 30 minutes
PER SERVING: 620cals, 53g fat, 26g carbohydrate

SERVES 6

8 large egg yolks

75g (3oz) golden caster sugar plus 2 level tsp

450ml (¾ pint) milk

450ml (¾ pint) double cream

125g (4oz) plain chocolate, preferably 70% cocoa solids, finely chopped

1 level tbsp instant coffee powder or granules, preferably espresso

1 To make the ice cream, beat the egg yolks and the 75g (3oz) caster sugar until well blended. Bring the milk and cream to the boil, pour over the yolk mixture and mix together. Pour into a pan and cook, stirring constantly, over a low heat until thick. Strain and divide the custard between two bowls.

2 Add the plain chocolate to one of the custards, whisking until melted. Dissolve the coffee in 1tbsp of boiling water and add to the remaining custard with 2 level tsp caster sugar. Cool and put in freezerproof containers; cover and freeze for 2–3 hours or until firm. Transfer the custards to a food processor and whiz until smooth. Put back in the containers and freeze for 30 minutes or until firm.

3 To serve, remove from the fridge for 20–30 minutes to soften.

TURKISH DELIGHT CRÈME BRÛLÉE

PREPARATION TIME: 15 minutes,
plus 20 minutes infusion and overnight chilling
COOKING TIME: 10 minutes
PER SERVING: 820cals, 68g fat, 47g carbohydrate

SERVES 6

1 vanilla pod, split lengthways

750ml (1¼ pints) double cream

6 pieces of Turkish delight cut into small pieces (optional)

8 large egg yolks

75g (3oz) golden caster sugar

2tbsp rosewater

Demerara sugar for sprinkling

1 Using a sharp knife, scrape the seeds out of the vanilla pod and put in a heavy-based pan with the cream. Bring to the boil slowly and put to one side for 20 minutes. If using, put the pieces of Turkish delight into the base of six 150ml (¼ pint) capacity earthenware dishes.

2 In a separate bowl, beat together the egg yolks, caster sugar and rosewater. Pour the vanilla-flavoured cream on to the egg mixture and mix together until thoroughly combined.

3 Return the cream and egg mixture to the heavy-based pan and cook, stirring constantly, over a low to moderate heat until bubbles start to appear on the surface, but don't allow the custard to boil. Pour immediately into the earthenware dishes. Set aside to cool, then chill overnight. Don't cover the dishes as you want a skin to form on the top of the custard.

4 Sprinkle the demerara sugar liberally over the custards. Preheat the grill and, when hot, put the dishes underneath until the sugar has melted and is a deeper brown. Allow the dissolved sugar to set hard for 10 minutes before serving.

COOK'S TIP Fragrant essences such as rosewater and orange flower water are widely used in Moroccan cookery. They're available from Middle Eastern shops or from large supermarkets.

(Illustrated)

DRIED FRUIT SALAD WITH CINNAMON CREAM

PREPARATION TIME: 30 minutes,
plus overnight macerating and chilling
COOKING TIME: 30 minutes
PER SERVING: 470cals, 31g fat, 44g carbohydrate

SERVES 6

FOR THE DRIED FRUIT SALAD

1 level tbsp Earl Grey tea leaves

200g (7oz) ready-to-eat dried apricots, cut into chunks

150g (5oz) ready-to-eat dried prunes, cut into chunks

50g (2oz) each ready-to-eat dried figs and dates, cut into chunks

3tbsp Grand Marnier

Pared rind and juice of 1 lemon

Juice of 1 orange

1 vanilla pod, split lengthways

1 star anise

2 bananas, peeled and sliced

25g (1oz) golden icing sugar, sieved, to dust

1 level tsp ground cinnamon to dust

FOR THE CINNAMON CREAM

142ml carton double cream

250g (9oz) mascarpone cheese

½ level tsp ground cinnamon

Grated zest of 1 lemon and 1 orange

1 level tsp golden caster sugar

1 Pour 450ml (¾ pint) of boiling water over the tea leaves and leave to stand for 5 minutes. Put the dried fruits in a bowl, pour the strained tea over and add the Grand Marnier. Leave to macerate overnight.

2 Put the dried fruits and liquid in a pan with the lemon rind and juice, orange juice, vanilla and star anise. Bring slowly to the boil and simmer for 20 minutes. Remove and discard the lemon rind and star anise and put the fruits to one side to cool. Using a sharp knife, scrape the seeds out of the vanilla pod and into a bowl, cover and put to one side separately for the cinnamon cream.

3 To make the cinnamon cream, whip the cream until it just holds its shape, then whisk in the mascarpone. Mix in the ground cinnamon, lemon and orange zest, caster sugar and the reserved vanilla seeds. Cover and chill.

4 To assemble, drain the fruit and mix with the banana slices. Put on a large serving dish and top with the cinnamon cream. Dust with sieved icing sugar and ground cinnamon and serve.

TO PREPARE AHEAD Complete steps 1 and 2 up to two days ahead. Cover and chill the fruit. Complete step 3 up to one day ahead. Cover and chill.
TO USE Complete the recipe.

APPLE STRUDEL WITH MAPLE FUDGE SAUCE

PREPARATION TIME: 30 minutes
COOKING TIME: 40 minutes
PER SERVING FOR 6: 450cals, 20g fat,
67g carbohydrate
PER SERVING FOR 8: 340cals, 15g fat,
50g carbohydrate

SERVES 6–8

Grated zest and juice of 1 lemon
25g (1oz) fresh white breadcrumbs
2 level tbsp golden caster sugar
700g (1½lb) cooking apples, peeled, quartered and
   thickly sliced
6 sheets filo pastry
25g (1oz) butter, melted

FOR THE MAPLE FUDGE SAUCE
75g (3oz) butter
150g (5oz) light muscovado sugar
2tbsp maple syrup
75ml (3fl oz) double cream
Icing sugar to dust

1 Preheat the oven to 190°C (170°C fan oven) mark 5. Mix the lemon zest with the breadcrumbs and 1 level tbsp of the caster sugar. Drizzle the apple slices with a little lemon juice to prevent them from browning. Mix the apple with the breadcrumb mixture.

2 Lay three pieces of filo pastry side by side on a clean tea towel, overlapping the longest edges by 5cm (2in). Brush with a little melted butter. Put the three remaining sheets of filo on top and brush again.

3 Put the apple mixture on the filo pastry. Using the tea towel to help, roll the filo from the longest edge to form a thick roll. Roll it on to a non-stick baking sheet, seam-side down, curling it slightly if necessary to fit the sheet. Brush with the remaining melted butter and sprinkle with the remaining sugar.

4 Bake the strudel for 40 minutes or until the pastry is golden brown and the apples are soft. If necessary, cover the pastry loosely with foil to prevent it becoming too brown.

5 Meanwhile, make the Maple Fudge Sauce: melt the butter in a small heavy-based pan, then add the sugar and syrup and cook gently until the sugar dissolves completely. Stir in the cream and bring to the boil. Allow the sauce to cool slightly before serving with slices of strudel, dusted with icing sugar.

TO PREPARE AHEAD Prepare the apple strudel to the end of step 3 and prepare the sauce as in step 5 up to one day ahead. Cover both and chill.
TO USE Bake the strudel as in step 4 and warm the Maple Fudge Sauce. Serve as in step 5.

PRUNES IN BRANDY

PREPARATION TIME: 10 minutes,
plus 2–3 days soaking
PER SERVING: 100cals, 0g fat, 11g carbohydrate

SERVES 8

225g (8oz) pitted, ready-to-eat prunes
200ml (7fl oz) brandy

Put the prunes in a jar or bowl and cover with the brandy. Cover the jar with a lid or clingfilm and leave for two to three days. Serve either with the Cinnamon Cream (left) or warm custard, and cigarette russes biscuits.

FEBRUARY

The shortest month of the year, but the soil is waking up, bringing a welcome variety of new season's vegetables

FEBRUARY CARRIES ON FROM JANUARY in being a good month for fish, especially round fish throughout the month. Flat fish will start bearing roe as the month wears on, which makes for softer flesh, so look for the telltale bulge when you're buying. Round fish follow a different cycle, so they'll be good throughout. In February, as in January, look for cheaper alternatives to cod and haddock; whiting is particularly good now. Don't bother with shellfish other than bivalves: mussels, scallops and oysters are continuing their good run, but crab and lobster won't be at their best for a couple of months. At the other end of the price spectrum, don't neglect the cheap but delicious herring, which is nearing the end of its peak season, or the consistently excellent mackerel with which our waters abound. (Mackerel goes particularly well with rhubarb, whose sharpness cuts cleanly through the richness of this oily fish.) And finally: look out for whitebait, whose season begins now. See the box on page 35 for more information on this sometimes misunderstood term.

Fruit

Where fruit is concerned, February is best for imports: southern-hemisphere apples and grapes and exotica from around the globe. Apples can be excellent, especially if they're the ever-more-popular Braeburns. The other star this month is oranges, increasingly from Morocco rather than Spain. Moroccan navels can be almost as good as their more northerly counterparts, if normally somewhat smaller, with sweet flesh that makes them perfect for eating as is or using in salads. Or try them in the Caramel Oranges with Vanilla Mascarpone on page 50

Left: Caramel Oranges (see page 50)

INGREDIENTS OF THE MONTH

GAME

Hare
Wild duck
Wild geese

FISH

Bream
Cod
Haddock
Hake
Halibut
Lemon sole
Mackerel
Plaice
Shrimps
Sole
Whiting

VEGETABLES

Broccoli
Brussels sprouts

Cabbages
Celeriac
Jerusalem
 artichokes
Leeks
Mushrooms
Purple sprouting
 broccoli
Swede

FRUIT

Apples
Forced rhubarb
Grapes
Lemons
Lychees
Seville oranges

BEST BUY

Oranges
Broccoli

– they make a refreshing pudding. And speaking of oranges, this is also the marmalade month: the inimitable Seville oranges are around just briefly, and must be grabbed when you see them. The Mixed Fruit Marmalade on page 55 combines oranges, grapefruit and limes for a tangy preserve. Satsumas and clementines tail off in quality as the month wears on, and can't be taken on trust as in January. One other import worth seeking out is the Sharon fruit from Israel, a user-friendlier form of the astringent persimmon. Among home-grown fruit, forced rhubarb is in its season and should be exploited not just for fools and crumbles but as a base for sauces served with plainly cooked fish.

Vegetables

For vegetables, February looks a lot like January. Any type of cabbage will continue to be a good bet, and sprout tops are a delicious alternative to plain old sprouts if you're tiring of the little green globes. Root vegetables also maintain their quality, with parsnips particularly good this month. Good carrots and onions are mainstays of stews and sauces, and leeks and potatoes will make delicious soups. If you find it, Swiss chard is a wonderful vegetable with a flavour somewhat similar to that of spinach. The stems are the best part, unusually: they need long cooking to soften them up, while the green leaves should be treated like spinach. But February also sees the arrival of some really good imports from the Mediterranean, both Europe and north Africa. There may be beans, mangetout peas, good celery, excellent new potatoes, and even some tomatoes that actually have flavour and texture worth taking seriously. Salads may not be at their best, but stir-fries using these imports certainly are. And don't forget the excellent broccoli from Spain and elsewhere, which sees many a home cook through the winter.

Game

There is still a bit of game around in February, though the variety is now greatly diminished. Keep on the look-out for wild duck, pigeon and goose in the markets, and hare as well if you like that strong taste in stews and sauces. Some butchers will also be selling a few stragglers – pheasant especially – from the main season. If they haven't been frozen already, they're a good (usually cheapish) buy for filling the freezer so you can enjoy game for a few months more. All are likely to be older animals that take better to braising than roasting. If you want a bit of gamey flavour, you can get it from guinea fowl – a bird that deserves more recognition as a good alternative to the sometimes flavourless chickens that are too often sold in supermarkets. Look for birds from either the UK or France, and treat it as you would a chicken.

WHITEBAIT

Whitebait is not a type of fish but the small fry of several types of fish, especially sprats and herring. They are really tiny, sometimes no more than 3cm (1¼ in) in length, and must be very fresh if they're to show at their best: look for shiny, silvery skin and bright, clear eyes. Restaurants usually serve them deep-fried in batter, but they're just as good tossed in seasoned flour and shallow-fried. No sauce is necessary apart from a squeeze of lemon, and because of their tiny size they can be eaten whole without gutting. Even children who normally turn their noses up at fish often love the crunch of whitebait.

EGGS BENEDICT

PREPARATION TIME: 1 minute
COOKING TIME: 10 minutes
PER SERVING: 460cals, 32g fat, 28g carbohydrate

SERVES 2

1 English muffin, cut in half horizontally
Butter to spread
4 rashers of bacon, grilled until crispy
2 eggs, poached and well-drained
Jar of hollandaise sauce
Fresh parsley to garnish

1 Grill the muffin halves until golden brown, then spread with butter.
2 Top each half with two rashers of the bacon and a poached egg. Spoon over some of the hollandaise sauce and garnish with the parsley.

CHEESE FONDUE TARTS

PREPARATION TIME: 20 minutes,
plus 10 minutes chilling
COOKING TIME: 25 minutes
PER SERVING: 550cals, 41g fat, 27g carbohydrate

MAKES 12; SERVES 6

Plain flour to dust
425g (15oz) puff pastry
200g (7oz) each Jarlsberg and Gouda cheese, grated
1 garlic clove, crushed
142ml carton single cream
Juice of 1 small lemon
½ level tsp paprika
2 level tsp cornflour
50ml (2fl oz) vodka
2 level tbsp freshly chopped dill

1 Preheat the oven to 220°C (200°C fan oven) mark 7. On a floured surface, roll the pastry out to 3mm (⅛in) thick, cut out twelve 10cm (4in) rounds and put in a muffin tin. Prick the bases, chill for 10 minutes, line with greaseproof paper and fill with baking beans. Bake for 15–20 minutes, remove the paper and beans and bake for a further 5 minutes or until golden.
2 Put the cheeses, garlic, cream, lemon juice and paprika in a pan, heat and stir to make a smooth sauce. Mix the cornflour and vodka together, add to the pan and cook for 1–2 minutes. Stir in the dill.
3 Spoon the mixture into the pastry cases and serve warm.

COOK'S TIPS This recipe works best with the types of cheese used for fondues. Jarlsberg and Gouda are good.
● Serve these pastries with a crisp green salad.

JERUSALEM ARTICHOKE SOUP

PREPARATION TIME: 10 minutes
COOKING TIME: 45 minutes
PER SERVING: 350cals, 29g fat, 19g carbohydrate

SERVES 6

125g (4oz) butter
175g (6oz) onions, chopped
1 garlic clove, crushed
50g (2oz) celery, chopped
900g (2lb) Jerusalem artichokes, peeled and chopped
125g (4oz) carrots, peeled and chopped
300ml (½ pint) dry white wine
1 sachet bouquet garni
142ml carton double cream

1 Melt the butter in a large pan, add the onions and garlic and cook for 2 minutes. Add the remaining vegetables and cook for 5 minutes.

2 Add the wine, bring to the boil and simmer until reduced by half. Add 1.1 litres (2 pints) of water and the bouquet garni. Bring back to the boil then simmer until the vegetables are tender.

3 Cool slightly, remove the bouquet garni then blend in a liquidiser or food processor until smooth.

4 Gently reheat the soup in a pan, season with salt and freshly ground black pepper and add half the cream. Spoon into bowls, drizzle with the remaining cream.

5 Serve with toasted or crusty bread and optional garnish of thyme.

(Illustrated)

CREAMED CELERIAC AND FRESH PARMESAN SOUP

PREPARATION TIME: 25 minutes

COOKING TIME: 35 minutes

PER SERVING: 310cals, 24g fat, 16g carbohydrate

SERVES 8

2tbsp oil

175g (6oz) onions, roughly chopped

1 garlic clove, crushed

450g (1lb) each celeriac and potatoes, peeled and
    roughly chopped

1.1 litres (2 pints) vegetable stock

Bouquet garni

568ml carton milk

284ml carton double cream

1tbsp lemon juice

8 level tbsp grated Parmesan cheese

Toasted Parmesan cheese to garnish (see Cook's Tip)

Parmesan Puffs to serve (see below)

PARMESAN PUFFS

PREPARATION TIME: 10 minutes

COOKING TIME: 15 minutes

PER SERVING: 160cals, 13g fat, 8g carbohydrate

SERVES 8

40g (1½oz) butter, melted

2 large eggs

75g (3oz) self-raising flour

125ml (4fl oz) milk

3 tbsp double cream

25g (1oz) Parmesan cheese, grated

1 level tbsp freshly chopped herbs

25g (1oz) white vegetable fat, melted

1 Heat the oil in a large pan then add the onions and garlic. Cook slowly for 4—5 minutes or until golden brown.

2 Add the celeriac, potatoes, vegetable stock and bouquet garni, bring to the boil and simmer for 20—25 minutes or until the celeriac and potatoes are tender. Remove the pan from the heat, cool slightly and discard the bouquet garni. Blend the soup in batches until smooth. Put back in the pan.

3 Add the milk, cream and lemon juice and season with salt and freshly ground black pepper. Simmer for a further 10 minutes.

4 To serve, put 1 level tbsp of grated Parmesan in the bottom of each serving bowl. Ladle in the soup, grind over some black pepper and garnish with the toasted Parmesan. Serve with warm Parmesan Puffs.

TO FREEZE Complete the recipe to the end of step 3. Cool, pack and freeze.

TO USE Thaw the soup overnight in the fridge. Bring slowly to the boil, whisking. Dilute with a little milk if necessary. Complete as above.

COOK'S TIP To make the toasted Parmesan, sprinkle 25g (1oz) finely grated Parmesan cheese on a baking sheet. Put under a hot grill until melted and golden. Cool, then crumble and store in an airtight container for up to one week.

1 Preheat the oven to 230°C (210°C fan oven) mark 8. Blend all the ingredients except the vegetable fat to make a smooth batter.

2 Put ½ tsp vegetable fat into each hole of a mini-muffin tin and heat until almost smoking. Fill with the batter and cook for 10—15 minutes or until well risen. Serve warm.

TO FREEZE Complete the recipe to the end of step 2. Cool, pack and freeze.

TO USE Put on a baking sheet and reheat at 180°C (160°C fan oven) mark 4 for 5—10 minutes.

BRUSCHETTA WITH OLIVE TAPENADE AND ANTIPASTI

PREPARATION TIME: 5 minutes

COOKING TIME: 5 minutes

PER SERVING WITHOUT ANTIPASTI: 200cals, 8g fat, 23g carbohydrate

SERVES 6

1 ciabatta loaf, sliced on the diagonal into 12 slices

A little olive oil to brush

Black olive paste (tapenade)

Selection of antipasti, such as marinated red peppers, artichokes, baby onions and aubergines

A few fresh basil sprigs to serve

1 Brush each side of the ciabatta slices with oil. Heat a griddle pan until hot and toast the ciabatta on each side.

2 Spread one side with olive paste. Arrange the antipasti on a large serving plate, garnish with the basil and let everyone help themselves.

(Illustrated)

BEEF, MUSHROOM AND RED WINE CASSEROLE

PREPARATION TIME: 20 minutes
COOKING TIME: 1 hour 5 minutes
PER SERVING: 680cals, 44g fat, 16g carbohydrate

MAKES 2 MEALS FOR 4

6tbsp groundnut or vegetable oil

40g (1½oz) butter

1.6kg (3½lb) braising steak, cut into 4cm (1½in) cubes
(see Cook's Tip)

2 x 200g (7oz) packs bacon lardons or streaky bacon
rashers cut into strips

700g (1½lb) onions, sliced

3 garlic cloves, crushed

700g (1½lb) small carrots, peeled and cut in half
lengthways

2 level tbsp tomato purée

2 level tbsp plain flour

450ml (¾ pint) red wine

600ml (1 pint) beef stock

Bouquet garni, including 1–2 strips of orange zest

12 juniper berries, crushed or chopped

450g (1lb) shiitake, large flat or chestnut mushrooms

1 Preheat the oven to 170°C (150°C fan oven) mark 3. Heat 2tbsp of the oil in each of two large flameproof casseroles, then divide the butter between them. When foaming, add enough beef to cover the base of each casserole. Brown the beef over a high heat on all sides, then put to one side. Repeat if necessary until all the beef has been browned. (If you have a large frying pan, use this as well to speed up the process.)

2 Divide the bacon between the casseroles and fry until golden, then add the onions, garlic, carrots and tomato purée. Cook over a moderate heat until lightly browned. Sprinkle in the flour, cook for 1–2 minutes, stirring, then pour in the wine. Mix until smooth, bring to the boil and bubble for 2–3 minutes. Return the beef to the casseroles, pour in enough stock to barely cover, tuck in the bouquet garni, add the juniper berries and season with salt and freshly ground black pepper. Bring to the boil, cover and cook in the oven for 1 hour or until tender.

3 Meanwhile, heat the remaining oil in a large frying pan, add the mushrooms and stir-fry until just cooked. When the beef is tender, remove the bouquet garni and add the mushrooms to the casseroles.

COOK'S TIP For a flavour boost, toss the raw beef in 2 level tbsp of steak seasoning before cooking.

(Illustrated)

TURKISH LAMB STEW

PREPARATION TIME: 10 minutes
COOKING TIME: 1 hour 30 minutes–2 hours
PER SERVING: 360cals, 18g fat, 24g carbohydrate

SERVES 4

2tbsp olive oil

400g (14oz) lean lamb fillet, cubed

1 red onion, sliced

1 garlic clove, crushed

1 potato, cubed

400g can chopped plum tomatoes

1 red pepper, deseeded and sliced

200g (7oz) canned chickpeas

1 aubergine, cut into chunks

200ml (7fl oz) lamb stock

1tbsp red wine vinegar

1 level tsp each freshly chopped thyme, rosemary and oregano

8 black olives, halved and pitted

1 Heat 1tbsp of the oil in a flameproof casserole and, over a high heat, brown the lamb. Turn down the heat and add the remaining oil, the onion and garlic, then cook until soft.

2 Preheat the oven to 170°C (150°C fan oven) mark 3. Add the potato, tomatoes, red pepper, chickpeas, aubergine, stock, vinegar and fresh herbs to the pan. Season with salt and freshly ground black pepper, stir and bring to the boil. Cover, put in the oven and cook for 1–1½ hours or until tender.

3 About 15 minutes before the end of cooking time, add the olives. Serve with rice and green vegetables.

GRILLED COD WITH BLACK-OLIVE OIL

PREPARATION TIME: 5 minutes
COOKING TIME: 45 minutes
PER SERVING: 440cals, 29g fat, 13g carbohydrate

SERVES 6

75g (3oz) black olives, pitted
175ml (6fl oz) olive oil
1 garlic clove, crushed
350g (12oz) baby potatoes
700g (1½lb) trimmed leeks, well washed and thickly sliced
6 cod fillet portions or Icelandic sea fish, weighing 1kg
   (2¼lb) in total
Fresh chives to garnish

1 Put the olives, 125ml (4fl oz) of the oil and the garlic in a food processor and season with salt and freshly ground black pepper in a food processor. Whiz for 1–2 minutes or until the mixture resembles a chunky purée. Cover and put to one side.

2 Cook the potatoes in boiling salted water until just tender, about 15–20 minutes. Drain and cut into wedges.

3 Heat the remaining oil in a large frying pan. Add the potato wedges and cook for 5–10 minutes or until golden brown on each side, stirring occasionally. Drain on kitchen paper, season and put to one side in a warm place. Add the leeks to the pan and cook for 3–4 minutes or until tender then season. Return the potatoes to the pan.

4 Put the cod fillets on a baking tray and season with freshly ground black pepper. Spoon 2tsp of the olive purée over each fillet. Cook under a hot grill for about 8 minutes or until the flesh turns opaque. Spoon a further 1tsp of the olive purée on to each fillet and put back under the grill for 1 minute to warm through.

5 Stir the leek and potato mixture in the frying pan over a medium heat for 1–2 minutes, to heat through. Divide the mixture among the plates and put a cod fillet on top. Garnish with chives and serve immediately.

SEAFOOD SPAGHETTI WITH PEPPER AND ALMOND SAUCE

PREPARATION TIME: 20 minutes
COOKING TIME: 20 minutes
PER SERVING: 370cals, 9g fat, 47g carbohydrate

SERVES 4

1 small red pepper – around 150g (5oz)
1 fresh red chilli
50g (2oz) toasted, blanched almonds
2–3 garlic cloves, crushed
2tbsp red wine vinegar
350ml (12fl oz) tomato juice
4 level tbsp freshly chopped parsley
225g (8oz) dried spaghetti
450g (1lb) mixed prepared cooked seafood, such as
   prawns, mussels and squid (see Cook's Tip)
Freshly chopped chilli to garnish

1 Put the pepper and chilli under the grill and cook, turning occasionally, until the skins char and blacken. Put in a bowl, cover with clingfilm and cool slightly. Pull off the skins. Halve the peppers and chilli and discard the seeds, then put the flesh into a large food processor bowl.

2 Add the nuts, garlic, vinegar, tomato juice and half the parsley and season with salt and freshly ground black pepper. Whiz until almost smooth. Transfer to a pan.

3 Cook the pasta in boiling salted water. Drain and toss in the rest of the fresh parsley then season and cover.

4 Meanwhile, gently heat the sauce until it simmers then add the seafood. Simmer for 3–4 minutes or until heated through, stirring frequently. Adjust the seasoning and serve immediately over the spaghetti. Garnish with freshly chopped chilli.

COOK'S TIP Hot chillies can sometimes irritate the skin so wear rubber gloves when handling them.

PORK WITH SPICED BUTTER

PREPARATION TIME: 5 minutes

COOKING TIME: 20 minutes

PER SERVING: 350cals, 19g fat, 17g carbohydrate

SERVES 6

300ml (½ pint) cider

3 level tbsp mixed peppercorns, crushed

6 level tbsp each brown sugar and wholegrain mustard

75g (3oz) butter, softened

6 pork chops – around 175g (6oz) each

1. Put the cider in a small pan and boil for 15 minutes.
2. Meanwhile, combine the peppercorns with the sugar, mustard and butter.
3. Season the chops with salt and freshly ground black pepper and cook under a preheated grill for 5 minutes on one side. Turn over, spread each chop with the butter, then cook for a further 5 minutes or until golden and cooked through.
4. Pour the grill pan juices into the cider and heat for 2–3 minutes. Pour over the pork chops and serve.

ROAST FIELD MUSHROOMS WITH RED WINE RISOTTO

PREPARATION TIME: 25 minutes

COOKING TIME: 25–30 minutes

PER SERVING: 660cals, 32g fat, 70g carbohydrate

SERVES 6

6 large flat mushrooms

4tbsp olive oil

2 shallots, peeled and finely chopped

50g (2oz) pitted Kalamata olives, roughly chopped

1 garlic clove, crushed

75g (3oz) fresh breadcrumbs

1 tbsp freshly chopped parsley

1 tbsp freshly chopped lemon thyme plus extra sprigs
   to garnish

2 tbsp red wine

75g (3oz) freshly grated Parmesan cheese

FOR THE RISOTTO

125g (4oz) butter

1 onion, finely chopped

1 stick celery, finely chopped

300ml (½ pint) red wine

450g (1lb) risotto rice

1.4 litres (2½ pints) hot vegetable stock

1. Preheat the oven to 180°C (160°C fan oven) mark 4. Cut the stems out of the mushrooms, chop, and put to one side. Lay the mushrooms stalk side up in a single layer in a shallow ovenproof dish. Season with salt and freshly ground black pepper.
2. Heat half the oil in a pan, add the shallots and cook until soft. Add the mushroom stalks and olives, and cook, stirring, until the onion is golden. Add the garlic, cook for 1 minute and remove from the heat. Stir in the breadcrumbs, parsley, thyme and wine and season with salt and freshly ground black pepper.
3. Pile the stuffing mixture into the mushrooms, pressing down lightly. Sprinkle with 2tbsp of the Parmesan and put the rest to one side for the risotto. Drizzle with the remaining oil and roast for 25–30 minutes, until the mushrooms are tender and the stuffing is golden brown.
4. Meanwhile, make the risotto. Melt half the butter in a large pan, and add the onion and celery. Cook gently for 10 minutes until soft. Add the wine, bring to the boil, and reduce to half the original volume.
5. Add the rice and stir to coat with the liquid. Add a ladleful of hot stock and stir until absorbed by the rice. Continue adding the stock, ladleful by ladleful, until the rice is tender and creamy. This will take about 20 minutes. Season well then stir in the remaining butter and Parmesan. Cover the pan and leave to rest for 5 minutes.
6. Serve the risotto on warm plates or bowls, and top each with a roasted mushroom.

PASTA WITH PINENUTS AND PARMESAN

PREPARATION TIME: 5 minutes
COOKING TIME: 5–6 minutes
PER SERVING: 290cals, 9g fat, 44g carbohydrate

SERVES 6

350g (12oz) dried pasta noodles, preferably vermicelli
50g (2oz) pinenuts or flaked almonds, toasted
50g (2oz) freshly grated or pared Parmesan cheese

Cook the pasta in boiling salted water for 5–6 minutes, or according to the packet instructions, until just tender. Drain well, toss in the pinenuts and Parmesan and serve.

CARROT AND CELERIAC SALAD

PREPARATION TIME: 20 minutes
PER SERVING: 150cals, 11g fat, 9g carbohydrate

SERVES 4

2tsp hoisin sauce
4tsp rice wine vinegar
2tsp soy sauce
1tbsp peanut oil
1tsp sesame oil
2tsp runny honey
225g (8oz) each carrot and celeriac or mooli, peeled, coarsely grated or shredded
75g (3oz) roasted, salted peanuts, finely chopped
50g (2oz) alfalfa or 125g (4oz) beansprouts

1 Put the hoisin sauce in a large bowl. Add the vinegar, soy sauce, oils and honey. Season with salt and freshly ground black pepper. Whisk together.
2 Add the carrot and celeriac or mooli to the bowl with the peanuts. Mix well. Stir in the alfalfa or beansprouts and serve immediately.

PARMESAN AND MUSTARD PARSNIPS

PREPARATION TIME: 20 minutes
COOKING TIME: 40–50 minutes
PER SERVING: 190cals, 13g fat, 11g carbohydrate

SERVES 8

700g (1½lb) small parsnips, peeled and halved
50g (2oz) butter
2tbsp olive oil
100g (3½oz) freshly grated Parmesan cheese
5 level tbsp English mustard powder

1 Put the parsnips in a pan of salted water, cover and bring to the boil. Boil for 5 minutes. Drain well and keep warm.
2 Preheat the oven to 200°C (180°C fan oven) mark 6. Put the butter and oil in a roasting tin and heat in the oven for 5 minutes.
3 Mix together the Parmesan and mustard powder and season well with salt and freshly ground black pepper. Coat the still-warm parsnips in the mixture, pressing the coating on well.
4 Cook in the preheated roasting tin for 30–40 minutes or until golden.

HONEY-GLAZED SHALLOTS

PREPARATION TIME: 15 minutes

COOKING TIME: 28 minutes

PER SERVING: 110cals, 6g fat, 12g carbohydrate

SERVES 6

700g (1½lb) shallots, blanched in boiling water and
    peeled

40g (1½oz) butter

1½tbsp runny honey

Juice of ½ lemon

1½tbsp Worcestershire sauce

1½tbsp balsamic vinegar

1 Put the shallots in a pan with just enough cold water to cover. Bring to the boil then simmer for 5 minutes. Drain well and return to the pan. Add the butter to the pan with all the remaining ingredients and stir until the shallots are coated with the glaze.

2 Cover and cook over a low heat, stirring occasionally, for 20 minutes or until the shallots are tender. Remove the lid and continue to cook for a further 2–3 minutes until any remaining liquid is thick and syrupy.

TO PREPARE AHEAD Complete the recipe up to one day ahead. Cool, cover and chill.

TO USE Reheat gently over a low heat.

(Illustrated)

PAN-FRIED POTATOES

PREPARATION TIME: 10 minutes
COOKING TIME: 30 minutes
PER SERVING: 400cals, 24g fat, 43g carbohydrate

SERVES 6

1.6kg (3½lb) potatoes, peeled and halved
150ml (¼ pint) vegetable oil
75g (3oz) butter
Fresh marjoram and sea salt to garnish

1 Cook the potatoes in a large pan of boiling salted water for about 15–20 minutes or until tender. Drain and cut into walnut-sized chunks.
2 Heat the oil and butter in a large frying pan and cook the warm potatoes in batches, tossing them frequently, for about 10 minutes or until they are evenly golden. Spoon on to sheets of kitchen paper to drain off excess fat. (See Cook's Tip.)
3 Garnish the potatoes with marjoram and sea salt, then serve.

TO PREPARE AHEAD Complete the recipe up to 4 hours ahead.
TO USE To reheat the potatoes, put them on a baking sheet and warm in the oven at 220°C (200°C fan oven) mark 7 for 10–15 minutes.
COOK'S TIP For a great variation, sprinkle over 25g (1oz) finely grated Parmesan cheese when the potatoes are cooked.

COLCANNON

PREPARATION TIME: 10 minutes
COOKING TIME: 30 minutes
PER SERVING FOR 4: 290cals, 12g fat, 41g carbohydrate
PER SERVING FOR 6: 200cals, 8g fat, 27g carbohydrate

SERVES 4–6

900g (2lb) potatoes, cut into chunks
50g (2oz) butter
250g (9oz) curly kale, finely sliced
100ml (3½fl oz) milk

1 Cook the potatoes in boiling water for 15–20 minutes or until tender.
2 Meanwhile, melt the butter in a frying pan and stir-fry the kale for 3 minutes.
3 Drain the potatoes, then tip them back into the pan and put over a medium heat for 1–2 minutes to dry off. Tip into a colander and cover with a lid to keep warm.
4 Pour the milk into the potato pan and bring to the boil. Remove from the heat, add the potatoes and mash thoroughly. Add the kale and any butter from the pan and mix together. Season well with salt and freshly ground black pepper and serve.

SEEDED RICE

PREPARATION TIME: 2 minutes
COOKING TIME: 20 minutes
PER SERVING: 220cals, 10g fat, 33g carbohydrate

SERVES 6

250g (9oz) basmati rice
3tbsp olive oil
1 level tbsp sesame seeds
2 level tbsp mustard seeds
1 level tbsp cumin seeds
2 level tbsp each freshly chopped coriander and parsley

1 Cook the rice according to the packet instructions. Drain and rinse in hot running water. Tip into a serving dish and put to one side.
2 Meanwhile, heat the oil in a small pan and add the sesame seeds. Fry until golden, then add the mustard and cumin seeds. Cover the pan and cook for 2–3 minutes or until the seeds start popping.
3 Stir the cooked seeds into the rice with the coriander and parsley. Season well with salt and freshly ground black pepper and serve.

CREAMY LEEKS

PREPARATION TIME: 15 minutes,

plus 15 minutes cooling

COOKING TIME: 20 minutes

PER SERVING: 120cals, 11g fat, 4g carbohydrate

SERVES 6

700g (1½lb) trimmed leeks, well washed and thickly sliced

25g (1oz) salted butter

100ml (3½fl oz) crème fraîche

Freshly grated nutmeg to serve

1 Cook the leeks in a pan of boiling salted water for 7–10 minutes until just tender. Drain and plunge immediately into icy cold water. After 15 minutes, drain again and dry well with several layers of kitchen paper. Put the leeks in a food processor and whiz until roughly chopped. Remove half and put to one side, then whiz the remainder until smooth.

2 Heat the butter in a frying pan, add all the leeks and stir over a high heat. Add the crème fraîche and season with salt and freshly ground black pepper then stir until hot and bubbling. Spoon into a serving dish and serve with a generous grating of nutmeg.

(Illustrated)

BREAD AND BUTTER PUDDING

PREPARATION TIME: 10 minutes,
plus 30 minutes soaking
COOKING TIME: 45–55 minutes
PER SERVING: 300cals, 14g fat, 35g carbohydrate

SERVES 6

50g (2oz) butter, softened
6 slices white bread
25g (1oz) each currants and sultanas
3 medium eggs
568ml carton full-fat milk
50g (2oz) light muscovado sugar
Pinch of ground mixed spice
Single cream to serve

1 Lightly grease a 1.1 litre (2 pint) ovenproof dish with a little of the butter. Use the rest to spread evenly over the bread then cut each slice in half diagonally. Arrange in the dish, each slice slightly overlapping the last, and sprinkle the currants and sultanas over the top.

2 Beat together the eggs, milk, sugar and ground mixed spice in a bowl then pour over the bread. Leave to soak for 30 minutes (see Cook's Tip). Preheat the oven to 180°C (160°C fan oven) mark 4.

3 Bake the pudding in the oven for 45–55 minutes or until golden brown but still slightly moist in the centre. Serve with a drizzle of single cream.

COOK'S TIP Leaving the prepared pudding to soak for half an hour before you bake it is the key to ensuring a brilliant result.

(Illustrated)

STICKY MARMALADE PUDDING

PREPARATION TIME: 20 minutes
COOKING TIME: 1 hour 15 minutes
PER SERVING: 370cals, 20g fat, 45g carbohydrate

SERVES 8

175g (6oz) butter
175g (6oz) light muscovado sugar
Around 300g (11oz) marmalade (or see page 55 for a
    mixed fruit marmalade recipe)
2 seedless oranges, peeled, all pith removed and sliced
    thinly into rounds
2 large eggs, beaten
175g (6oz) self-raising flour
1½ level tsp ground ginger
40g (1½oz) stem ginger, finely chopped
Homemade vanilla custard to serve

1 Preheat the oven to 180°C (160°C fan oven) mark 4. Line the base of a round 23cm (9in) wide, minimum 5cm (2in) deep tin with non-stick baking parchment. Warm together 50g (2oz) each of the butter and sugar and half the marmalade. Spoon into the tin. Arrange the orange slices over the base of the tin.

2 Beat together the remaining butter and sugar. Gradually beat in the eggs. Sift the flour and ground ginger and fold into the mixture with the remaining marmalade and the stem ginger. Spread over the oranges.

3 Stand the tin on a baking sheet and bake for 1 hour 10 minutes or until just firm to the touch. If necessary, cover with foil.

4 Loosen around the edges of the tin then invert the pudding on to an edged serving plate. Serve warm with custard.

TO PREPARE AHEAD Complete the recipe to the end of step 3 up to one day ahead. Loosen the edges and turn the pudding out on to an ovenproof dish, cool, cover and store in a cool place.
TO USE Cover with foil; reheat at 180°C (160°C fan oven) mark 4 for about 40 minutes.

CARAMELISED APPLE MERINGUE

PREPARATION TIME: 10 minutes
COOKING TIME: 2 hours 40 minutes
PER SERVING: 460cals, 34g fat, 37g carbohydrate

SERVES 6

2 large egg whites

125g (4oz) golden caster sugar

50g (2oz) butter

700g (1½lb) eating apples, such as Granny Smith,
    peeled, cored and sliced

284ml carton double cream

50g (2oz) flaked almonds, toasted

Icing sugar to decorate

Apple and Calvados Sauce to serve (see below)

APPLE AND CALVADOS SAUCE

PREPARATION TIME: 1 minute
COOKING TIME: 10 minutes
PER SERVING: 60cals, trace fat, 15g carbohydrate

600ml (1 pint) apple juice

2 level tsp arrowroot

Calvados to taste

1 Preheat the oven to 140°C (120°C fan oven) mark 1. Put the egg whites in a large clean grease-free bowl and whisk until stiff. Add 50g (2oz) of the sugar and continue whisking until stiff and glossy. Using a large spoon, fold in the remaining sugar.

2 Line two baking sheets with baking parchment and spread six small thin circles of meringue mixture, each around 9cm (3½in) across, on to each baking sheet.

3 Bake for 2–2½ hours or until dry. Lift off the paper and store in an airtight container interleaved with baking parchment until required.

4 Melt a third of the butter in a large frying pan and fry a third of the apples for 3–4 minutes or until golden brown. Remove and cool. Repeat with the remaining butter and apples. Whip the cream.

5 To serve, sandwich the cream and apples between two meringue discs per person, sprinkle with the almonds and dust with icing sugar. Pour round the Apple and Calvados Sauce and serve.

1 Put the apple juice into a pan and bring to the boil then bubble to reduce by half.

2 Blend the arrowroot with 1tbsp of water and whisk into the juice. Return to the boil, stirring, then put to one side.

3 When cooled, add Calvados to taste.

CARAMEL ORANGES WITH VANILLA MASCARPONE

PREPARATION TIME: 15 minutes
COOKING TIME: 5 minutes
PER SERVING: 380cals, 16g fat, 49g carbohydrate

SERVES 6

1 vanilla pod, split lengthways

200g tub mascarpone cheese

150ml (¼ pint) Cointreau

175g (6oz) golden caster sugar

6 oranges, peeled, all pith removed and sliced
    into rounds

1 Using a small sharp knife, scrape the seeds from the vanilla pod into a bowl. Add the mascarpone and 1tbsp of the Cointreau to the bowl and mix everything together. Cover and chill.

2 Put the remaining Cointreau and the sugar in a frying pan and heat gently to dissolve. Bring to the boil and cook to a light caramel. Add the oranges and cook for 2–3 minutes, then cool and chill until needed. Warm through, if liked, and serve with the vanilla mascarpone.

(Illustrated on page 32)

RUM AND RAISIN ICE CREAM

PREPARATION TIME: 40 minutes

COOKING TIME: 5 minutes

FREEZING TIME: 8 hours or overnight

PER SERVING: 480cals, 37g fat, 28g carbohydrate

MAKES 1.1 LITRES (2 PINTS); SERVES 8

250g (9oz) Australian muscat raisins (also known as Lexia raisins)

100ml (3½fl oz) dark rum

4 large egg yolks

3tbsp golden syrup

1tbsp treacle

568ml carton double cream, whipped until it falls in soft ribbons

Ice cubes for the ice bowls

Bay leaves

Juniper berries

1 Put the raisins in a pan, add the rum and bring to the boil. Turn off the heat and leave to soak while you're making the ice cream. This will soften and plump up the fruit.

2 Put the egg yolks, syrup and treacle in a small bowl. Whisk with an electric mixer for 2–3 minutes until it has a mousse-like consistency. Pour into the cream and whisk for 3–4 minutes until thick.

3 Set the freezer to fast freeze (or turn to coldest setting). Pour the mixture into a 2 litre (3½ pint) roasting tin and freeze for 45 minutes–1 hour or until it begins to harden around the edges.

4 Add the soaked fruit and any remaining liquid to the ice cream and mix well. Put back in the freezer for 45 minutes. Spoon into a 1.7 litre (3 pint) sealable container and freeze for at least 2 hours.

5 To make ice bowls, put a layer of ice cubes into four plastic 1 litre (1¾ pint) bowls. Tape a round 600ml (1 pint) bowl on top of each. Put the bay leaves and juniper berries down the sides. Add more ice cubes and fill with water. Freeze overnight.

6 To assemble, take the ice bowls out of the freezer, then remove the tape and top container. Gently squeeze the outer container so that the ice bowl drops out. Sit it upright. Scoop the ice cream into balls and serve in the ice bowls.

COOK'S TIP Bear in mind that most freezers will only have enough room to make four ice bowls at a time.

(Illustrated)

CHOCOLATE CRÊPES WITH A BOOZY SAUCE

PREPARATION TIME: 5 minutes, plus 20 minutes standing
COOKING TIME: 10 minutes
PER SERVING: 550cals, 32g fat, 52g carbohydrate

SERVES 6

150g (5oz) plain flour, sifted
2 medium eggs
450ml (¾ pint) milk
Sunflower oil for frying
150g (5oz) unsalted butter
150g (5oz) light muscovado sugar plus extra to sprinkle
6tbsp brandy
75g (3oz) dark chocolate, minimum 70% cocoa solids, roughly chopped

1 Put the flour and a pinch of salt in a bowl, make a well in the centre and add the eggs. Use a balloon whisk to mix the eggs with a little of the flour, then gradually add the milk to make a smooth batter. Cover and leave to stand for about 20 minutes.

2 Pour the batter into a jug. Heat 1tsp of oil in a 23cm (9in) pancake pan, then pour 100ml (3½fl oz) of batter into the centre of the pan. Tip the pan around so the mixture coats the base and fry for 1–2 minutes until golden underneath. Use a palette knife to flip over and fry on the other side. Tip on to a plate, cover with a piece of greaseproof paper and repeat with the remaining batter, using more oil as necessary.

3 Put the butter in a frying pan with the sugar and melt over a low heat to mix together. Add the brandy and stir.

4 Divide the chocolate between the crêpes. Fold each in half, then in half again.

5 Slide each pancake into the pan and cook for 3–4 minutes to melt the chocolate, turning halfway through to coat with the sauce. Serve the crêpes drizzled with sauce and sprinkled with extra sugar.

(Illustrated)

VANILLA PANNA COTTA

PREPARATION TIME: 20 minutes, plus 20 minutes infusing and overnight chilling
COOKING TIME: 10 minutes
PER SERVING: 540cals, 54g fat, 10g carbohydrate

SERVES 8 (SEE COOK'S TIP)

1 vanilla pod, split lengthways
900ml (1½ pints) extra-thick double cream
Finely grated zest of 1 lemon and ½ tsp juice
50g (2oz) golden caster sugar
Oil to grease
2tbsp dark rum
2 level tsp powdered gelatine

1 Using a small sharp knife, scrape out the seeds from the vanilla pod and put in a heavy-based pan. Add the cream, lemon zest and caster sugar. Slowly bring to simmering point, then remove from the heat, cover and put to one side for 20 minutes. Grease and base-line eight 150ml (¼ pint) dariole moulds or ramekins.

2 Pour the rum into a small heatproof bowl, sprinkle over the gelatine and leave to soak for 1–2 minutes. Put the bowl over a pan of simmering water until the gelatine has dissolved. Immediately stir the gelatine and lemon juice into the cream mixture. Divide between the moulds, put on a tray and chill overnight.

3 To serve, dip the moulds for 2–3 seconds in hot water and turn out on to serving plates.

TO PREPARE AHEAD Complete the recipe to the end of step 2 up to 24 hours ahead. Cover and chill.
TO USE Complete the recipe.
TO FREEZE Complete the recipe to the end of step 2, pack and freeze.
TO USE Thaw for 4 hours. Complete the recipe.
COOK'S TIP This recipe freezes well so it's worth making the full amount and freezing any that you don't need.

MAKING MARMALADE AND JAM

WATCHPOINTS

TIPS

- Before you start, put four saucers in the fridge to chill ready to repeat testing for setting as needed.
- A large preserving pan with a wide open top is essential for its size and shape – it helps the evaporation process, ensuring the finished preserve isn't too runny. Stainless steel or non-stick pans are best.
- Preserving sugar is a superior-quality coarse-grain sugar that gives a clear set ideal for jellied preserves, but it's not essential for marmalade and jam and it's much more pricey than granulated sugar.
- Jam sugar is not the same as preserving sugar – it's a granulated sugar with added pectin and citric acid to aid the setting of fruits that have a naturally low pectin content such as strawberries and cherries.

SETTING AGENTS

- Preserving sugar produces less scum, dissolves easily and produces sparkling clear jellies and jams. Jam sugar is used for fruits with low pectin and acid level.
- Pectin makes preserves set when fruit is heated with sugar. However, many summer fruits are low in natural pectin, so if your jam or marmalade is not setting, add extra lemon juice – a good natural source of pectin. Alternatively, use an artificial pectin – add one sachet per 1kg (2¼lb) granulated sugar.

SETTING POINT

When marmalade or jam reaches setting point it's ready to pot. Test regularly for a set; if the preserve is boiled for too long it darkens and caramelises. There are two good ways of testing this stage:

- spoon a little marmalade or jam on to a chilled plate, then chill for 1–2 minutes. If it crinkles when you run your finger through it, setting point has been reached
- take the guesswork out of getting the perfect set by using a sugar or jam thermometer – check the recipe for the ideal temperature.

POTTING TIPS

- Before use, wash jars in hot water, drain, then leave to dry in a warm oven. Boil the lids. Alternatively, a fast wash in the dishwasher is ideal.
- Always pour hot preserves into warm jars.
- Always fill to the rim to allow for shrinkage on cooling.
- Cover with waxed discs, waxed side down, and dampened Cellophane covers, dampened side up.
- For longer-term storage, cover with screw-on lids, too.
- For best results, store preserves in a cool dark place.

MIXED FRUIT MARMALADE

PREPARATION TIME: 2 hours
COOKING TIME: Around 2 hours 30 minutes
PER 1 LEVEL TBSP: 40cals, 0g fat,
11g carbohydrate

MAKES 4KG (9LB)

2 each unwaxed Seville oranges, yellow grapefruit
   and limes
4 large unwaxed lemons
3kg (6½lb) preserving or granulated sugar

1 If you can't get unwaxed fruit, rub with a tiny drop of washing-up liquid, rinse well and dry. Weigh the fruit – you need around 1.6kg (3½lb) in total – then cut in half. Squeeze by hand or with an electric juicer to extract as much juice as possible, then pour into a jug through a sieve to catch any pips. Put the pips to one side.

2 Cut the halves into quarters. Cut away the membrane and add to the pips, then cut away a thin layer of pith and add to the pips. Chop the peel into thin strips and tip into a preserving pan. Cut out a 35.5cm (14in) square of muslin, pile the pips, membrane and pith in the middle, gather up and tie with a 45.5cm (18in) piece of string.

3 Tie the muslin bag to the pan handle, so it hangs near the bottom of the pan. Add the juice and 3 litres (5¼ pints) of cold water. Bring to the boil, then simmer for 2 hours without a lid or until the peel is very, very tender and the liquid has reduced. Skim off any scum during cooking and discard.

4 Preheat the oven to 110°C (90°C fan oven) mark ¼. Warm the sugar in a large roasting tin for 20 minutes. Add to the pan and stir until dissolved. Rest a warmed sugar thermometer in the liquid, bring to the boil, then reduce the heat and bubble until the temperature registers 104°C 'jam stage'. Cook at this temperature for about 10 minutes.

5 Meanwhile, put four saucers in the freezer ready to test for setting. Take the pan off the heat and put 1tsp marmalade on the saucer, then put back in the freezer for 1–2 minutes. Tip the saucer up – the marmalade is ready when it doesn't move. If it does move, continue to boil, testing at 5 minute intervals as you go.

6 Position a non-stick funnel on top of clean, warm jars and use a ladle to pour in the marmalade. Cover with waxed discs, wax side down. Wipe a clean damp cloth over Cellophane discs and use to top jars, damp side up, to create a tight seal. Secure with elastic bands. Label and store in a cool, dark place for up to one year.

COOK'S TIP If you chop the peel by hand, rather than in a processor, it produces the perfect shred.

MARCH

A lean month, often wild and windy, March should herald the approach of spring with its promise of good things to come

ARCH, SO THE SAYING GOES, comes in like a lion and goes out like a lamb. The weather may not always bear this out, but the vegetable markets usually do: this is the in-between month, too late for many of winter's glorious root vegetables and brassicas, too early for the fresh, cheering arrivals of spring. It's often a case of making do if you're a stickler for home-grown produce, or of relying on imported produce. There may still be good root veg around, though you'll have to check carefully for signs of the softness that can indicate a spongy, watery interior; parsnips and Jerusalem artichokes in particular may be good. Potatoes, of course, should be fine whether from the UK or abroad; new potatoes from Cyprus are especially good choices now.

Curly kale, a member of the cabbage family, is a good choice among greens, as are broccoli imports from Spain and elsewhere. At the beginning of the month, spinach is likely to come from overseas but UK crops will start appearing as March heads towards April. In the absence of a wide vegetable choice, don't forget the humble onion – tasty small new crops should be coming into the market, and enliven just about any dish. Bake or braise them on their own, or use them in dishes like the French Onion Tarts with Warm Tomato and Olive Salad on page 60. And finally, take advantage of the wonderful leeks (see box on page 59), which are one of the month's few vegetable star attractions. They're combined with fish and shellfish for a great party dish in the Creamy Fish Gratin on page 66, or try the Smoked Ham, Leek and Mushroom Pie on page 68.

Left: French Onion Tarts with Warm Tomato and Olive Salad (see page 60)

INGREDIENTS OF THE MONTH

FISH
Brill/Flounder
Hake/John Dory
Mackerel
Monkfish
Mussels
Oysters
Plaice
Scallops
Skate
Sole
Wild salmon

VEGETABLES
Broccoli
Chicory
Curly kale
Leeks
Potatoes

Spinach
Watercress

FRUIT
Apples
Grapes
Limes
Mangoes
Oranges
Papaya
Passion fruit
Rhubarb
Sharon fruit

BEST BUY
Leeks

Fruit

For fruit, there's essentially nothing but imports to rely on – and that's no terrible thing, because there are some good ones about. Oranges from Morocco remain a good buy, as do Israeli Sharon fruit and exotic travellers from the southern hemisphere such as mangoes, papaya and passion fruit. Grapes are another good bet, especially the green ones. And don't forget about the last of the season's forced rhubarb – use it to make the Rhubarb and Cinnamon Pie on page 77.

Fish

March is the last month for good supplies of a few of our best fish – and you should make the most of them.

Brill and John Dory both come to the end of their main season now, and both, though pricey, are worth seeking out. Brill is usually ranked after turbot among flat fish, but some people think it's just as good – and it's cheaper, if not cheap. A small one will feed two or sometimes even just one, while larger fish can be a meal for four or sometimes six people at a special dinner party. Big John Dory are rare in retail markets – they usually go to restaurants – but small fish serving one or two are not uncommon. They have a huge amount of waste, and they are always expensive anyway, but their flavour is incomparable.

This is the end of the scallop season, but there may still be good skate around with a wonderful flavour and texture, and not that expensive when you consider the quality. Try the Skate with Black Butter and Rocket Mash on page 64. There may also be good hake and whiting, though their season too is usually considered to end in February. If you need special fish for a dinner party, farmed sea bass is sometimes very good and a lot cheaper than line-caught fish. And don't forget the lemon sole, which is nowhere near as good as Dover but still excellent at its best for grilling, baking or poaching.

LEEKS

Leeks are a member of the allium family, which also includes onions and garlic, but generally have far less of the smelly qualities that make onions and garlic such a tricky proposition for people who worry about their breath on a crowded train the morning after. Most sold here are grown here, though you will also find imports – especially of 'baby' leeks, rarely worth the money charged for them. As the home-grown leeks get to the end of their season, which they are in March, they can be large and tough, with an inedibly 'woody' core and usually a stronger taste. Small to medium-size specimens are best, and preferably without too much of the green tops: these are not suitable for eating, though they can be used to flavour stock. Leeks have a reputation for being difficult to clean; many recipes tell you to cut a slit down the centre after the green part has been trimmed, and then run water into the separated layers. In fact, some leeks come into the market almost free of grit in the edible white sections, and can be 'cleaned' just by cutting off the green part. Check the leeks you're using before you make that slit. Some very small leeks can be successfully grilled or stir-fried, but generally speaking it is better to cook them in a moist environment – steaming, poaching, braising or cooking with meat in a casserole – as well as using them, naturally, for soups.

FRENCH ONION TARTS
WITH WARM TOMATO AND OLIVE SALAD

PREPARATION TIME: 35 minutes,
plus 1 hour chilling
COOKING TIME: 1 hour 10 minutes
PER SERVING: 770cals, 62g fat, 40g carbohydrate

SERVES 6

50g (2oz) small pitted black olives

3tbsp olive oil

1tbsp balsamic or red wine vinegar

350g (12oz) plum tomatoes, sliced

225g (8oz) plain flour plus extra to dust

225g (8oz) butter, diced and chilled

450g (1lb) large onions, halved and sliced

2 level tsp freshly chopped thyme

142ml carton double cream

2 large eggs, separated

200g (7oz) feta cheese, crumbled

50g (2oz) Emmenthal cheese, grated

Fresh thyme sprigs to garnish

1 Put the olives in a large bowl with the oil and vinegar and season with salt and freshly ground black pepper. Arrange the tomatoes in an ovenproof dish, season with pepper and spoon over the olive dressing. Cover and put to one side.

2 To make the pastry, put the flour and 175g (6oz) of the butter in a food processor and whiz until the mixture resembles fine crumbs. Pulse the mixture, adding, one spoonful at a time, approximately 3tbsp of iced water until it forms a ball. Wrap and chill for 30 minutes.

3 Roll the pastry out on a lightly floured surface and line six 8cm (3¼in) base measurement, 3cm (1¼in) deep, individual loose-bottomed tart tins. Prick the bases well and chill for 30 minutes.

4 Melt the remaining butter in a large heavy-based pan. Add the onions, seasoning and thyme. Cover and cook slowly over a gentle heat, stirring occasionally, for 30 minutes or until very soft and golden. Remove the lid, increase the heat and cook until all the pan juices have evaporated. Stir in the cream and leave to cool.

5 Preheat the oven to 200°C (180°C fan oven) mark 6. Line the pastry cases with greaseproof paper and baking beans and cook for 10 minutes; remove the paper and beans and cook for a further 10 minutes or until the pastry is golden and cooked through.

6 Combine the egg yolks and the two cheeses with the onion mixture and season well.

7 Whisk the egg whites in a clean grease-free bowl until stiff, then fold into the onion mixture.

8 Spoon the mixture into the cooked pastry cases and cook on the top shelf of the oven for 20 minutes or until the filling is risen and puffed up. Put the tomatoes in the oven 10 minutes before the end of the cooking time.

9 To serve, turn the tarts out of the tins, garnish with fresh thyme and serve with a spoonful of the warm tomato and olive salad.

TO FREEZE Complete the tart recipe to the end of step 8. Cool, pack and freeze.

TO USE Reheat the tarts from frozen at 200°C (180°C fan oven) mark 6 for 25–30 minutes. Prepare the tomato and olive salad. Cover the tarts with foil for the last 10 minutes. Warm the tomatoes in the oven as per recipe. Serve as in step 9.

(Illustrated on page 56)

EASY GARLIC BREADSTICKS

PREPARATION TIME: 5 minutes
COOKING TIME: 15–20 minutes
PER SERVING: 220cals, 12g fat, 26g carbohydrate

MAKES 6 BREADSTICKS

1 ready-to-bake baguette
1 garlic clove, crushed
5tbsp olive oil

1 Preheat the oven to 200°C (180°C fan oven) mark 6. Cut the baguette lengthways into three, then put each slice flat and cut in half lengthways to create six breadsticks. Arrange the sticks on a baking sheet.

2 Mix the garlic with the oil and spread this over the cut sides of the breadsticks. Sprinkle with coarse sea salt and bake for 15–20 minutes until crisp and golden brown. Serve the breadsticks warm or cold with soup.

CHICKEN LIVER PATE WITH GARLIC MUSHROOMS

PREPARATION TIME: 30 minutes,
plus at least one day chilling
COOKING TIME: 30 minutes
PER SERVING: 350cals, 30g fat, 2g carbohydrate

SERVES 8

FOR THE PÂTÉ

75g (3oz) butter
125g (4oz) streaky bacon, roughly chopped
125g (4oz) shallots, blanched in boiling water, peeled and roughly chopped
225g (8oz) button mushrooms, roughly chopped
450g (1lb) chicken livers, rinsed and membranes removed
3tbsp each balsamic vinegar and brandy
2 garlic cloves, crushed
2 level tsp freshly chopped thyme
125ml (4fl oz) double cream

FOR THE GARLIC MUSHROOMS

50g (2oz) butter
350g (12oz) button mushrooms, roughly chopped
3 garlic cloves, crushed
Toasted walnut bread and salad leaves to serve

1 Melt the butter in a large heavy-based frying pan. Add the bacon, shallots and mushrooms and cook, stirring, for 10 minutes. Stir in the chicken livers and cook for 5 minutes or until they change colour. Pour in the vinegar and brandy, bring to the boil and bubble for 2–3 minutes.

2 Strain the chicken liver mixture through a colander, reserving the juices. Return the juices to the pan, then add the garlic, thyme and cream. Bring to the boil and bubble for 10 minutes or until the sauce is reduced and syrupy. Season well with salt and freshly ground black pepper.

3 Put the chicken livers and sauce in a food processor, then pulse until the mixture forms a rough purée. Turn into a bowl, cover and chill for at least 8 hours until firm (see Cook's Tips).

4 To make the garlic mushrooms, melt the butter in a frying pan, add the mushrooms and cook on a high heat, stirring, for 5 minutes. Add the garlic, cook for 1 minute and season well.

5 To serve, put a spoonful of pâté on each slice of toasted walnut bread and spoon the hot garlic mushrooms over. Serve with salad leaves.

TO FREEZE Complete the recipe to the end of step 3. Put the pâté in a freezerproof container, cover and freeze.
TO USE Thaw overnight at cool room temperature and complete the recipe.
COOK'S TIPS As an alternative, spoon the pâté into ramekins. Melt unsalted butter in a pan and spoon off the clear melted butter, discarding the sediment left behind. Pour a thin layer of this clarified butter over the pâté, cover with foil and chill for up to four days.
• This pâté improves with keeping, so try to make it ahead.

WATERCRESS SOUP WITH PARMESAN AND POPPY SEED CRISPS

PREPARATION TIME: 15 minutes

COOKING TIME: 30 minutes

PER SERVING: 460cals, 29g fat, 32g carbohydrate

SERVES 6

FOR THE PARMESAN CRISPS

125g (4oz) freshly grated Parmesan cheese

½ tsp poppy seeds

FOR THE SOUP

250g (9oz) watercress, trimmed and coarse stalks discarded

75g (3oz) butter

1 onion, finely chopped

700g (1½lb) potatoes, cut into small pieces

900ml (1½ pints) milk

900ml (1½ pints) vegetable stock

284ml carton single cream

1 To make the Parmesan crisps, preheat the oven to 200°C (180°C fan oven) mark 6 and line two baking sheets with baking parchment. Put heaped tablespoons of Parmesan evenly spaced on the sheets and spread each one out slightly. Sprinkle with poppy seeds and bake for 5–10 minutes until lacy and golden. Leave on the tray for 2–3 minutes to cool and firm up slightly, then use a palette knife to transfer to a cooling rack.

2 To make the soup, reserve a few watercress sprigs for garnish and roughly chop the rest.

3 Melt the butter in a large pan, add the onion and cook gently for 8–10 minutes until soft. Add the potatoes and cook for 1 minute, then pour in the milk and stock and bring to the boil. Reduce the heat and cook for 15–20 minutes until tender.

4 Take off the heat, stir in the watercress and blend in batches until smooth. Pour the soup into a clean pan, add the cream and season with salt and freshly ground black pepper. Heat through and serve garnished with the reserved watercress sprigs.

COOK'S TIP The secret of keeping the brilliant colour is to stir the leaves into the hot soup and blend straight away – cook the watercress for too long and it will lose its vibrancy.

MUSHROOM SAMOSAS

PREPARATION TIME: 40 minutes
COOKING TIME: 50 minutes
PER SERVING: 260cals, 11g fat, 36g carbohydrate

SERVES 6

2.5cm (1in) piece fresh root ginger, peeled and finely
    chopped
3 garlic cloves, crushed
2 level tbsp natural yogurt
25g (1oz) butter
125g (4oz) onion, finely chopped
1 level tsp cumin seeds
½ level tsp turmeric
Pinch of cayenne pepper
225g (8oz) button mushrooms, roughly chopped
125g (4oz) potato, finely diced
125g (4oz) frozen petits pois
2 level tbsp freshly chopped coriander
Around 300g (11oz) filo pastry
Oil to brush

1 Combine the ginger and garlic with the yogurt and put to one side.
2 Heat the butter in a medium-sized pan. Add the onion and cook for 5–7 minutes or until soft. Add the spices and cook for 30 seconds. Add the mushrooms and cook over a high heat, stirring, for 2 minutes or until all the liquid has evaporated. Add the yogurt mixture, potatoes and 150ml (5fl oz) of water and bring to the boil. Cover and simmer, stirring occasionally, for 25–30 minutes or until the potatoes are cooked and nearly all the liquid has been absorbed. Add the petits pois 5 minutes before the end. Set aside to cool, add the coriander and season with salt and freshly ground black pepper. Preheat the oven to 200°C (180°C fan oven) mark 6.
3 Cut the filo pastry into rectangles 30.5x12.5cm (12x5in) (see Cook's Tip). Keep covered. Brush a rectangle lightly with oil, fold in half lengthways to form a strip 6.5cm (2½in) wide and brush again with oil. Put about 2 level tsp of the mushroom mixture in the bottom left-hand corner, fold the filo over to form a triangle and continue to fold until the filling is enclosed in several layers. Brush with oil. Repeat with the remaining filling and filo. Cook for 10 minutes or until a deep golden brown. Allow to cool a little before serving, as the filling becomes very hot, then serve with the spiced yogurt.

COOK'S TIP Filo pastry comes in several sizes. Cut squares accurately to waste as little pastry as possible.

BROCCOLI AND GOAT'S CHEESE FRITTATA

PREPARATION: 10 minutes
COOKING TIME: 20 minutes
PER SERVING: 350cals, 27g fat, 2g carbohydrate

SERVES 4

8 large eggs
2tbsp freshly chopped parsley
1tbsp freshly chopped tarragon
350g (12oz) broccoli, trimmed
2tbsp extra-virgin olive oil
1 garlic clove, crushed
1 small green or red chilli, deseeded and finely chopped
150g (5oz) soft rindless goat's cheese
25g (1oz) pitted black olives (optional)

1 Beat the eggs, herbs, salt and freshly ground black pepper together in a small bowl and set aside. Peel and thinly slice the broccoli stalk and cut the florets into small pieces.
2 Heat the oil in a large non-stick frying pan, add the broccoli, garlic and chilli and fry over a low heat, stirring frequently, for 5 minutes. Cover and cook for a further 5 minutes until the broccoli feels tender when pierced with a knife.
3 Crumble over the goat's cheese and stir in the olives, if using, then pour in the beaten egg mixture, making sure it reaches the edge of the pan.
4 Cook the frittata over a medium heat for 6–8 minutes, then carefully slide out on to a plate. Flip the frittata back into the pan (see Cook's Tip) and cook the other side for 2–4 minutes. Serve hot or warm, with a salad and some crusty bread.

COOK'S TIP If you don't want to try flipping the frittata, after 6 minutes' cooking time put the pan under a preheated grill for 2–3 minutes until the top is set.

SKATE WITH BLACK BUTTER AND ROCKET MASH

PREPARATION TIME: 40 minutes
COOKING TIME: 40 minutes
PER SERVING: 870cals, 56g fat, 65g carbohydrate

SERVES 6

1.8kg (4lb) floury potatoes, such as Maris Piper, peeled
   and cut into chunks
3 garlic cloves, peeled
200ml tub crème fraîche
2 x 100g bags rocket
125g (4oz) plain flour to dust
6 x 175g (6oz) skate wings
300g (11oz) butter
30 caper berries
6tbsp white wine vinegar
1 lemon, cut into wedges

1 Put the potatoes and garlic in a large pan of cold salted water, cover and bring to the boil. Cook for 15 minutes or until tender. Drain, return the potatoes and garlic to the pan, then add the crème fraîche and mash until smooth. Season well with salt and freshly ground black pepper. Chop 100g (3½oz) of the rocket and stir into the mash. Put the lid on to keep it warm.

2 Meanwhile, cook the skate. Preheat the oven to 140°C (120°C fan oven) mark 1. Put the flour on a plate and season well, then dip each skate wing into it, covering both sides evenly with flour.

3 Melt 125g (4oz) of the butter in a large frying pan and fry the skate over a medium heat, in batches of two, for 5 minutes on each side, making sure the butter doesn't burn. Put the skate wings on a baking sheet and keep them warm in the oven – but don't throw away the butter in the frying pan.

4 Add the remaining butter to the frying pan and melt over a gentle heat. Add the caper berries and wine vinegar and stir well until heated through. Season well and serve poured over the skate with a wedge of lemon, some rocket mash and the remaining rocket.

(Illustrated)

PORK ESCALOPES WITH DOUBLE CHEESE CRUST

PREPARATION TIME: 10 minutes
COOKING TIME: 10 minutes
PER SERVING: 400cals, 25g fat, 8g carbohydrate

SERVES 4

4 ready-sliced pork escalopes – around 125g (4oz) each
1½ slices white bread, processed into breadcrumbs
50g (2oz) strong tasty hard cheese, such as mature
   Cheddar or Gruyère, coarsely grated
25g (1oz) butter, melted
175g (6oz) soft goat's cheese, such as Chavroux
Lemon slices to serve

1 Put the escalopes between two sheets of clingfilm and bat out with a rolling pin. (Taking time to do this now cuts down on the cooking time and makes a larger surface for the cheese crust.) Season with plenty of freshly ground black pepper.

2 Mix together the breadcrumbs, grated cheese and melted butter.

3 Grill the pork for 3–4 minutes, fairly close to the heat, until it changes colour and feels firm. Spread the goat's cheese roughly over the pork, leaving it thick in places. Sprinkle the breadcrumb mixture on top and pop under the grill, slightly further away from the heat, for 3–4 minutes or until the cheese is bubbling and the breadcrumbs are golden. Serve each escalope with a slice of lemon.

CREAMY FISH GRATIN

PREPARATION TIME: 30 minutes
COOKING TIME: 1 hour 40 minutes
PER SERVING: 620cals, 38g fat, 19g carbohydrate

SERVES 8

125g (4oz) butter

175g (6oz) leeks, well washed and roughly chopped

450ml (¾ pint) fresh fish stock or good-quality liquid stock
    made up to 450ml (¾ pint)

300ml (½ pint) vermouth

4tbsp Pernod (see Cook's Tips)

350g (12oz) each monkfish and salmon fillet, cut into
    large pieces (see Cook's Tips)

225g (8oz) raw prawns, peeled and deveined

225g (8oz) raw scallops, halved

175g (6oz) onions, chopped

100g (3½oz) plain flour

142ml carton double cream

450ml (¾ pint) milk

75g (3oz) each Parmesan and Gruyère cheese, grated

1 level tbsp Dijon mustard

4 large eggs, separated

15g (½oz) coarse breadcrumbs

Fresh dill sprigs to garnish

1 Melt 25g (1oz) of the butter in a pan. Add the leeks and cook, stirring, for 4–5 minutes or until golden. Pour in the stock, vermouth and Pernod and bring to the boil. Add the monkfish and salmon and simmer for 2–3 minutes, then add the prawns and scallops and simmer for another 3 minutes. Remove the fish, reserve the liquor, and then wipe out the pan.

2 Add 50g (2oz) of the butter and the onions to the wiped-out pan and cook for 10 minutes or until soft and golden. Stir in 50g (2oz) of the flour and cook for another minute. Pour in the reserved poaching liquor and the cream, whisking to prevent lumps forming, then bring to the boil and bubble hard for 10 minutes. Season with salt and freshly ground black pepper. Put the fish and leeks in a 2.3 litre (4 pint) deep ovenproof dish, then pour the hot sauce over the top. Put to one side while you make the topping.

3 Melt 25g (1oz) of the butter in a large pan, add the remaining flour and cook, stirring, for 1 minute. Pour in the milk and, whisking continuously, bring the mixture to the boil; season. Stir in 125g (4oz) of the grated cheeses and the mustard. Cool slightly then stir in the egg yolks. Season well.

4 Preheat the oven to 190°C (170°C fan oven) mark 5. Whisk the egg whites in a clean grease-free bowl to a soft peak and fold into the sauce. Spoon the soufflé topping over the fish and sprinkle with the remaining cheeses and the breadcrumbs.

5 Cook for 1 hour–1 hour 10 minutes or until the soufflé has risen and the fish is piping hot (see Cook's Tips). Garnish with dill to serve.

TO FREEZE Complete the recipe to the end of step 2. Cool, wrap and freeze.
TO USE Complete the recipe, cooking for 1 hour 50 minutes.
VARIATION Omit the soufflé topping and serve the fish mixture topped with puff pastry, cooked at 200°C (180°C fan oven) mark 6 for 15–20 minutes, or with Croquette Potatoes (see page 72).
COOK'S TIPS If you have ouzo or Pastis use it instead of Pernod.
● As a cheaper alternative, try cod or haddock, when in season, or smoked fish or shelled mussels.
● To test if the gratin is cooked, insert a skewer into the fish mixture. Leave for 30 seconds. The skewer should be hot to the touch.

(Illustrated)

SMOKED HAM, LEEK AND MUSHROOM PIE

PREPARATION TIME: 40 minutes,
plus 30 minutes chilling
COOKING TIME: 55 minutes
PER SERVING: 760cals, 50g fat, 57g carbohydrate

SERVES 8

FOR THE PASTRY

300g (11oz) butter, at room temperature

1 whole egg

2 medium egg yolks

550g (1¼lb) plain flour, sifted

½ level tsp salt

FOR THE FILLING

50g (2oz) butter

450g (1lb) trimmed leeks, well washed and thinly sliced

225g (8oz) chestnut mushrooms, sliced

125g (4oz) Gruyère cheese, grated

50g (2oz) Parmesan cheese, grated

225g (8oz) sliced oak-smoked cooked ham, diced

4tbsp wholegrain mustard

200ml tub fromage frais

1 medium egg, beaten, to glaze

1 To make the pastry, put the butter, whole egg and yolks in a food processor and whiz until pale – it may look curdled but don't worry. Add the flour and salt and pulse until the mixture just comes together. Add 2–3tbsp of iced water, whiz for 1 second, then tip the dough out into a bowl and use your hands to bring the dough together. Divide in two, one slightly larger than the other. Wrap, cover and chill for 30 minutes.

2 Preheat the oven to 200°C (180°C fan oven) mark 6. Roll out the smaller piece of dough on greaseproof paper into a large rectangle measuring 23x28cm (9x11in). Gather up any trimmings, cover and put to one side. Slide the dough on to a baking sheet. Prick all over with a fork and bake for 10–15 minutes. Cool.

3 To make the filling, melt the butter in a frying pan, add the leeks and mushrooms and cook for about 10 minutes until soft. Stir in the cheeses, and season well with salt and freshly ground black pepper. Spread half of this mixture over the cooked pastry base, leaving a 1cm (½in) border around the edge. Cover with the ham.

4 Mix the mustard with the fromage frais, season, and spread over the ham. Top with the remaining leek and mushroom mixture. Lightly brush the edges with water.

5 Roll out the remaining dough on a large piece of greaseproof paper. This pastry is very short and crumbly so ask someone to help you lift the greaseproof on top of the pie. Use a palette knife to loosen the dough from the paper then carefully slide the paper out. Press the dough down to seal, then trim and put any excess to one side. Crimp the edges.

6 Roll out the spare pastry and cut out six or eight diamonds. Brush with a little water and put on top of the pie. Brush all over with beaten egg, then bake for 35 minutes until the pastry is golden and crisp. Serve the pie warm or cold.

STEAK AND ONION PUFF PIE

PREPARATION TIME: 5 minutes,
plus 30 minutes chilling
COOKING TIME: 2 hours 15 minutes
PER SERVING: 930cals, 51g fat, 63g carbohydrate

SERVES 4

3tbsp vegetable oil
2 onions, sliced
900g (2lb) casserole beef
3 level tbsp plain flour plus extra to dust
500ml (18fl oz) hot beef stock
2 fresh rosemary sprigs, bruised
500g pack puff pastry
1 medium egg, beaten, to glaze

1 Preheat the oven to 170°C (150°C fan oven) mark 3. Heat 1tbsp of the oil in a casserole dish and sauté the onions for 10 minutes or until golden. Lift out and put to one side.

2 In the same pan, sear the beef in batches until brown all over, using the rest of the oil as necessary. Lift out and put to one side.

3 Add the flour to the pan and cook for 1–2 minutes to brown. Return the onions and beef to the pan, add the hot stock and rosemary and season well with salt and freshly ground black pepper. Cover and bring to the boil, then cook in the oven for 1½ hours or until the meat is tender.

4 About 30 minutes before the end of the cooking time, lightly dust a surface with flour and roll out the puff pastry. Cut out the lid using a 1.1 litre (2 pint) deep pie dish or four 300ml (½ pint) dishes. Put on a baking sheet and chill for 30 minutes.

5 Remove the dish from the oven then increase the heat to 220°C (200°C fan oven) mark 7. Pour the beef mixture into the pie dish or dishes, brush the edge with water then put the pastry lid on top and press down lightly to seal the pie. Lightly score the top with a small sharp knife and brush with the beaten egg.

6 Put the dish back on the baking sheet and put back in the oven for 30 minutes or until the pastry has risen and is golden.

CRISP CHICKEN LIVER RISOTTO

PREPARATION TIME: 15 minutes
COOKING TIME: 40 minutes
PER SERVING: 920cals, 46g fat, 81g carbohydrate

SERVES 4

50g (2oz) Italian salami, sliced
225g (8oz) streaky bacon rashers, thinly sliced
100g (3½oz) butter
225g (8oz) fresh chicken livers, halved if large
225g (8oz) onions, roughly chopped
375g (12oz) risotto (arborio) rice
2 level tbsp tomato purée
1.4–1.7 litres (2½–3 pints) chicken or vegetable stock
200ml (7fl oz) white wine
2 level tbsp freshly chopped rosemary
25g (1oz) grated Parmesan cheese, plus extra to serve
Rosemary sprigs to garnish

1 Preheat the oven to 200°C (180°C fan oven) mark 6. Put the salami and bacon in an even layer in a large roasting tin and cook in the oven for 15–20 minutes or until crisp and brown. Drain on kitchen paper.

2 Meanwhile, melt 25g (1oz) of the butter in a large pan, add the livers and fry briskly for 2–3 minutes. Drain and put to one side, then wipe out the pan. Add the remaining butter to the pan and cook the onions over a medium heat for 10 minutes until soft. Stir in the rice and tomato purée and cook for 1 minute. Bring the stock and wine to the boil together and pour a ladleful of hot liquid into the rice. Bubble gently until absorbed, stirring. Keep adding stock, one ladle at a time stirring until each one is absorbed: this should take about 20 minutes – the risotto will become thick and creamy and the rice tender. Add more stock if the risotto looks dry (the amount needed will vary depending on the absorbency of the rice).

3 To serve, discard any juices from the chicken livers, then add to the risotto with the chopped rosemary and Parmesan cheese. Break the crisp salami and bacon into pieces and add to the pan and season with salt and freshly ground black pepper. Stir for 1 minute over the heat, then garnish with rosemary sprigs to serve.

BAKED COUSCOUS WITH SPICED CHICKEN

PREPARATION TIME: 15 minutes,
plus minimum 20 minutes marinating
COOKING TIME: 25–30 minutes
PER SERVING: 620cals, 28g fat, 60g carbohydrate

SERVES 6

12 boneless, skinless chicken thighs (see Cook's Tip)

3 level tbsp medium-hot curry powder

2 level tbsp paprika

1 level tsp ground cinnamon

10 garlic cloves, crushed

6tbsp olive oil

450g (1lb) – or 600ml (1 pint) in a measuring jug –
     couscous

600ml (1 pint) hot chicken or vegetable stock

50g (2oz) sultanas

75g (3oz) butter, diced

5tbsp fresh coriander, roughly chopped

1 Put the chicken into an ovenproof dish and season generously with salt and freshly ground black pepper. Add the curry powder, spices, garlic and oil and mix well. Cover and leave to marinate, chilled, for at least 20 minutes and up to 24 hours.

2 Preheat the oven to 200°C (180°C fan oven) mark 6. Put the couscous into an ovenproof serving dish and cover with the stock. Add 1 level tsp salt, stir and leave for 5 minutes to allow the liquid to be absorbed.

3 Bake the chicken for 5 minutes. Meanwhile, add the sultanas to the couscous and dot the butter over the top. Cover with foil and bake on the shelf below the chicken for a further 20–25 minutes until the chicken is cooked right through.

4 To serve, add the chicken and juices to the couscous and mix, then sprinkle the coriander on top. To keep the dish warm, cover with foil, reduce the oven temperature to 150°C (130°C fan oven) mark 2 and leave the dish in the oven for 10 minutes.

COOK'S TIP Buy chicken thighs with bones and skin on, saving a few extra pennies, and allow more preparation time.

(Illustrated)

RED SPICED LAMB

PREPARATION TIME: 5 minutes
COOKING TIME: 2 hours 25 minutes
PER SERVING: 400cals, 25g fat, 4g carbohydrate

SERVES 6

2.5cm (1in) piece fresh root ginger, peeled and roughly
    chopped
8 garlic cloves, crushed
225g (8oz) onion, roughly chopped
4tbsp oil
1.1kg (2½lb) boned leg of lamb or stewing beef, cut into
    4cm (1½in) cubes
10 cardamom pods
2 bay leaves
6 whole cloves
10 peppercorns
2.5m (1in) stick cinnamon
1 level tsp coriander seeds
2 level tsp cumin seeds
4 level tsp ground paprika
1 level tsp cayenne pepper
6 level tbsp natural yogurt
600–750ml (1–1¼ pints) lamb or beef stock
1 level tsp salt

1. Pour 4tbsp of water into a blender or food processor, add the ginger, garlic and onion and whiz until smooth.
2. Preheat the oven to 180°C (160°C fan oven) mark 4. Heat the oil in a large flameproof casserole and brown the meat in small batches (see Cook's Tips) then put to one side. Add a little more oil if necessary and stir in the cardamom pods, bay leaves, cloves, peppercorns and cinnamon. Cook until the cloves begin to swell and the bay leaves to colour, then add the onion paste and cook, stirring all the time, for 4 minutes, or until most of the liquid has evaporated. Add the remaining spices, the meat and juices and cook, stirring, for 1 minute. Add the yogurt a spoonful at a time, cooking and stirring after each addition. Stir in just enough stock to cover the meat. Add the salt and bring to the boil.
3. Cover and cook in the oven for 1½–2 hours or until the meat is very tender. Spoon off any excess fat before serving.

COOK'S TIPS The meat should be well browned, so that the juices have a rich, dark colour. Frying the onion paste gives the sauce body and rich colour.
● When serving, warn your guests to watch out for the whole spices.

RICE AND LENTIL PILAF

PREPARATION TIME: 10 minutes
COOKING TIME: 40 minutes, plus 10 minutes resting
PER SERVING: 340cals, 8g fat, 59g carbohydrate

SERVES 6

50g (2oz) butter
225g (8oz) onion, finely chopped
1 level tsp cumin seeds
350g (12oz) basmati rice, rinsed and drained
600ml (1 pint) chicken stock
420g can lentils or chick peas, drained and rinsed

1. Heat the butter in a large heavy-based pan. Add the onion and cook for 5–7 minutes or until golden and soft. Add the cumin seeds and 1 level tsp salt and cook for a further minute. Add the rice and cook, stirring, for 2–3 minutes or until all the grains are coated in butter.
2. Add the stock and lentils or chick peas. Bring to the boil, cover tightly and simmer gently for 20–25 minutes. Remove from the heat and leave to rest, covered, for another 10 minutes.
3. Adjust the seasoning and serve.

CROQUETTE POTATOES

PREPARATION TIME: 10 minutes,
plus at least 4 hours chilling
COOKING TIME: 30 minutes
PER SERVING: 140cals, 8g fat, 14g carbohydrate

MAKES ABOUT 16

700g (1½lb) large floury potatoes, cut into large chunks
4tbsp milk
25g (1oz) butter
4 large eggs
2 level tbsp each freshly chopped chives and parsley or
   tarragon
50g (2oz) plain flour
125g (4oz) white breadcrumbs
Butter and oil for frying

1 Cook the potatoes in boiling salted water until tender, then drain and dry well. Mash with the milk and butter and season generously with salt and freshly ground black pepper.
2 Lightly beat two of the eggs and add to the mash with the chopped herbs. Put the mixture in a rectangular 16x25.5cm (6½x10in) non-stick tin, cover carefully and chill for at least 4 hours or overnight.
3 Divide the mixture into about 16, then roll into little barrel shapes. Put the flour in a shallow bowl and season well. Beat the remaining eggs in another shallow bowl. Roll each croquette first in the flour, then in the beaten egg and then in the breadcrumbs.
4 Fry in batches in a mixture of butter and oil until the croquettes are golden brown. Drain on kitchen paper. Keep them warm while you cook the remaining croquettes.

TO FREEZE Complete the recipe; leave the croquettes to cool. Open-freeze, then wrap and put back in the freezer.
TO USE Put the croquettes on a cooling rack over a baking sheet and cook from frozen at 200°C (180°C fan oven) mark 6 for about 25 minutes.

SPICED POTATOES

PREPARATION TIME: 5 minutes
COOKING TIME: 1 hour
PER SERVING: 150cals, 8g fat, 20g carbohydrate

SERVES 6

2 level tbsp coriander seeds
1 level tbsp black peppercorns
2tsp mustard seeds
700g (1½lb) potatoes, unpeeled, cut into large chunks
Around 3tbsp olive oil
2 spring onions, chopped

1 Coarsely crush the coriander, peppercorns and mustard seeds in a pestle and mortar or a strong bowl with the end of a rolling pin.
2 Cook the potatoes in boiling salted water until just tender, then drain well.
3 Preheat the oven to 200°C (180°C fan oven) mark 6. Fry the crushed spices in oil for 1 minute. Add the hot potatoes, some coarse sea salt and the spring onions and mix well.
4 Put in a shallow ovenproof serving dish and cook for about 40 minutes, or until beginning to crisp. Serve immediately.

CARROTS WITH CUMIN AND ORANGE

PREPARATION TIME: 10 minutes

COOKING TIME: 10 minutes

PER SERVING: 40cals, trace fat, 8g carbohydrate

SERVES 6

200ml (7fl oz) hot chicken or vegetable stock

Finely grated zest and juice of 1 orange

1 level tbsp golden caster sugar

2 level tsp cumin seeds

450g (1lb) spring carrots, trimmed and cut in half lengthways

1 bay leaf

1 Put the stock in a pan, and add the orange zest and juice, sugar and cumin seeds. Add the carrots, bay leaf and stock to the pan, cover and simmer for 5 minutes.

2 Remove the lid and cook for a further 5 minutes until the carrots are tender and all the liquid is absorbed. Serve garnished with the bay leaf.

(Illustrated)

CELERIAC DAUPHINOISE

PREPARATION TIME: 20 minutes

COOKING TIME: 1 hour 25 minutes

PER SERVING: 380cals, 28g fat, 26g carbohydrate

SERVES 6

700g (1½lb) potatoes, peeled and thinly sliced

450g (1lb) celeriac, peeled and thinly sliced

2 bay leaves

568ml carton milk

2 garlic cloves, crushed

284ml carton double cream

25g (1oz) diced butter

1 Put the potatoes and celeriac in a large pan with the bay leaves and milk. Bring just to the boil, reduce the heat and cook for 5–8 minutes until tender. Drain, then discard the milk and bay leaves.

2 Preheat the oven to 180°C (160°C fan oven) mark 4. Season the potatoes and celeriac well, then arrange in layers in a buttered 1.4 litre (2½ pint) gratin dish. Add the garlic and cream and dot with the butter. Cover with foil and bake for 1 hour. Remove the foil and bake for another 15–20 minutes, until golden, then serve.

SAVOY CABBAGE

PREPARATION TIME: 5 minutes

COOKING TIME: 5 minutes

PER SERVING: 100cals, 7g fat, 7g carbohydrate

SERVES 4

½ Savoy cabbage, washed and shredded

25g (1oz) butter or 2tbsp groundnut oil

FOR THE DRESSING

150g (5oz) pan-fried lardons

3 level tbsp toasted pinenuts

OR

1 level tbsp sesame seeds

1tbsp light soy sauce

1 Stir-fry the cabbage in the butter or oil for 5 minutes, then season generously with salt and freshly ground black pepper.

2 Add one of the following:
Add the lardons and pinenuts, drizzle with the balsamic vinegar and serve.
Or sprinkle with the sesame seeds, drizzle over the soy sauce and serve.

GOLDEN PASSION FRUIT TART

PREPARATION TIME: 10 minutes,
plus 1 hour chilling
COOKING TIME: 1 hour 25 minutes,
plus 2 hours chilling
PER SERVING: 500cals, 32g fat, 49g carbohydrate

SERVES 8

8 large, ripe passion fruit
225g (8oz) plain flour
50g (2oz) golden icing sugar
Finely grated zest of 1 orange
150g (5oz) butter, diced and chilled
5 large eggs
150g (5oz) golden caster sugar
200ml (7fl oz) double cream
Mango and Citrus Sauce to serve (see below)
Whipped cream to serve

MANGO AND CITRUS SAUCE

PREPARATION TIME: 20 minutes
PER SERVING: 30cals, 0g fat, 7g carbohydrate

2 large, ripe mangoes, peeled and flesh roughly chopped
1 orange, peeled and flesh chopped
Juice of 1 lemon

1 Halve the passion fruit, scoop out the flesh and put to one side.
2 To make the pastry, put the flour, icing sugar and the grated orange zest in a food processor with the butter. Whiz until the mixture resembles fine crumbs. Lightly beat one egg and add all but 1tbsp to the pastry mixture. (Cover and chill the remaining beaten egg.) Pulse until the mixture comes together in a ball. Wrap in clingfilm and chill for 30 minutes. Roll the dough out on a lightly floured surface and use to line a 23cm (9in) fluted loose-bottomed tart tin. Prick the base well and line with greaseproof paper and baking beans. Chill for 30 minutes. Preheat the oven to 200°C (180°C fan oven) mark 6.
3 Bake the tart case for 10 minutes, then remove the paper and beans and cook for a further 10 minutes. Brush with the reserved beaten egg to seal the base, and cook for a further 2 minutes.
4 Wipe out the food processor, add the passion fruit pulp and the caster sugar, then whiz for 1 minute or until the flesh comes away from the seeds. With the machine running, add the remaining four eggs and the double cream, then strain through a fine sieve. Fill the tart case with the passion fruit mixture and bake at 140°C (120°C fan oven) mark 1 for 1 hour or until the filling has just set in the middle. Set aside to cool, then chill for 2 hours.
5 Leave the tart to cool – the passion fruit mixture will firm further on cooling, then serve with the Mango and Citrus Sauce and whipped cream.

TO FREEZE Complete the recipe to the end of step 3. Cool, pack and freeze.
TO USE Thaw overnight at cool room temperature and complete the recipe from step 4.

Put the mango and orange flesh in a food processor and pulse until smooth, then sieve. Add lemon juice to taste and serve with the Golden Passion Fruit Tart.

TO FREEZE Complete the recipe. Cool, pack and freeze.
TO USE Thaw the sauce overnight at cool room temperature.

LIME MERINGUE TARTS

PREPARATION TIME: 50 minutes,
plus 30 minutes chilling
COOKING TIME: 40 minutes
PER SERVING: 580cals, 33g fat, 62g carbohydrate

SERVES 6

FOR THE PASTRY

75g (3oz) unsalted butter, diced and chilled, plus
    extra to grease
125g (4oz) plain flour, sifted, plus extra to dust
50g (2oz) pistachio nuts
50g (2oz) golden icing sugar
2 medium eggs

FOR THE FILLING

4 medium eggs
Grated zest and juice of 5 limes – around 150ml (¼ pint)
    juice
200g (7oz) golden caster sugar
142ml carton double cream

1 Grease and flour six 8 x 2.5cm (3¼ x 1in) tartlet tins. To make the pastry, whiz the pistachios in a food processor for 30 seconds. Add the flour, a pinch of salt and the butter and pulse until the mixture resembles crumbs. Add the icing sugar and pulse to mix. Separate the eggs, put one egg white to one side for the meringue and freeze the other for future use. Add the yolks to the mixture and pulse until it just holds together.

2 Turn the dough on to a lightly floured surface and knead gently to bring the mixture together. Roll out the pastry and use to line the tins, pressing well into the edges. Trim off excess pastry. Cover with clingfilm and chill for 30 minutes. Preheat the oven to 190°C (170°C fan oven) mark 5.

3 Put the tins on a baking sheet, line with greaseproof paper and fill with baking beans. Bake for 10 minutes. Remove the paper and beans and bake for 10–12 minutes until just cooked. Remove from the oven.

4 Meanwhile, make the filling: separate three of the eggs and freeze the whites for future use. Put the remaining egg and the three yolks into a small pan, add the lime zest and juice, 150g (5oz) of the caster sugar and the cream. Cook over a medium heat for 5 minutes, stirring regularly, until the custard has thickened and is smooth. Pour the filling into a large bowl and allow to cool.

5 Lower the oven temperature to 180°C (160°C fan oven) mark 4. Spoon the lime filling into the pastry cases. Put the one reserved egg white into a clean grease-free bowl and whisk until it stands in stiff peaks. Add the remaining sugar a little at a time and continue to beat until the mixture is stiff and shiny. Put into a piping bag fitted with a round 1cm (½in) nozzle and pipe around the edge of the tarts. Bake the tarts for 10 minutes or until the meringue is firm to the touch. Serve warm or cold.

(Illustrated)

SQUIDGY CHOCOLATE AND BANANA ROLL

PREPARATION TIME: 25 minutes

COOKING TIME: 25 minutes

PER SLICE: 440cals, 29g fat, 36g carbohydrate

SERVES 6

4 level tbsp cocoa powder, sifted

150ml (¼ pint) milk

4 medium eggs, separated

125g (4oz) golden caster sugar plus 2 level tbsp to dust

250g tub mascarpone cheese

1tbsp maple syrup

3tbsp double cream

1 banana, sliced

1tsp vanilla extract

1 Line a 33x23cm (13x9in) Swiss roll tin with baking parchment.

2 Mix the cocoa powder with 3tbsp of the milk to form a paste. Heat the remaining milk in a small pan, then slowly pour on to the cocoa paste and stir together to combine evenly. Cool for 10 minutes. Preheat the oven to 180°C (160°C fan oven) mark 4.

3 Whisk the egg yolks with 125g (4oz) sugar in a freestanding mixer until pale, thickened and mousse-like. Gradually whisk in the cooling chocolate milk.

4 Whisk the egg whites in a clean grease-free bowl until stiffly peaking. Gently fold one third into the chocolate mixture, to loosen slightly, then fold in the remainder.

5 Turn into the prepared Swiss roll tin and bake for 25 minutes until the mixture has risen and is just firm to the touch. Turn out on to a sheet of baking parchment dusted with 2 level tbsp of golden caster sugar and remove the baking parchment. Cover with a warm damp clean tea towel to prevent the sponge from drying out. (You can keep it like this for up to 8 hours.)

6 Put the mascarpone into a bowl, stir in the maple syrup and cream. Put the bananas into a small bowl, pour on the vanilla extract and stir to mix.

7 Remove the tea towel from the chocolate sponge and, using a palette knife, spread half the mascarpone cream over the sponge. Sprinkle on the banana. Starting at the shortest edge and, using the paper underneath to help you, gently roll up the chocolate sponge. Slide on to the serving plate and eat within 3 hours, with the rest of the mascarpone cream.

RHUBARB AND CINNAMON PIE

PREPARATION TIME: 15 minutes

COOKING TIME: 50 minutes

PER SERVING: 570cals, 26g fat, 83g carbohydrate

SERVES 4

175g (6oz) plain flour

125g (4oz) butter

150g (5oz) golden caster sugar

700g (1½lb) rhubarb, washed and cut into bite-sized chunks

2 level tbsp cornflour

½ level tsp cinnamon

A little milk and sugar for glazing

Vanilla ice cream to serve

1 Put the flour, butter and 25g (1oz) of the sugar in a processor and whiz until the pastry comes together to form a ball. If it is slightly sticky, roll in some flour and chill for 20 minutes or until it is firm enough to handle.

2 Roll out the pastry into a large circle, making sure you leave the edges ragged and uneven. It should be large enough to line a 23cm (9in) round greased ovenproof dish with sides at least 5cm (2in) deep, and to allow the edges of the pastry to drape over the sides of the dish.

3 Preheat the oven to 200°C (180°C fan oven) mark 6. Toss the rhubarb in the remaining sugar, the cornflour and cinnamon and spoon into the dish. Bring the pastry edges up and over the fruit, leaving a gap in the centre to reveal the filling. Glaze with milk and sprinkle with sugar.

4 Put on a baking sheet and bake for about 50 minutes or until the pastry is golden brown and the juice is bubbling up around the pastry. Serve hot with ice cream.

PASSION FRUIT CREME CARAMEL

PREPARATION TIME: 10 minutes

COOKING TIME: 1 hour,

plus minimum 2 hours chilling

PER SERVING: 320cals, 18g fat, 34g carbohydrate

SERVES 6

A little butter to grease

4 large eggs plus 1 large yolk

175g (6oz) golden caster sugar

142ml carton double cream

150ml (¼ pint) full-fat milk

10 large passion fruit

1 Preheat the oven to 150°C (130°C fan oven) mark 2. Grease six 150ml (¼ pint) dariole moulds. Whisk together the eggs, yolk and 100g (3½ oz) of the sugar. Add the cream and milk and mix well to make a custard. Strain into a large jug. Halve six of the passion fruit and scoop out the flesh to make 150ml (¼ pint) pulp. Add to the custard and mix together.

2 Put the remaining sugar into a small pan and add 3tbsp of cold water. Heat gently, stirring from time to time to dissolve the sugar, then bring to the boil over a medium heat, cooking to a pale golden syrup. Reduce the heat a little and boil steadily for around 5 minutes until a dark brown caramel forms. Add 2tbsp of cold water – stand well back as the caramel splutters. When this stops, pour the caramel into the dariole moulds, then pour the custard on top.

3 Put the moulds in a roasting tin and half-fill with boiling water. Cover the tin with foil and bake for 50 minutes until the custards are firm. Leave in the tin with the water to cool, then remove and chill for at least 2 hours.

4 Slice each of the remaining passion fruit into six wedges. Turn out the caramels and serve with passion fruit wedges.

(Illustrated)

CINNAMON AND NUTMEG ICE CREAM

PREPARATION TIME: 10 minutes

COOKING TIME: 5 minutes

FREEZING TIME: 6 hours

PER SERVING: 290cals, 24g fat, 17g carbohydrate

SERVES 8

½ level tsp each ground cinnamon and nutmeg

50g (2oz) golden caster sugar

142ml carton double cream

250g (9oz) tub mascarpone cheese

400g carton fresh custard sauce

1 Put the cinnamon, nutmeg, sugar and cream in a small pan. Bring slowly to the boil, then put to one side to cool.

2 Put the mascarpone in a large bowl and beat until smooth.

3 Stir in the fresh custard sauce and the cooled spiced cream. Pour the mixture into a shallow freezer container and freeze for 2–3 hours. Beat to break up the ice crystals and freeze for a further 2–3 hours before using. (The ice cream will keep in the freezer for up to one month.)

CARDAMOM AND PISTACHIO ICE CREAM

PREPARATION TIME: 10 minutes

COOKING TIME: 10 minutes

FREEZING TIME: 6 hours

PER SERVING: 460cals, 24g fat, 47g carbohydrate

SERVES 6

50g (2oz) shelled pistachio nuts

3 litres (5¼ pints) whole milk

14 cardamom pods

125g (4oz) golden caster sugar

1 Preheat a grill and toast the pistachios, cool, then roughly chop. Cover and put to one side. Put the milk and cardamom pods in a large heavy-based pan. Bring to the boil, then simmer vigorously until reduced to 750ml (1¾ pints). Strain the milk, discarding the cardamom, and stir in the sugar and nuts.

2 Cool quickly and freeze the mixture in an ice-cream machine or pour into a freezeproof container, cover and freeze. Allow to stand at room temperature for 30 minutes before serving.

APRIL

*With the daffodils in full bloom, the buds bursting
on the trees and the days growing ever longer, this is an
exciting month of change*

APRIL SEES THE ARRIVAL OF ONE OF the greatest foods produced in the UK, and one of the few farmed meats in which seasons really do matter: new season's lamb, or spring lamb as it is sometimes called. The strong taste and relatively dark, chewy flesh of last month's lamb – from animals around a year old – gives way to pink, tender meat with a delicate flavour that's sometimes appreciated even by people who think they don't like lamb. See the box on page 83 for more information.

Fish

April is also the first month for another great seasonal delicacy, wild salmon or sea trout. Salmon is farmed so extensively all year round that we can forget it has a natural life-cycle, and the wild variety is vastly superior in taste, leanness and texture: once you've made the comparison, you will see this instantly. The problem is scarcity, which translates into expense. Wild salmon are threatened by all manner of perils, from poaching to pollution, and it's increasingly hard to find them. The cost at the beginning of the season is always high, but usually comes down somewhat if there are good supplies. If supplies are low, the price will stay high right until the season's end in August. Sea trout is less highly prized than wild salmon, but unjustly so: this is a magnificent fish which can be treated in any way you would treat salmon, and doesn't cost nearly as much. Buy it whenever you spot it. Both wild salmon and sea trout will make the Herby Salmon Fishcakes on page 92 taste even

Left: Herb-Scented Lamb with Balsamic Dressing (see page 90)

INGREDIENTS
OF THE MONTH

FISH
Crab
Flounder
Hake
Mackerel
Plaice
Prawns
Salmon
Sole
Trout

VEGETABLES
Broccoli
Carrots
Chicory
Leeks

New potatoes
Spinach
Sweet potatoes
Watercress

FRUIT
Apples
Bananas
Grapefruit
Grapes
Lemons
Limes
Rhubarb

BEST BUY
Spring lamb

more delicious. The other fishy star of the month is crab, which is now reappearing and ranks among the best things that seafood lovers can buy. If you want to cook with them, buy live crabs from a good fishmonger who regularly gets in fresh supplies. Crabs should be lively on the fishmonger's slab, and should feel heavy for their weight. Hen crabs have more white meat than cock crabs, and can be identified by picking them up and turning them over. The 'apron' on the belly of a hen crab is shaped like a V, while on cock crabs it has a long, pointed shape. Eat them on their own, with lemon or mayonnaise, or use them in a dish like the Crab and Tomato Soup on page 86.

Vegetables

As far as veg are concerned, the April supplies will be dominated mostly by the same things that were good in March: broccoli (including purple sprouting – try it stir-fried, see page 95), carrots, leeks and various imports from Europe and north Africa. Cauliflower may also be of prime quality, and English spinach will be coming on the scene as the month wears on. Another candidate to consider is asparagus. You will probably have noticed asparagus in the markets all year round, with imports coming from as far away as Peru. Purists rightly reject them, waiting for next month's beginning of the English asparagus season, but it's possible, if you really love this vegetable, to make an exception for imports from Spain. They start in early- or mid-April, and they are sometimes very good. There may also be really good courgettes appearing in the markets now, and sweet potatoes for cooking indoors or out, as in the Barbecued Sweet Potato Wedges on page 97.

Fruit

Fruit supplies will also be dominated by imports. Oranges are likely to be past their best, but other citrus fruits

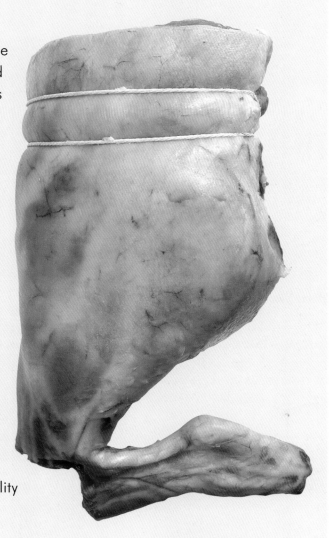

are good: you may be able to use grapefruit in place of oranges for some recipes.

The chief UK fruit this month is the first of the outdoor rhubarb, put to excellent use in Rhubarb and Apple Cobbler (page 100).

SPRING LAMB

Much of the best lamb comes from the southwest counties and from Wales, and these will probably be among the first areas supplying butchers with new season's lamb. Most good supermarkets will be selling it, but it's really worth looking around for small specialist suppliers. Supermarkets tend not to get the best meat in any case, and with a product capable of such distinction it is worth finding the best. Mail-order firms, selling direct from a farm or from a group of local farms, are often the best place to shop.

Some have a minimum order too large for many people's needs, so you should consider splitting your order with friends. If you like looking at meat before you buy, choose lamb that has a delicate pink colour in the flesh and fat that's creamy or ivory rather than yellow. The delicacy of spring lamb – and the expense, it has to be said – makes it more suitable for fairly simple treatment which allows the quality of the main ingredient to show through.

PRAWN, GRAPEFRUIT AND WATERCRESS SALAD

PREPARATION TIME: 15 minutes,
plus minimum 2 hours marinating
PER SERVING: 320cals, 30g fat, 5g carbohydrate

SERVES 4

2 pink grapefruit

1 level tsp French mustard

9tbsp olive oil

5–6 cooked prawns per person, approximately
   175g (6oz) total weight

2 bunches – around 100g (½oz) – watercress, washed
   and drained

1 Remove the zest from the grapefruit. Put in a small pan of cold water and bring to the boil. Drain and put to one side. Holding the grapefruit over a bowl to catch the juice, carefully cut the pith from the fruit with a sharp serrated-edged knife. Cut the flesh into segments by cutting down between the flesh and the membrane, then squeeze the central membrane to extract the juice. Put the grapefruit segments and juice to one side.

2 Put the mustard and some salt and freshly ground black pepper in a small bowl and add 6tbsp of the grapefruit juice. Whisk together well. Whisk in the oil. Spoon 4tbsp of the dressing over the prawns, then cover and leave to marinate in the fridge for at least 2 hours or overnight.

3 Toss together the watercress, grapefruit segments, strips of zest, prawns and remainder of the dressing. Serve immediately.

TO PREPARE AHEAD Complete the recipe to the end of step 2 up to one day ahead. Cover and keep chilled.
TO USE Complete the recipe.

(Illustrated)

THAI CHICKEN WONTONS

PREPARATION TIME: 15 minutes
COOKING TIME: 5 minutes
PER SERVING FOR 12: 140cals, 6g fat,
11g carbohydrate
PER SERVING FOR 14: 120cals, 5g fat,
9g carbohydrate

SERVES 12–14

3 large red chillies, finely chopped

3 kaffir lime leaves, finely chopped

6 spring onions, finely chopped

2 x 15cm (6in) lemongrass stalks, finely chopped

450g (1lb) boneless, skinless chicken fillet, roughly
   chopped

Small handful fresh coriander sprigs

3 garlic cloves, crushed

3tbsp coconut milk

225g (8oz) filo pastry

1 large egg, beaten

Oil for frying

Sweet chilli dipping sauce to serve

1 Put the chillies, lime leaves, spring onions, lemongrass and chicken in a food processor with the coriander, garlic and coconut milk and season with salt and freshly ground black pepper. Whiz for 2–3 minutes.

2 Cut the filo into thirty 15cm (6in) squares (see Cook's Tips). Keep the filo squares covered with clingfilm as you work on each one. Brush each square with the beaten egg. Put 2 level tsp of the chicken mixture in the centre of each square. Scrunch the edges together roughly to seal. Set aside while you complete the remaining wontons.

3 Deep-fry the wontons in the oil for 4–5 minutes (see Cook's Tips) or until they are pale golden brown and cooked through, then drain on kitchen paper. Pile the wontons up on a serving dish and serve with the Sweet Chilli Dipping Sauce. Alternatively, cool and leave for up to 1 hour.

COOK'S TIPS Look for packets of fresh Thai herbs, containing chillies, lemongrass and coriander.
● Filo pastry comes in several sizes. Cut squares accurately to waste as little pastry as possible.
● Keep the wontons well apart in the hot oil so that they do not stick together.
● Freeze leftover coconut milk for up to three months.

CRAB AND TOMATO SOUP

PREPARATION TIME: 40 minutes

COOKING TIME: 45 minutes

PER SERVING: 300cals, 18g fat, 25g carbohydrate

SERVES 6

1 dressed crab – around 200g (7oz) (see Cook's Tip)

4tbsp olive oil

125g (4oz) onion, chopped

1 stick celery, chopped

4tbsp port

1.1 litres (2 pints) vegetable stock

550g bottle or carton passata or creamed tomatoes

3 level tbsp mayonnaise

1 level tsp tomato ketchup

1 garlic clove, crushed

A few drops each of Tabasco sauce and Worcestershire sauce

1 small French stick, thinly sliced and toasted on one side

50g (2oz) Emmenthal cheese, grated

Single cream to garnish

1 Separate the white and brown crab meat and put to one side. Roughly crush the shell.

2 Heat 2tbsp of the oil in a large pan, add the crab shell and the onion and celery and cook for 5 minutes, stirring all the time. Add the port and bring to the boil. Bubble until all the liquid has evaporated. Pour in the stock and passata or creamed tomatoes and bring to the boil. Add the brown crab meat, then simmer, covered for 30 minutes.

3 Strain the crab stock through a sieve, pressing to extract the juices. Discard the shell and vegetables.

4 Wipe out the pan, return the soup and bring back to the boil. Whisk in the mayonnaise, tomato ketchup, garlic, a few drops of Tabasco and Worcestershire sauce and season with salt and freshly ground black pepper.

5 Drizzle the remaining oil over the untoasted sides of the bread and sprinkle with the grated cheese. Cook under the grill until bubbling.

6 Stir the flaked white crab meat into the soup and heat through for 1–2 minutes. Ladle the hot soup into warmed, ovenproof bowls, garnish with a swirl of single cream, float the warm croûtes on top and serve.

COOK'S TIP Dressed crabs are available in most supermarkets, with the white and dark meat neatly separated

BAKED EGGS WITH THYME AND GARLIC

PREPARATION TIME: 10 minutes

COOKING TIME: 25 minutes

PER SERVING: 310cals, 29g fat, 3g carbohydrate

SERVES 4

142ml carton double cream

4 fresh thyme sprigs

4 garlic cloves, peeled

Few strands of saffron (optional)

125g (4oz) onions, finely chopped

25g (1oz) butter plus extra for baking

4 large eggs

Fresh thyme sprigs to garnish

Garlic bread to serve

1 In a small pan, heat the cream to simmering point with two of the thyme sprigs, the garlic and saffron, if using. Take off the heat and leave to infuse for 10 minutes.

2 Preheat the oven to 170°C (150°C fan oven) mark 3. Meanwhile, fry the onions in the butter with the remaining thyme for 7–10 minutes or until the onions are very soft. Season with salt and freshly ground black pepper, then spoon into four ovenproof cups or dishes. Crack an egg into each, then top each yolk with a knob of butter. Cook in the oven for 10 minutes.

3 Strain the cream and season. Pour over the eggs and cook for a further 4–5 minutes.

4 Garnish with the thyme and serve with garlic bread.

CARROT ROULADE WITH
EGG AND WATERCRESS MAYONNAISE

PREPARATION TIME: 15 minutes

COOKING TIME: 20 minutes

PER SERVING: 640cals, 59g fat, 9g carbohydrate

SERVES 6

FOR THE ROULADE

2tbsp freshly grated Parmesan cheese

1tbsp freshly chopped coriander plus extra leaves to
    decorate

125g (4oz) butter

700g (1½lb) carrots, peeled and finely grated

6 medium eggs, separated

FOR THE FILLING

6 medium eggs, hard-boiled

2 bunches watercress, washed and stalks removed

200g (7oz) good-quality mayonnaise

1 Preheat the oven to 200°C (180°C fan oven) mark 6. Line a 33x23cm (13x9in) Swiss roll tin with baking parchment. Sprinkle the Parmesan over the top and arrange the coriander leaves on top.

2 Melt the butter in a frying pan, add the carrots, and cook gently for about 10 minutes, until soft. Drain in a sieve. Transfer to a bowl and beat in the egg yolks, then season with salt and freshly ground black pepper.

3 Whisk the egg whites in a clean grease-free bowl until stiff, and fold into the carrot mixture with the chopped coriander. Spoon into the prepared tin, spreading the mixture evenly with a palette knife. Bake for 10–12 minutes, until golden and springy to the touch.

4 To make the filling, chop the eggs, and finely chop one bunch of the watercress. Mix with the mayonnaise and season to taste. Turn the roulade out on to a sheet of greaseproof paper. Spread the egg mayonnaise over, leaving a 1cm (½in) border around the edge.

5 Starting from one of the shorter sides, and using the paper to help, roll the roulade up. (See Cook's Tip.)

6 To serve, trim the edges and cut into six thick slices. Put, cut-side up, on a serving plate and garnish with the remaining bunch of watercress.

COOK'S TIP If you chill the roulade for about 20 minutes before serving it will be easier to slice. This can be done in advance – keep the slices covered in the fridge, and remove 10 minutes before serving.

WARM GOAT'S CHEESE AND SMOKED SALMON CROUTES

PREPARATION TIME: 20 minutes
COOKING TIME: 12 minutes
PER SERVING: 210cals, 11g fat, 14g carbohydrate

SERVES 6

75g (3oz) ricotta cheese
75g (3oz) soft goat's cheese
Grated zest of 1 lemon
1 large egg, beaten
6 slices French bread – each around 1cm (½in) thick (see Cook's Tip)
2tbsp olive oil
6 slices smoked salmon – around 200g (7oz) total weight
2 level tbsp freshly chopped chives
Salad leaves drizzled with olive oil and balsamic vinegar to serve
Grated lemon zest and lemon wedges to garnish

1 Put the cheeses, lemon zest and egg in a bowl. Season with freshly ground black pepper and beat together. Drizzle the French bread with half the oil and place under a hot grill for 1–2 minutes until golden, then turn over and repeat on the other side.

2 Preheat the oven to 200°C (180°C fan oven) mark 6. Twist the slices of smoked salmon and place one on each croûte, then top with the goat's cheese mixture.

3 Cook for 6 minutes or until the salmon is hot. Place under a preheated grill for 1–2 minutes to brown. Sprinkle with chives and serve immediately with the dressed salad leaves and garnished with grated lemon zest and lemon wedges.

TO PREPARE AHEAD Complete the recipe to the end of step 2 up to 12 hours ahead. Cover and chill.
TO SERVE Complete the recipe.
COOK'S TIP To save time, use ready-made garlic bread instead of making the croûtes. If you decide to do this, simply omit the French bread and the oil.

(Illustrated)

PARSLEY, WALNUT AND ORANGE CHICKEN

PREPARATION TIME: 15 minutes
COOKING TIME: 40 minutes
PER SERVING: 550cals, 45g fat, 4g carbohydrate

SERVES 6

9tbsp extra-virgin olive oil
125g (4oz) onion, finely chopped
75g (3oz) walnuts, finely chopped
Grated zest and juice of 1 large orange
6 level tbsp freshly chopped parsley
1 level tbsp cranberry sauce
1 large egg, beaten
6 chicken breasts, with skin
1 level tbsp Dijon mustard
Fresh herbs sprigs to garnish

1 Heat 3tbsp of the oil in a small pan and add the onion. Cover and cook for 10 minutes or until soft, then cool. In a bowl, combine the walnuts, orange zest, parsley, cranberry sauce and beaten egg and season well with salt and freshly ground black pepper. Stir in the cooled onion mixture and put to one side.

2 Preheat the oven to 200°C (180°C fan oven) mark 6. Gently ease up the chicken skin over the breast and push in the stuffing. Re-shape the chicken and put in a large roasting tin. Spread with the mustard and season. Drizzle over 2tbsp of the oil and roast for 25–30 minutes, basting occasionally. Put to one side to cool (see Cook's Tip).

3 When the chicken is cold, slice thickly and arrange in a serving dish. Whisk together 2tbsp of orange juice with the remaining oil and some seasoning. Add the strained cooking juices, pour over the chicken, garnish with herb sprigs and serve.

COOK'S TIP This dish can be cooked ahead and served cold at lunch – but if serving hot, keep the chicken warm while making the dressing, then serve.

ROASTED POUSSINS WITH PANCETTA, ARTICHOKE AND NEW POTATO SALAD

PREPARATION TIME: 20 minutes,
plus overnight marinating
COOKING TIME: 1 hour 40 minutes
PER SERVING: 540cals, 39g fat, 13g carbohydrate

SERVES 6

5 large, fresh rosemary sprigs
Grated zest of 1 lemon
4tbsp white wine vinegar
150ml (¼ pint) white wine
4 garlic cloves, crushed
3 level tbsp freshly chopped oregano
290g jar antipasto artichokes
3 poussins – around 450g (1lb) each
½ level tsp cayenne pepper
450g (1lb) new potatoes, halved or quartered
225g (8oz) pancetta or prosciutto or streaky bacon,
   roughly chopped
350g (12oz) peppery salad leaves, washed and dried

1 Remove the leaves from the sprigs of rosemary and put in a large bowl with the lemon zest, vinegar, wine, garlic, oregano and 4tbsp of oil from the antipasto artichokes. Stir well.
2 Using a fork, pierce the skin of the poussins in five or six places, then season well with freshly ground black pepper and the cayenne pepper. Put the birds, breast-side down, in the bowl and spoon the marinade over. Cover and chill overnight.
3 Preheat the oven to 200°C (180°C fan oven) mark 6. Boil the potatoes for 2 minutes in salted water then drain.
4 Lift the poussins from the marinade and put, breast-side up, in a large roasting tin. Scatter the potatoes, pancetta and artichokes around them and pour the marinade over. Cook for about 1 hour 30 minutes, basting occasionally or until golden and cooked through.
5 Remove the poussins and cut each in half lengthways; keep them warm. Toss the salad leaves with about 5tbsp of the warm cooking juices. Arrange the leaves on warm plates, then top with the potatoes, pancetta, artichokes and poussin halves. Serve immediately.

(Illustrated)

HERB-SCENTED LAMB WITH BALSAMIC DRESSING

PREPARATION TIME: 20 minutes
COOKING TIME: 35 minutes
PER SERVING: 420cals, 34g fat, 2g carbohydrate

SERVES 6

Around 50g (2oz) each fresh thyme and rosemary sprigs
3 best-end fillets of lamb – around 800g (1¾lb) total
   weight – trimmed, silvery membrane removed
6 unpeeled garlic cloves
150ml (¼ pint) olive oil
150g (5oz) spring onions, thinly sliced
225g (8oz) cherry tomatoes
3tbsp balsamic vinegar
300ml (½ pint) lamb or chicken stock
1 level tbsp freshly chopped thyme

(Illustrated on page 80)

1 Put two to three sprigs of the thyme and rosemary on a board, put one lamb fillet over them, season with freshly ground black pepper, then top with a further two to three herb sprigs. Tie the herbs and lamb into a bundle with string, secured at about 4cm (1½in) intervals. Repeat the process with the remaining lamb and herbs.
2 Preheat the oven to 200°C (180°C fan oven) mark 6. Put the lamb in a roasting tin with the garlic cloves, drizzle with 4tbsp of the oil and season with freshly ground black pepper. Cook for about 25 minutes for medium, or 35 minutes for well done.
3 Remove the lamb from the roasting tin and put to one side in a warm place covered with foil. Put the pan juices and garlic cloves into a bowl on one side. Heat the remaining oil in the roasting tin, then add the reserved garlic cloves, the spring onions and tomatoes. Fry gently for 5 minutes, lift out and put to one side. Pour the balsamic vinegar into the tin and bubble to reduce by half. Add the stock and reserved pan juices, bring to the boil and bubble for 5–10 minutes. Add the freshly chopped thyme and return the garlic cloves, spring onions and tomatoes to the tin.
4 Remove the string from the meat and cut the meat into thick slices. Garnish with the herbs and serve drizzled with the warm dressing.

HERBY SALMON FISHCAKES

PREPARATION TIME: 5 minutes
COOKING TIME: 1 hour
PER SERVING: 720cals, 45g fat, 35g carbohydrate

SERVES 4

900g (2lb) floury potatoes such as Maris Piper, peeled
    and quartered
900g (2lb) salmon fillets
Juice of 1 lemon
4 level tbsp mayonnaise
Pinch of cayenne pepper
2 level tbsp freshly chopped herbs such as tarragon, basil
    or parsley
2tbsp chilli oil

1 Put the potatoes in cold salted water, cover and bring to the boil. Turn the heat down and simmer for around 20 minutes or until tender. Drain well, put the pan back on the heat to dry the potatoes, then mash.

2 Meanwhile, put the salmon in a pan with 600ml (1 pint) of cold water and half the lemon juice. Cover and bring to the boil, then simmer for 1 minute. Turn off the heat and leave to cool for 20–30 minutes.

3 Preheat the oven to 200°C (180°C fan oven) mark 6. Drain the fish, remove the skin and discard, then flake the fish. Add to the potato along with the remaining lemon juice, the mayonnaise, cayenne and the chopped herbs. Season well with salt and freshly ground black pepper and mix together.

4 Line a large baking sheet with a non-stick Teflon liner. Put a 7.5cm (3in) plain cooking ring on the tray and fill with some of the mixture. Lift off, then repeat to make eight cakes. Drizzle with chilli oil and bake for 25 minutes or until golden.

(Illustrated)

STIR-FRIED VEGETABLES WITH OYSTER SAUCE

PREPARATION TIME: 30 minutes
COOKING TIME: 12–15 minutes
PER SERVING: 300cals, 15g fat, 21g carbohydrate

SERVES 4

FOR THE SAUCE
100ml (3½fl oz) vegetable stock
2tbsp oyster sauce
1tbsp light soy sauce
2 level tsp clear honey
1 level tsp cornflour

FOR THE STIR-FRIED VEGETABLES (SEE COOK'S TIP)
Oil for deep-frying
175g (6oz) tofu, drained, dried and cut into large cubes
2 garlic cloves, thinly sliced
1 green pepper, deseeded and sliced
225g (8oz) broccoli, cut into small florets, stalk sliced
125g (4oz) yard-long beans or French beans, trimmed and
    cut into short lengths
50g (2oz) bean sprouts, washed and dried
50g can straw mushrooms, drained
125g (4oz) canned water chestnuts, drained
2 level tbsp freshly chopped coriander to garnish

1 Blend all the ingredients for the sauce together until smooth and put to one side.

2 Heat a 10cm (4in) depth of oil in a deep pan until a cube of bread dropped into the oil browns in 30 seconds. Add the tofu and deep-fry for 1–2 minutes until golden. Drain and put to one side.

3 Heat 2tbsp of the oil, add the garlic and fry for 1 minute then discard. Add the pepper, broccoli and beans and stir-fry for 3 minutes. Add the bean sprouts, mushrooms and water chestnuts and stir-fry for 1 minute.

4 Add the tofu and sauce to the vegetables and simmer, covered, for 3–4 minutes. Garnish with the coriander and serve with Thai rice or rice noodles.

COOK'S TIP Tofu, straw mushrooms and water chestnuts are available from supermarkets. Yard-long beans, found in ethnic shops, are similar to French beans but longer, as the name suggests.

GRILLED LAMB WITH GARLIC AND LEMON

PREPARATION TIME: 5 minutes
COOKING TIME: 15 minutes
PER SERVING: 300cals, 17g fat, 0g carbohydrate

SERVES 6

900g–1.1kg (2–2½lb) boneless leg steaks of lamb
Grated zest and juice of 1 lemon
3 garlic cloves, sliced
150ml (5fl oz) olive oil
Fresh flat-leafed parsley and lemon slices to garnish

1 Put the lamb in a foil-lined grill pan. Add the lemon zest and juice, the garlic and oil and season with freshly ground black pepper.
2 Grill for about 7–10 minutes on each side, until well-charred and just cooked through. Season with salt, garnish with the parsley and lemon slices and serve.

VERY EASY FOUR-CHEESE GNOCCHI

PREPARATION TIME: 2 minutes
COOKING TIME: 20 minutes
PER SERVING: 580cals, 24g fat, 75g carbohydrate

SERVES 4

2 level tsp salt
2 x 350g packets fresh gnocchi
500g tub fresh four-cheese sauce
2 x 240g packets sunblush tomatoes
4 level tbsp freshly torn basil leaves
2 level tbsp freshly grated Parmesan cheese
25g (1oz) butter, chopped

1 Bring two large pans of water to the boil, add 1tsp salt and one packet of gnocchi to each and cook according to the instructions on the pack or until all the pieces have floated to the surface. Drain well and put back into one pan.
2 Preheat the grill. Pour the cheese sauce and tomatoes over the gnocchi and heat gently, stirring, for 2 minutes. Season with salt and freshly ground black pepper then add the basil and stir again.
3 Put into individual heatproof bowls, sprinkle over the Parmesan and dot with the butter. Grill for 3–5 minutes or until golden and bubbling, then serve.

SALT-CRUSTED NEW POTATOES

PREPARATION TIME: 2 minutes

COOKING TIME: 45 minutes

PER SERVING: 120cals, 3g fat, 24g carbohydrate

SERVES 6

900g (2lb) small new or salad potatoes

1½ tbsp olive oil

1½ level tbsp coarse sea salt

1 level tbsp freshly ground coarse black pepper

1 Preheat the oven to 200°C (180°C fan oven) mark 6. Toss the potatoes with the oil until well coated. Add the salt and pepper and toss again to coat each potato lightly.

2 Roast for about 45 minutes or until tender. Serve at once.

STIR-FRY PURPLE SPROUTING BROCCOLI

PREPARATION TIME: 2 minutes

COOKING TIME: 5–11 minutes

PER SERVING: 150cals, 14g fat, 3g carbohydrate

SERVES 2

1 tbsp oil

15g (½oz) butter

1 mild red chilli, finely sliced

1 lemongrass stalk, finely sliced

2 garlic cloves, finely sliced

200g (7oz) purple-sprouting broccoli,
   thick stems halved

1 Heat the oil and butter in a wok, then add the chilli, lemongrass and garlic and cook for 1 minute.

2 Add the broccoli and continue to stir-fry for 5–10 minutes or until tender.

(Illustrated)

BRAISED CHICORY IN WHITE WINE

PREPARATION TIME: 5 minutes

COOKING TIME: 1–1½ hours

PER SERVING: 80cals, 7g fat, 3g carbohydrate

SERVES 6

50g (2oz) butter, softened

6 heads of chicory, trimmed

100ml (3½fl oz) white wine

Chives to garnish

1 Preheat the oven to 190°C (170°C fan oven) mark 5. Grease a 1.7 litre (3 pint) ovenproof dish with 15g (½oz) of the butter.

2 Put the chicory into the dish, season with salt and freshly ground black pepper, add the wine and dot the remaining butter over the top.

3 Cover with foil and cook for 1–1½ hours or until very soft. Garnish with chives and serve.

(Illustrated)

CRISPY POTATOES WITH ROSEMARY

PREPARATION TIME: 2 minutes
COOKING TIME: 45 minutes
PER SERVING: 200cals, 4g fat, 38g carbohydrate

SERVES 6

1.4kg (3lb) new potatoes
6tbsp olive or vegetable oil
4 garlic cloves
1 sprig of fresh or 1 level tbsp dried rosemary

1 Preheat the oven to 200°C (180°C fan oven) mark 6. Cook the potatoes in boiling water for 5 minutes, then drain.
2 Heat the oil in a roasting tin in the oven for 2 minutes. Add the potatoes, whole garlic and the rosemary and cook for 35–40 minutes, turning the potatoes occasionally, until golden brown and crisp. Drain on absorbent kitchen paper and sprinkle with salt.

BARBECUED SWEET POTATO WEDGES

PREPARATION TIME: 15 minutes
COOKING TIME: 35–50 minutes
PER SERVING: 130cals, 4g fat, 24g carbohydrate

SERVES 8

Juice of ½ lemon
900g (2lb) white-fleshed sweet potatoes
Bamboo skewers, soaked in warm water for 5 minutes
2 garlic cloves, crushed
4tbsp olive oil

1 Bring a pan of salted water to the boil. Add the lemon juice and sweet potatoes and cook for 15–20 minutes or until almost tender. Drain and cool.
2 Cut the potatoes into thick wedges and push three on to each bamboo skewer.
3 Mix the garlic and oil and brush over the potatoes. Cook over medium-hot coals for 20–30 minutes until tender and lightly browned.

TO PREPARE AHEAD Parboil the sweet potatoes and cool quickly under cold running water up to three hours before. Keep in cold water until ready to cook.
COOK'S TIP See Barbecue Tips on page 142.

CARROTS AND PARSNIPS

PREPARATION TIME: 10 minutes
COOKING TIME: 15 minutes
PER SERVING: 100cals, 1g fat, 20g carbohydrate

SERVES 6

700g (1½lb) parsnips, peeled and cut into long, thin batons
700g (1½lb) carrots, peeled and cut into long, thin batons

1 Cook the parsnips and carrots in boiling salted water until tender, but still retaining their bite – about 10 minutes.
2 Drain, season with salt and freshly ground black pepper and serve.

BAKED BANANAS

PREPARATION TIME: 5 minutes
COOKING TIME: 25 minutes
PER SERVING: 310cals, 17g fat, 35g carbohydrate

SERVES 6

5 cardamom pods
Juice of 3 oranges and 1 lemon
6 level tbsp dark muscovado sugar
125g (4oz) butter
4tbsp rum or brandy
6 bananas, peeled and quartered

1 Preheat the oven to 200°C (180°C fan oven) mark 6. Remove the papery cardamom pods and crush the black seeds. Measure the orange and lemon juice – there should be about 300ml (½ pint) of orange juice and 2tbsp of lemon juice.
2 Combine the cardamom seeds, juices, sugar, butter and rum or brandy in a pan and heat gently until the butter has melted.
3 Put the bananas in a shallow ovenproof dish, pour over the juice mixture and bake for 20 minutes or until the bananas are soft. Serve immediately on their own or with ice cream.

COCONUT- AND LIME-SCENTED FRUITS

PREPARATION TIME: 10 minutes
COOKING TIME: 10 minutes
PER SERVING: 180cals, 8g fat, 27g carbohydrate

SERVES 8

125g (4oz) golden caster sugar
Juice of 3 limes
400ml can coconut milk
1 small mango and papaya, peeled and roughly chopped
125g (4oz) kumquats, quartered
2 or 3 slices fresh or canned pineapple, roughly chopped
1 banana, roughly chopped
Lime slices to decorate

1 Put the sugar, 5tbsp of the lime juice and the coconut milk in a large frying pan. Bring to the boil and bubble for 5 minutes. Add the mango and papaya and poach in the syrup for 1 minute. Lift out the fruits with a slotted spoon and put to one side.
2 Add the kumquats to the pan and simmer in the syrup for 3 minutes. Add the pineapple, kumquats and syrup to the mango and papaya.
3 Stir the banana into the fruits, decorate with lime slices and serve.

COFFEE SEMIFREDDO

PREPARATION TIME: 20 minutes
FREEZING TIME: 6 hours
PER SERVING: 340cals, 29g fat, 15g carbohydrate

SERVES 6

2tbsp sambucca or amaretto plus extra to serve
2 level tbsp instant espresso coffee, dissolved in 125ml (4fl oz) of water
75g (3oz) golden caster sugar
3 large egg yolks
284ml carton double cream, whipped into soft peaks
40g (1½oz) ground almonds, lightly toasted and cooled

1 Stir the sambucca or amaretto liqueur into the dissolved coffee to mix.
2 In a large bowl, whisk together the sugar and egg yolks until light and fluffy. Gradually whisk the coffee into the egg mixture.
3 Gently fold the cream and almonds into the mixture until all the ingredients are combined.
4 Line the bases of six individual 150ml (¼ pint) pudding moulds with greaseproof paper, then divide the mixture among them.
5 Freeze the ice creams for at least 6 hours. To serve, upturn the moulds on to individual plates and drizzle a little sambucca or amaretto around each one. Eat immediately, before they melt.

ITALIAN EASTER TART

PREPARATION TIME: 50 minutes,
plus 30 minutes chilling
COOKING TIME: 1 hour, plus 15 minutes cooling
PER SERVING: 730cals, 31g fat, 95g carbohydrate

SERVES 6

FOR THE PASTRY

250g (9oz) plain flour plus extra to dust
100g (3½oz) butter, chilled and cut into cubes
100g (3½oz) golden icing sugar, sifted
Grated zest of 1 orange
1 large egg yolk
¼ tsp vanilla extract

FOR THE FILLING

75g (3oz) arborio (risotto) rice (see Cook's Tips)
750ml (1¼ pints) milk
15g (½oz) butter
50ml (2fl oz) brandy
2tbsp orange flower water
Grated zest and juice of 1 orange
75g (3oz) raisins
½ level tsp ground cinnamon
1 vanilla pod, halved lengthways
500g (1lb 2oz) ricotta cheese
125g (4oz) golden caster sugar
2 large eggs, separated
Icing sugar to dust

1 To make the pastry, put the flour, butter, icing sugar and orange zest in a processor and whiz until the mixture resembles coarse crumbs. Add the egg yolk, vanilla extract and a few drops of cold water and pulse until the mixture forms a dough. Wrap in clingfilm and chill for 30 minutes.

2 Preheat the oven to 200°C (180°C fan oven) mark 6. Roll out two-thirds of the pastry on a floured surface and use to line a 23cm (9in) loose-bottomed fluted tart tin. Prick the pastry base and cover with greaseproof paper and baking beans. Bake blind for 15 minutes. Remove the paper and beans and bake for a further 5–10 minutes or until the base is cooked through. Remove from the oven and reduce the heat to 180°C (160°C fan oven) mark 4.

3 Meanwhile, make the filling. Put the rice in a pan with 600ml (1 pint) of the milk, the butter, brandy, orange flower water, orange zest and juice, raisins, cinnamon and vanilla pod. Bring slowly to the boil and simmer, stirring occasionally, for 20 minutes or until the rice is cooked and creamy. Remove from the heat, stir in the remaining milk and remove the vanilla pod.

4 Put the ricotta cheese, caster sugar and egg yolks in a bowl and beat until light and fluffy, then fold into the rice. Whisk the egg whites in a clean grease-free bowl until stiff peaks form and gently fold into the rice and ricotta mixture. Spoon the filling into the pastry case and level the surface.

5 Roll out the remaining pastry, cut into 5mm (¼in) strips and use to form a lattice top for the tart. Bake in the oven for 20 minutes, then increase the temperature to 190°C (170°C fan oven) mark 5 and bake for 15 minutes. The pastry should be golden and the filling just set. Cool for 10–15 minutes, then remove from the tart case. Dust with icing sugar and serve warm.

TO PREPARE AHEAD Complete the recipe to the end of step 2 up to three days ahead. Store the pastry case in an airtight container, wrap the pastry trimmings in clingfilm and chill. One day ahead, make the filling, spoon into a bowl, cover with clingfilm and chill.

TO USE Spoon the filling into the pastry case and complete step 5.

COOK'S TIPS: Carnaroli rice is another type of risotto rice that would work well.

• Never wash risotto rice. The fine coating of starch on each grain helps to create its characteristic creamy texture when cooked.

DATE AND GINGER CAKE

PREPARATION TIME: 20 minutes

COOKING TIME: About 1 hour

PER SERVING: 210cals, 8g fat, 36g carbohydrate

MAKES ABOUT 16 SLICES

½ level tsp bicarbonate of soda

50ml (2fl oz) milk

125g (4oz) butter plus extra to grease

125g (4oz) light muscovado sugar

2 large eggs, beaten

150g (5oz) golden syrup

150g (5oz) treacle

125g (4oz) stoned dates, roughly chopped

50g (2oz) stem ginger in syrup, roughly chopped

225g (8oz) plain flour, sifted

1½ level tsp ground ginger

1 Preheat the oven to 150°C (130°C fan oven) mark 2. Grease and line a 23cm (9in) square cake tin with non-stick baking parchment. Stir the bicarbonate of soda into the milk.

2 Beat together the butter and sugar until pale and light. Slowly add the beaten eggs and then stir in the syrup, treacle, milk, dates and stem ginger.

3 Fold in the flour, ground ginger and a pinch of salt. Pour into the tin and bake for 1 hour or until a skewer inserted into the cake comes out clean. Leave in the tin for 1 hour. Turn out on to a wire rack.

4 When cool, wrap in greaseproof paper and store.

TO PREPARE AHEAD/FREEZE Complete the recipe up to one week ahead. Store in a tin or in the freezer.

(Illustrated)

RHUBARB AND APPLE COBBLER

PREPARATION TIME: 5 minutes

COOKING TIME: 30–40 minutes, plus standing

PER SERVING: 390cals, 14g fat, 63g carbohydrate

SERVES 6

900g (2lb) rhubarb, cut into 2.5cm (1in) lengths

450g (1lb) cooking apples, peeled, cored, quartered and sliced

6 level tbsp golden caster sugar

4 level tbsp plain flour

1 level tbsp cornflour

½ level tsp ground ginger

A knob of softened butter

Grated zest of 1 orange

TO MAKE THE COBBLER DOUGH

150g (5oz) plain flour

2 level tsp baking powder

60g (2½oz) softened butter

3 level tbsp golden caster sugar

125ml (4fl oz) buttermilk (or whole milk with a generous squeeze of lemon juice)

2tbsp double cream

1 level tsp demerara sugar

1 Preheat the oven to 220°C (200°C fan oven) mark 7. Mix together the rhubarb, apples, sugar, flour, cornflour, ginger, butter and orange zest. Put into a 25.5cm (10in) shallow ovenproof dish and put to one side.

2 To make the cobbler dough, sift the flour, baking powder and a pinch of salt into a bowl. Rub in the softened butter until the mixture resembles fine breadcrumbs. Stir in the caster sugar and buttermilk (or milk with lemon juice). Spoon the dough on to the rhubarb in small mounds, making sure it doesn't completely cover the fruit. Mix the cream with the demerara sugar and drizzle on top.

3 Put the dish on a baking tray and bake for 10 minutes, then lower the heat to 190°C (170°C fan oven) mark 5 and bake for a further 20–30 minutes or until puffed and brown and the fruit is just soft. Remove from the oven and leave to stand for 10 minutes, then serve warm with cream.

LEMON AND SAFFRON CAKE

PREPARATION TIME: 30 minutes,
plus 30 minutes cooling and 30 minutes soaking
COOKING TIME: 1 hour
PER SERVING FOR 8: 670cals, 26g fat,
108g carbohydrate
PER SERVING FOR 10: 540cals, 21g fat,
87g carbohydrate

SERVES 8–10

175g (6oz) unsalted butter, softened, plus extra to grease
Grated zest and juice of 1½ lemons
275g (10oz) golden caster sugar
5 large eggs, separated
3 level tbsp ground almonds
275g (10oz) self-raising flour, sifted
Crème fraîche or mascarpone cheese to serve

FOR THE SYRUP

150ml (¼ pint) lemon juice – around 3½ lemons
350g (12oz) golden caster sugar
Large pinch of saffron (optional)
Lemon slices and rose petals to decorate (optional)

1 Preheat the oven to 170°C (150°C fan oven) mark 3. In a large mixing bowl, beat together the butter, lemon zest and caster sugar until thoroughly combined, then mix in the lemon juice, a tablespoon at a time. Beat in the egg yolks together with the ground almonds, then fold in the flour.

2 Whisk the egg whites in a large clean grease-free bowl until soft peaks form. Stir a quarter of the egg whites into the butter mixture, then gently fold in the remainder with 2tbsp of cold water.

3 Pour the mixture into a greased, base-lined 23cm (9in) spring-release cake tin and smooth the top. Bake for 50–60 minutes or until the cake is cooked in the centre – a skewer inserted in the middle should come out clean. Leave the cake in the tin and allow to cool for 30 minutes.

4 Meanwhile, make the syrup. Put the lemon juice, caster sugar, saffron and 300ml (½ pint) of water into a heavy-based pan. Dissolve the sugar over a low heat, then bring to the boil. Set aside until the cake is cool.

5 Leaving the cake in the tin, put the tin on a baking tray with a lip. Drizzle the lemon syrup over the cake and leave to soak in for 30 minutes. Unmould the cake, slice and, if you like, decorate with lemon slices and rose petals. Serve with crème fraîche or mascarpone cheese.

(*Illustrated*)

SHORTBREAD DISCS

PREPARATION TIME: 20 minutes,
plus 1 hour chilling
COOKING TIME: 15 minutes plus 10 minutes cooling
PER SERVING: 300cals, 18g fat, 34g carbohydrate

SERVES 6

150g (5oz) plain flour, sieved, plus extra to dust
125g (4oz) unsalted butter, diced
25g (1oz) ground semolina
50g (2oz) golden caster sugar plus extra to dust
¼ tsp vanilla extract

1 Put the flour, butter, semolina, sugar and vanilla extract in a food processor and pulse until the mixture just comes together to form a ball. If you don't have a food processor, put the flour, semolina, sugar and vanilla extract in a bowl and rub the butter into it until it comes together in a ball. Wrap and chill the dough for 30 minutes.

2 Roll out the dough on a lightly floured worksurface until 5mm (¼in) thick. Stamp out with a 4.5cm (1¾in) diameter plain cutter. Put on a non-stick baking sheet and chill for 30 minutes.

3 Preheat the oven to 190°C (170°C fan oven) mark 5. Dust the rounds with caster sugar and bake for 15 minutes or until pale golden. The discs may not look cooked, but they'll become crisp as they cool down. Cool for 10 minutes on the baking sheet, then transfer to a cooling rack.

TO PREPARE AHEAD/FREEZE Complete the recipe. Store in an airtight container for up to one week, or wrap and freeze for up to three months.
TO USE Thaw at cool room temperature for 2–3 hours before serving.

MAY

*As summer approaches, long warm days
tempt us outdoors for al fresco
meals and picnics*

MAY IS A GOOD MONTH for veggie-lovers, the first in a while to throw up new and welcome produce. And there are two undisputed champions this month: asparagus and Jersey Royals. You can, of course, buy asparagus at any time of year, and new potatoes as well, but English asparagus and the unique Jersey Royals rank among the world's great delicacies. Both will be at their most expensive early in the season, and will come down in price as the month wears on. But they're worth every penny for their unique flavour.

Jersey Royals range in size from little more than an olive to something closer to a size 1 egg. They have a creamy texture and complex flavour that are equalled nowhere else – even though we get good new potatoes from all around the Mediterranean as well as our own farms. Jersey Royals should always, like any potato, be squeezed between thumb and forefinger to check for freshness; if there's any 'give', they are not fresh enough. Don't be alarmed if the skin seems to be falling off: this is standard for Jersey Royals and not a sign of a fault. Prepare them by washing only: the skin has flavour as well as nutrients, and shouldn't be peeled or scraped. If they're very gritty, a preliminary soak in warm water will help with cleaning. For a different way to cook them try the Jersey Royals with Mint and Petits Pois, where they're sliced and sautéed (see picture opposite).

For buying tips on asparagus, see the box on page 107, and for a light and summery starter try the Warm Asparagus and Herb Mousses on page 111 or, for something more substantial, the Salmon and Asparagus Terrine, on page 110.

Left: Jersey Royals with Mint and Petits Pois (see page 120)

INGREDIENTS OF THE MONTH

FISH

Crab

Flounder

Haddock

Herring

Lobster

Monkfish

Plaice

Sole

Trout

Wild salmon

Broad beans

Cauliflower

Chicory

Jersey Royal
   potatoes

Leeks

Spinach

Watercress

FRUIT

Rhubarb

VEGETABLES

Asparagus

Avocados

BEST BUY

Jersey Royal
   potatoes

Asparagus

Vegetables

While Jersey Royals and asparagus are the stars of the season, May is just a good month in general for veg: the real beginning of summer as far as the table is concerned. There will be the first broad beans, at their smallest, most tender and sweetest; it's almost always worth the extra work to skin them before serving, but the smallest may not need this treatment. Other stars: tasty spring greens, the first of the new crops of turnips, cauliflower and more purple sprouting broccoli; and, towards the end of the month, the first of the British-grown peas. Peas must be eaten as soon as possible after picking, so it's dodgy to jump the gun on peas by buying the Spanish imports that precede the native crop. There should also be some small leeks coming into the market, much better for steaming or stir-frying than their over-sized brethren. Good watercress will add a welcome green crunch to salads, though it's also good for stir-frying or as a base for fish or chicken. Spring greens, and spring cabbage varieties such as Primo, are also coming along. Radishes will begin to appear as well – delicious just dipped into a little coarse salt, with or without butter. And UK spinach will also be putting in its first appearance, for cooking or eating in salads, though imports from Spain and/or Italy will also continue to be a good buy. May is also likely to be the last month for Hass avocados, the best variety.

Fruit

Other fruits are also nearly all imported, (we'll start to see some good cherries around) apart from rhubarb. There should be good mangoes and pineapples around and bananas are ever-reliable.

Meat and Fish

New season's lamb remains the top choice in meat this month – and may well be coming down in price as supplies increase. Try the Rack of Lamb with Mushroom and Port Sauce on page 115. You could also take advantage of the cheaper price by stocking the freezer. Crab, salmon and sea trout are also still in their best season, and prices for wild fish may have dropped somewhat. Flatfish are also looking good now; seek out less expensive varieties like flounder and witch sole alongside the costlier Dover sole and plaice. And whitebait is still in season, but not for long. Now is the time to get your last fix if you have a taste for it.

ASPARAGUS

Asparagus should be bought, if possible, on the day you plan to eat it. Those hard, bright spears lose some of their lustre after even a day in the fridge. If you do buy more than you can use in one day, keep them loosely wrapped in the vegetable drawer of the fridge. When you're buying, look closely at the individual spears and squeeze them if you can. They should be rock-hard, like any good vegetable, with no sign of wrinkling, and a spear, when held by the end and shaken, should not be flexible enough to bend. The root-ends may be white, where they didn't receive any sunlight, but if there's too much white you will lose a lot when trimming. The green part of the spears should be truly green, with no hints of the brown or yellow that indicate something less than fully fresh; you'll often find these signs on the tiny leaves. And when you get the asparagus home, remember that it has probably been grown in sandy soil which may cling to it stubbornly. A good soak will remove grit. If you sometimes see imperfect asparagus (broken spears, irregular sizes, etc.), you can use them for soups, or for making the Asparagus Risotto on page 113.

SWEET RED ONION AND GORGONZOLA SALAD

PREPARATION TIME: 20 minutes,
plus 15 minutes cooling
COOKING TIME: 25 minutes
PER SERVING: 370cals, 33g fat, 10g carbohydrate

SERVES 6

4tsp olive oil

3 medium red onions – total weight around 500g
   (1lb 2oz) – cut into wedges, keeping root area intact

2 level tsp light muscovado sugar

2tbsp balsamic vinegar

275g (10oz) mixed salad leaves, washed and dried

200g (7oz) Gorgonzola, crumbled

FOR THE DRESSING

2tsp runny honey

½tsp Dijon mustard

2tbsp red wine vinegar

6tbsp extra-virgin olive oil

1 Heat the oil in a large frying pan, add the onion wedges in a single layer, cover with a lid and cook over a low to moderate heat for 15 minutes or until the onions have softened and are beginning to brown on the underside.
2 Sprinkle the sugar over, cover the pan and cook for a further 10 minutes until the exposed side is beginning to caramelise. Add the balsamic vinegar and cook uncovered until most of the vinegar has evaporated and the onions are sticky.
3 To make the dressing, put the honey, mustard and vinegar into a bowl, season with salt and freshly ground black pepper and whisk together. Whisk in the oil to form an emulsion.
4 Put the salad leaves in a bowl with the onions and Gorgonzola and toss together. Divide between six plates, then pour the dressing over to moisten.

(Illustrated)

AVOCADO SALAD

PREPARATION TIME: 5 minutes
PER SERVING: 370cals, 37g fat, 7g carbohydrate

SERVES 6

3 ripe avocados, thinly sliced

3 oranges, peeled, pith removed and segmented

275g (10oz) mixed salad leaves

1 small bunch watercress, washed and drained

Juice of 2 limes

9tbsp olive oil

1 level tsp crushed chillies

1 Put the avocado slices, orange segments, salad leaves and watercress in a bowl.
2 Mix together the lime juice, oil and chillies, season with salt and freshly ground black pepper and toss through the ingredients in the bowl. Serve at once.

SALMON AND ASPARAGUS TERRINE

PREPARATION TIME: 40 minutes,
plus overnight chilling
COOKING TIME: 1 hour 5 minutes
PER SERVING: 280cals, 19g fat, 1g carbohydrate

SERVES 10

75g (3oz) butter, plus extra to grease

1 medium red chilli, deseeded and finely diced

1 garlic clove, chopped

½ lemongrass stalk, finely chopped

250g (9oz) asparagus spears, trimmed and woody stems
    removed

250g (9oz) smoked salmon

4 level tbsp fresh dill, roughly chopped, plus extra sprigs to
    garnish

1kg (2¼ lb) skinless salmon fillet, bones removed

1 Melt the butter in a pan over a low heat. Bring to the boil and skim off any scum until clear. Pour into a bowl leaving the milky residue behind (discard this) and add the chilli, garlic and lemongrass. Leave to infuse.

2 Bring a large pan of cold salted water to the boil and cook the asparagus for 2–3 minutes. Drain and refresh under cold running water.

3 Grease and line a 900g (2lb) loaf tin with foil and grease the foil. Line the tin with smoked salmon, reserving some, and sprinkle over 1 level tbsp of the dill. Drizzle with a little infused butter and season with salt and freshly ground black pepper.

4 Preheat the oven to 180°C (160°C fan oven) mark 4. Cut the salmon fillet in half to fit in the loaf tin, put one piece inside, sprinkle with 1 level tbsp of the dill and drizzle with a little infused butter. Layer up the terrine with the asparagus and the other salmon half, sprinkling 1 level tbsp of the dill and some infused butter between each layer and seasoning well. Add the rest of the smoked salmon and cover with foil.

5 Put the loaf tin in a roasting tin and half fill with hot water. Cook for 50–60 minutes or until a skewer inserted in the middle for 30 seconds comes out warm.

6 Cool, weight down with two cans and put in the fridge overnight.

7 Turn out the terrine, slice and serve garnished with dill.

POLENTA WITH MIXED MUSHROOMS

PREPARATION TIME: 10 minutes
COOKING TIME: 20 minutes
PER SERVING: 190cals, 11g fat, 18g carbohydrate

SERVES 8

50g (2oz) butter

1.1kg (2½lb) assorted mushrooms

1 red chilli, deseeded and finely chopped

3 garlic cloves, finely sliced

100g (3½oz) sun-dried tomatoes, roughly chopped

1 level tsp fresh thyme

1kg roll ready-made polenta

3tbsp olive oil

Truffle oil (optional)

Thyme sprigs to garnish

1 To make the sauce, melt half the butter in a deep-sided frying pan or wok. Add half the mushrooms and cook over a high heat until all the liquid has evaporated, then put to one side. Repeat with the remaining butter and mushrooms. Add the chilli and garlic to the pan and cook for 2 minutes. Add the sun-dried tomatoes to the mushrooms with the thyme and season with salt and freshly ground black pepper.

2 Slice the polenta into 16 pieces, about 1cm (½ in) thick. Heat the oil in a non-stick frying pan and, in batches, fry the polenta on each side for 3–4 minutes or until golden.

3 To serve, arrange two slices of polenta per person on each plate, top with the mushroom sauce and drizzle with truffle oil, if using. Garnish with fresh thyme.

TO PREPARE AHEAD Complete the recipe to the end of step 1 up to one day ahead, cover and chill.

TO USE Complete the recipe, adding 2tbsp of cold water to the mushrooms when you reheat them in a frying pan.

COOK'S TIP The mushroom mixture also works well served over grilled slices of Italian bread, seasoned with olive oil and sea salt.

WARM ASPARAGUS AND HERB MOUSSES

PREPARATION TIME: 20 minutes
COOKING TIME: 1 hour
PER SERVING: 620cals, 62g fat, 5g carbohydrate

SERVES 6

75g (3oz) butter
450g (1lb) small asparagus spears, trimmed and
   woody stems removed
3 large eggs and 2 egg yolks
2 level tsp freshly chopped chervil or tarragon
2 level tsp freshly chopped chives
568ml carton double cream
2 shallots, peeled and finely chopped
150ml (¼ pint) dry white wine
150ml (¼ pint) vegetable stock
Sprigs of fresh chervil to garnish

1 Melt 25g (1oz) of the butter and grease six 150ml (¼ pint) ramekins and chill them. Put to one side 12 small asparagus spears for garnish and roughly chop the remainder.

2 Bring a large pan of salted water to the boil, add the chopped asparagus and cook for 4–5 minutes or until tender. Drain, plunge into iced water and drain again. Cook the reserved asparagus spears for 1–2 minutes, cover and put to one side. Put the chopped asparagus in a food processor or blender with the eggs and yolks and whiz until smooth. Sieve and stir in the chopped herbs and 450ml (¾ pint) of the cream and season well with salt and freshly ground black pepper.

3 Preheat the oven to 180°C (160°C fan oven) mark 4. Pour the asparagus mixture into the ramekins and put in a large roasting tin with enough boiling water to come halfway up the sides of the ramekins. Cover the tin loosely with foil. Cook for 30–40 minutes or until just set.

4 Melt the remaining butter in a pan, add the shallots and cook, stirring, for 10 minutes, until soft. Add the wine and stock, bring to the boil and simmer for 10 minutes. Add the remaining cream, season and simmer for 10 minutes.

5 To serve, reheat the asparagus spears in the hot sauce for 1 minute. Turn the ramekins out on to six heated plates and spoon round the sauce and asparagus spears. Garnish with the chervil.

(Illustrated)

SPICY MONKFISH STEW

PREPARATION TIME: 10 minutes
COOKING TIME: 30 minutes
PER SERVING: 160cals, 3g fat, 18g carbohydrate

SERVES 6

1 tbsp olive oil

1 onion, finely sliced

1 tbsp tom yum soup paste

450g (1lb) potatoes, cut into 2cm (¾in) chunks

400g can chopped tomatoes in rich tomato juice

600ml (1 pint) hot fish stock

450g (1lb) monkfish, cut into 2cm (¾in) chunks

200g bag washed ready-to-eat baby spinach

1 Heat the oil in a pan and fry the onion over a medium heat for 5 minutes, until golden.

2 Add the tom yum paste and potatoes and stir-fry for 1 minute. Add the tomatoes and hot stock, season well with salt and freshly ground black pepper and cover. Bring to the boil then simmer, partially covered, for 15 minutes or until the potatoes are just tender.

3 Add the monkfish to the pan and continue to simmer for 5–10 minutes or until the fish is cooked. Add the baby spinach leaves and stir through until wilted.

4 Spoon the fish stew into warmed bowls and serve immediately with crusty bread.

(Illustrated)

TAGLIATELLE WITH
SUMMER VEGETABLES AND HERB SAUCE

PREPARATION TIME: 20 minutes,
plus 4 hours infusing
COOKING TIME: 20 minutes
PER SERVING FOR 4: 680cals, 34g fat,
83g carbohydrate
PER SERVING FOR 6: 450cals, 23g fat,
55g carbohydrate

SERVES 4–6

25g (1oz) mixed fresh herbs, such as basil, chervil, chives,
   dill and parsley, roughly chopped
1 level tbsp fresh oregano
125ml (4fl oz) extra-virgin olive oil
700g (1½ lb) mixed summer vegetables: cherry tomatoes
   (optional), courgettes, thinly sliced, asparagus spears,
   trimmed, shelled broad beans and/or peas, baby
   carrots, peeled
2 shallots, peeled and finely chopped
1 garlic clove, crushed
400g (14oz) dried tagliatelle
6tbsp single cream
Parmesan cheese shavings to serve (optional)

1 Put the fresh herbs and oregano in a bowl. Add all but 2tbsp of the oil.
   Stir well then put to one side for a few hours, if possible.
2 Blanch all the vegetables (except the tomatoes) separately, in a large pan
   of lightly salted boiling water for 1–3 minutes, depending on the size
   and the vegetable (see Cook's Tip). Drain, refresh under cold water and
   pat dry.
3 Heat the remaining oil in a large frying pan, add the shallots and garlic
   and sauté for 5 minutes. Add the vegetables and tomatoes and stir-fry
   over a gentle heat then add the herb mixture.
4 Meanwhile, cook the pasta in a large pan of boiling salted water until al
   dente – tender yet still with a slight bite.
5 Drain the pasta, reserving 4tbsp of the cooking water. Add the pasta and
   water to the frying pan. Toss with the vegetables and herb sauce, stir in
   the cream and heat through briefly. Serve at once, seasoned and scattered
   with Parmesan shavings, if using.

COOK'S TIP The vegetables are listed in order of required blanching
time, from courgette slices (shortest) to baby carrots (longest).

ASPARAGUS RISOTTO

PREPARATION TIME: 5 minutes
COOKING TIME: 30 minutes
PER SERVING: 450cals, 21g fat, 49g carbohydrate

SERVES 4

50g (2oz) butter
2 shallots, peeled and diced
2 garlic cloves, crushed
225g (8oz) arborio rice
500ml (17fl oz) stock
2tbsp mascarpone cheese
75g (3oz) Parmesan cheese, finely grated, plus shavings
   to garnish
2tbsp freshly chopped parsley
400g (14oz) asparagus spears, trimmed and woody
   stems removed, blanched and halved

1 Melt the butter in a pan and sauté the shallots and garlic until soft. Stir in the
   rice, add the stock and bring to the boil. (Alternatively, follow the traditional
   method, see below.) Simmer for 12 minutes or until the rice is cooked.
2 Add the mascarpone, half the Parmesan and half the parsley to the pan.
   Season with salt and freshly ground black pepper, then stir in the
   asparagus and the remaining Parmesan and parsley. Spoon on to plates,
   garnish with the Parmesan shavings and serve.

TRADITIONAL METHODS

1 Traditional risotto can't be rushed – allow plenty of time to make it.
   The rice has to absorb the stock one ladleful at a time to achieve a
   creamy consistency.
2 Keep the stock heated in a pan at a low simmer so it doesn't boil away.
3 Spice up a basic risotto with favourite ingredients such as diced chorizo,
   a handful of finely sliced sun-dried tomatoes and a handful of freshly
   chopped basil.

STICKY PORK RIBS WITH APPLE, AVOCADO AND PECAN NUT SALAD

PREPARATION TIME: 25 minutes
COOKING TIME: 1 hour–1 hour 10 minutes
PER SERVING: 560cals, 31g fat, 39g carbohydrate

SERVES 4

1kg (2¼lb) lean pork spare ribs

1 onion, chopped

2 garlic cloves, crushed

300g jar hoisin sauce

2 level tbsp tomato purée

2tbsp cider vinegar

4 large celery sticks, washed and chopped

1 dessert apple, quartered, cored and sliced

25g (1oz) pecan nut halves

100g (3½oz) wild rocket

½ avocado, sliced

Juice of 1 orange

2tsp American mustard

1 Preheat the oven to 200°C (180°C fan oven) mark 6. Put the ribs in a pan, cover with water, bring to the boil and skim the surface. Cook for 10 minutes, then drain.

2 In a large roasting tin, mix together the onion, garlic, hoisin sauce, tomato purée and vinegar. Add the ribs and toss together well. Put in the oven and cook for 50 minutes–1 hour, turning every 15 minutes.

3 To make the salad, put the celery, apple, nuts, rocket and avocado in a bowl. Mix the orange juice and mustard together, season with salt and freshly ground black pepper and toss with the salad. Serve with the ribs.

(Illustrated)

RACK OF LAMB WITH MUSHROOM AND PORT SAUCE

PREPARATION TIME: 20 minutes

COOKING TIME: About 1 hour

PER SERVING: 300cals, 18g fat, 4g carbohydrate

SERVES 6

50g (2oz) butter

3 garlic cloves

225g (8oz) mixed mushrooms, such as shiitake, oyster
 and chanterelle, sliced

2 level tsp plain flour

200ml (7fl oz) port

450ml (¾ pint) red wine

900ml (1½ pints) chicken stock

2 level tsp redcurrant jelly

3 trimmed racks of lamb – around 900g (2lb) total weight

3tbsp olive oil

1 Heat the butter in a large frying pan. Crush 2 of the garlic cloves and add to the pan with the mushrooms and cook, stirring, for 4 minutes or until they have released their juices and started to colour. Stir in the flour and add the port, wine, stock and redcurrant jelly. Bring to the boil and bubble furiously for 20 minutes or until the sauce is reduced and syrupy. Season with salt and freshly ground black pepper and put to one side.

2 Trim the lamb of any excess fat or sinews and slice the remaining garlic clove. Make incisions in the flesh and stud with the garlic. Rub with 2tbsp of the oil and season.

3 Preheat the oven to 200°C (180°C fan oven) mark 6. Put the remaining oil in a roasting tin and put in the oven for 5 minutes to heat up. Put the lamb in the roasting tin, fat side down, and cook for 5 minutes to brown. Turn over, baste and put back in the oven for 20–25 minutes for pink lamb, depending on the thickness. Allow an extra 5 minutes for well done.

4 Carve the lamb and stir any roasting juices into the mushroom sauce. Serve with the sauce.

COOK'S TIP This sauce can be made up to one day ahead and then reheated.

(Illustrated)

CHICKEN WITH CRISP CIABATTA AND PARMA HAM

PREPARATION TIME: 45 minutes,
plus 15 minutes cooling
COOKING TIME: 1 hour 30 minutes
PER SERVING: 730cals, 52g fat, 24g carbohydrate

SERVES 6

2tbsp olive oil
4 medium leeks – around 800g (1lb 12oz) – well washed,
    trimmed and cut into 1cm (½in) slices
150ml (¼ pint) dry sherry
200ml (7fl oz) chicken stock
2 x 200ml tubs crème fraîche
2 level tsp plain flour
2 level tbsp wholegrain mustard
3 level tbsp freshly chopped sage
1 level tbsp freshly chopped flat-leafed parsley
4–5 large chicken breast fillets – around 700g (1½lb) total
    weight – cut into 1cm (½in) strips
100g (3½oz) Gruyère cheese, finely grated

FOR THE TOPPING

200g (7oz) ciabatta breadcrumbs
3tbsp olive oil
75g (3oz) Parma ham, roughly torn
2 level tbsp freshly chopped flat-leafed parsley

1 Heat the oil in a large non-stick frying pan, add the leeks and cook over a gentle heat for 15–20 minutes or until softened and tinged golden brown. Remove with a slotted spoon and put to one side. Add the sherry and stock, bring to the boil and bubble until reduced by about a quarter. Allow to cool.
2 Mix the crème fraîche, flour, mustard, sage and parsley together with some salt and freshly ground black pepper (watch the seasoning as the Parma ham and chicken stock are salty), then mix in the reduced stock, chicken and leeks.
3 Pour the chicken mixture into a 2.3 litre (4 pint) ovenproof dish. Sprinkle the grated cheese on top. Preheat the oven to 190°C (170°C fan oven) mark 5.
4 To make the topping, put the ciabatta crumbs in a bowl with the oil, Parma ham and parsley. Toss together and sprinkle over the chicken.
5 Cook for 50–60 minutes or until bubbling at the sides, hot to the centre and the topping is golden and crisp. If the top is becoming too brown, cover loosely with foil.

(Illustrated)

SPRING VEGETABLES IN TARRAGON DRESSING

PREPARATION TIME: 10 minutes
COOKING TIME: 15 minutes
PER SERVING: 120cals, 9g fat, 9g carbohydrate

SERVES 6

1tbsp white wine or cider vinegar
4tbsp oil
1 level tbsp freshly chopped tarragon
275g (10oz) small new potatoes
150g (5oz) each asparagus tips and mangetout

1 In a small bowl, whisk together the vinegar, oil and tarragon and season with salt and freshly ground black pepper. Cover and put to one side.
2 Cook the potatoes in boiling salted water for 10 minutes or until just tender. Drain and plunge into a bowl of iced water and cool. Bring a large pan of salted water to the boil. Add the asparagus spears and cook for 2–3 minutes until just beginning to soften. Drain and cool in iced water. Repeat this process with the mangetout.
3 To serve, drain the vegetables well and toss in the dressing.

NEW POTATOES WITH PEAS, PARSLEY AND BROAD BEANS

PREPARATION TIME: 5 minutes
COOKING TIME: 30 minutes
PER SERVING: 280cals, 10g fat, 41g carbohydrate

SERVES 4

700g (1½lb) small new potatoes
200g (7oz) each fresh shelled peas and broad beans
40g (1½oz) butter
Pinch of golden caster sugar
3 level tbsp freshly chopped flat-leafed parsley

1 Cook the potatoes in a large pan of boiling salted water for about 15 minutes or until tender, then drain and put to one side.
2 In the meantime, put the peas and beans in a large frying pan with the butter, sugar and 75ml (3fl oz) of water. Bring to the boil, cover and simmer for 10 minutes.
3 Remove the lid from the pan, stir in the potatoes and simmer until all the liquid has evaporated. Season well with salt and freshly ground black pepper, stir in the parsley and serve.

(Illustrated)

BUTTERED ASPARAGUS WITH ROASTED GARLIC

PREPARATION TIME: 5 minutes
COOKING TIME: 40 minutes
PER SERVING: 390cals, 27g fat, 28g carbohydrate

SERVES 6

6 garlic bulbs
3tbsp olive oil
125g (4oz) unsalted butter
1.4kg (3lb) asparagus spears, trimmed
Juice of ½ lemon
1 level tbsp freshly chopped chervil, plus six sprigs
   to garnish

1 Preheat the oven to 200°C (180°C fan oven) mark 6. Peel off the papery skin from each garlic bulb, put them in a roasting tin, drizzle with 1tbsp of water and the olive oil and season with salt and freshly ground black pepper. Cover with foil and roast for 40 minutes or until soft and golden.
2 Melt the butter in a small pan, bring to the boil, take off the heat and cool. Skim the scum from the surface and discard. Pour the clear butter into a bowl and discard the milky part at the bottom.
3 Cook the asparagus in a deep frying pan of boiling water for 4—5 minutes or until tender, then drain. Add the lemon juice to the butter, season, then add the chopped chervil.
4 Remove the garlic from the roasting tin and slice off the tops.
5 Put the asparagus and garlic bulbs in a serving dish, drizzle with butter and garnish with chervil sprigs. Squeeze the sweet garlic purée from individual cloves to enjoy with the asparagus.

SPINACH WITH TOMATOES

PREPARATION TIME: 10 minutes
COOKING TIME: 10 minutes
PER SERVING: 90cals, 7g fat, 3g carbohydrate

SERVES 6

50g (2oz) butter
2 garlic cloves, crushed
450g (1lb) baby plum tomatoes, halved
250g bag of washed baby spinach leaves
A large pinch freshly grated nutmeg

1 Melt 25g (1oz) of the butter in a pan and cook the garlic for 30 seconds—1 minute, until just soft.
2 Add the plum tomatoes and cook for 4—5 minutes.
3 Put the spinach leaves and a little water in a clean pan, cover and cook for 2—3 minutes. Drain well, chop roughly and stir into the tomatoes.
4 Add the remaining butter and gently heat through. Season well with salt and freshly ground black pepper, stir in a large pinch of freshly grated nutmeg and serve.

JERSEY ROYALS WITH MINT AND PETITS POIS

PREPARATION TIME: 15 minutes

COOKING TIME: 30 minutes

PER SERVING: 180cals, 7g fat, 27g carbohydrate

SERVES 6

3tbsp olive oil

900g (2lb) Jersey Royals, scrubbed and thickly sliced

175g (6oz) frozen petits pois

3 level tbsp freshly chopped mint

1 Heat half the oil in a large non-stick frying pan, add half the potatoes and cook for 5 minutes, turning, until brown on both sides. Remove the potatoes from the pan with a slotted spoon and put to one side.

2 Add the remaining oil to the pan along with the rest of the potatoes and brown in the same way.

3 Return the reserved potatoes to the pan and cook all of them together, covered loosely, for a further 10–15 minutes.

4 Meanwhile, cook the petits pois in a pan of boiling water for 2 minutes, then drain well. Add the petits pois to the potatoes and cook through for 2–3 minutes.

5 Toss the petits pois and potatoes with the mint, salt and freshly ground black pepper just before serving.

(Illustrated on page 104)

LEMON SPINACH

PREPARATION TIME: 5 minutes

COOKING TIME: 5 minutes

PER SERVING: 100cals, 8g fat, 2g carbohydrate

SERVES 6

50g (2oz) butter

4 garlic cloves, crushed

900g (2lb) young fresh spinach, well washed and drained, any large stalks discarded

3tbsp lemon juice

Grated nutmeg

1 Melt the butter in a very large pan, add the garlic and sauté for 1 minute. Add the spinach and stir well until coated in the garlic butter.

2 Cover tightly and cook for about 2 minutes or until the spinach has just softened but is still bright green.

3 Lift out of the pan using a draining spoon. Add the lemon juice and season with salt, freshly ground black pepper and some grated nutmeg. Serve immediately.

CRUSHED POTATOES WITH FETA AND OLIVES

PREPARATION TIME: 20 minutes

COOKING TIME: 15 minutes

PER SERVING: 410cals, 29g fat, 29g carbohydrate

SERVES 4

700g (1½lb) new potatoes, unpeeled

75ml (3fl oz) olive oil

75g (3oz) pitted black olives, shredded

2 level tbsp freshly chopped flat-leafed parsley

200g (7oz) feta cheese, crumbled

1 Cook the potatoes in their skins in a pan of boiling salted water for 15 minutes or until tender. Drain, put back in the pan and crush roughly.

2 Add the oil, olives, parsley and feta cheese. Season with salt and freshly ground black pepper and toss together – don't over-mix or the potatoes will become glutinous.

VANILLA CHILLED RISOTTO

PREPARATION TIME: 2 minutes

COOKING TIME: 55 minutes,

plus cooling and chilling

PER SERVING: 190cals, 13g fat, 15g carbohydrate

SERVES 10

900ml (1½ pints) whole milk

1 vanilla pod, split lengthways

75g (3oz) risotto rice

40g (1½oz) golden caster sugar

200ml (7fl oz) double cream

A little ground cinnamon

1 Pour the milk into a large pan, add the vanilla pod and bring slowly to the boil.

2 Stir in the rice, reduce the heat and simmer gently for about 40 minutes, stirring from time to time, until the rice is soft and most of the liquid has been absorbed. You might need to add a little more milk during the cooking time.

3 Stir in the sugar, remove the vanilla pod and set aside to cool.

4 Stir the cream into the cooled mixture, pour into a large bowl, cover and chill. To serve, sprinkle with a little ground cinnamon.

TO PREPARE AHEAD Complete the recipe, but don't sprinkle with cinnamon; cover and chill.

TO USE Complete the recipe as above.

TO FREEZE Complete the recipe but don't sprinkle with cinnamon, then pack and freeze.

TO USE Thaw overnight at cool room temperature. Complete the recipe.

MANGO AND LIME MOUSSE

PREPARATION TIME: 10 minutes,
plus 1 hour 20 minutes freezing and chilling
PER SERVING: 210cals, 14g fat, 17g carbohydrate

SERVES 6

Juice and finely grated zest of 2 limes plus zest of 1 lime
    to decorate
1 sachet (around 10g) gelatine
3 large eggs plus 2 large egg yolks
50g (2oz) golden caster sugar
300ml (½ pint) mango purée – around 2 large mangoes
100ml (3½fl oz) double cream, lightly whipped, plus extra
    to serve

1 Put the lime juice into a small heatproof bowl, then sprinkle over the gelatine and leave to soak for 10 minutes.
2 In a large bowl, whisk together the whole eggs, egg yolks and sugar until thick and mousse-like – this will take about 4–5 minutes.
3 Gently fold the mango purée, whipped cream and zest of 2 limes into the mousse mixture.
4 Dissolve the gelatine and lime juice mixture over a pan of boiling water, then carefully and lightly fold into the mango mixture, making sure everything is evenly combined.
5 Pour the mousse into glasses, put in the freezer for 20 minutes, then transfer to the fridge for at least 1 hour. Decorate with whipped double cream and the remaining lime zest. The mousses can be made the day before you plan to serve them.

(Illustrated)

GINGER CREAMS

PREPARATION TIME: 30 minutes, plus infusion
COOKING TIME: 1 hour 50 minutes
PER SERVING: 640cals, 39g fat, 66g carbohydrate

SERVES 6

350g (12oz) golden caster sugar
1cm (½in) piece fresh root ginger, peeled and grated, or
    1 level tsp ground ginger
375ml (13fl oz) double cream
300ml (½ pint) milk
125ml (4fl oz) ginger wine
3 eggs, plus 4 egg yolks
Desiccated or sliced coconut to decorate

1 Dissolve 225g (8oz) of the caster sugar in 50ml (2fl oz) of water over a low heat until clear and liquid. Bring to the boil and bubble for 5–6 minutes or until a golden caramel colour.
2 Add ¼tsp of water to the pan. Carefully swirl the caramel around the base and sides of six 150ml (5fl oz) heatproof moulds, then put to one side.
3 Whisk together the fresh ginger, if using, with the cream, milk and ginger wine. Pour into a small pan and warm over a gentle heat for 2–3 minutes (it should barely simmer). Whisk together the eggs, yolks and remaining 125g (4oz) caster sugar (add the ground ginger here, if using).
4 Pour the flavoured milk slowly on to the whisked egg mixture, stirring constantly, then strain the mixture into a large jug. Meanwhile, toast the desiccated or sliced coconut under the grill until it turns golden brown.
5 Preheat the oven to 150°C (130°C fan oven) mark 2. Pour the custard into the moulds set in a roasting tin. Add hot water to come halfway up the sides of the moulds. Bake for 1½ hours or until lightly set, then remove the moulds from the tin. When cool, cover with clingfilm and chill for at least 4 hours and up to two days.
6 To serve, run a clean finger lightly around the edge of the creams to loosen, then turn out on to serving plates. Decorate with toasted desiccated coconut slices dipped in caramel.

COOK'S TIP These creams are excellent made up to two days ahead and kept in the fridge, ready to serve.

CREME ANGLAISE TRIFLE

PREPARATION TIME: 20 minutes, plus 20 minutes infusing, 1 hour cooling and 3 hours chilling
COOKING TIME: 6 minutes
PER SERVING: 660cals, 34g fat, 67g carbohydrate

SERVES 4

450ml (¾ pint) whole milk
1 vanilla pod, split lengthways
1 large egg plus 2 large egg yolks
4 level tbsp golden caster sugar plus extra to sprinkle
200ml (7fl oz) double cream
200ml (7fl oz) crème de Cassis or sweet sherry
8 trifle sponges, Madeira sponge or madeleines
450g (1lb) cherries plus extra to decorate

1 Put the milk in a pan with the vanilla pod and bring slowly to the boil. Remove from the heat, then cover and leave to infuse for 20 minutes.
2 Whisk the egg, yolks and caster sugar together and add the milk. Return to a clean pan and cook gently without boiling until the custard thickens. Strain into a bowl and cool for 1 hour, then chill for 3 hours. To prevent a skin forming, sprinkle the surface with caster sugar.
3 Lightly whip the cream until just stiff, then whisk in the chilled custard. Pour 1tbsp crème de Cassis or sherry into the bottom of four tall glasses. Make layers with sponge cake, custard, stoned cherries and Cassis, finishing with the custard. Decorate with cherries.

TO PREPARE AHEAD Complete the recipe to the end of step 2. Cover and chill the custard for up to three days.
TO USE Complete the recipe.

(Illustrated)

MANGO TARTES TATIN

PREPARATION TIME: 20 minutes
COOKING TIME: 20–25 minutes
PER SERVING: 430 cals, 26g fat, 61g carbohydrate

SERVES 4

2 small ripe mangoes, peeled, the flesh cut away in one
   piece from each side of the stone (see Cook's Tip)
40g (1½oz) golden granulated sugar
40g (1½oz) butter
375g pack ready-rolled puff pastry

1 Slice each piece of mango along three-quarters of the length, so the slices are still joined together at the top.
2 Put the sugar into a large heavy-based frying pan. Heat very gently until it starts to dissolve and turn brown.
3 Add 25g (1oz) of the butter to the pan and stir well with a wooden spoon to make a caramel. Add the mango to the pan and toss gently to coat in the caramel. Cook for 2–3 minutes, pressing the fruit down firmly to fan out the slices. Remove from the heat.
4 Grease four 8cm (3¼in) individual tartlet tins with the remaining butter. Unroll the pastry and put one tin upside down on to it. Press a rolling pin over the tin to stamp out a pastry round. Repeat to make three more rounds. You can freeze any leftover pastry for future use.
5 Preheat the oven to 220°C (200°C fan oven) mark 7. Put one mango piece, curved side down, into each tin, pressing it gently so the slices fan out, then divide any remaining caramel among them.
6 Top the mango in each tin with one pastry round. Bake the tartlets in the oven for 20–25 minutes until the pastry is puffed up and golden brown.
7 To serve, turn the tartlets out on to plates with the mango uppermost.

COOK'S TIP To guarantee a superb flavour, choose ripe mangoes that give gently when you press them at the stem end.

CARAMELISED ORANGE TART

PREPARATION TIME: 25 minutes,
plus 15 minutes chilling
COOKING TIME: 45–50 minutes
PER SERVING FOR 6: 750cals, 39g fat,
95g carbohydrate
PER SERVING FOR 8: 570cals, 29g fat,
71g carbohydrate

SERVES 6–8

FOR THE PASTRY

225g (8oz) plain flour plus extra to dust

2 tbsp golden icing sugar

125g (4oz) butter, diced

1 medium egg yolk, beaten

FOR THE FILLING

Juice of 1 lemon

Juice of 1 orange

Grated zest of 2 oranges

75g (3oz) butter

225g (8oz) golden granulated sugar

3 medium eggs, beaten

75g (3oz) ground almonds

2tbsp orange liqueur

2 drops orange food colouring (optional)

TO DECORATE

100g (3½ oz) golden caster sugar for sprinkling

Pared zest of 1 orange, cut into slivers

1 To make the pastry, sift the flour with a pinch of salt and the icing sugar into a bowl. Add the butter, and, using your fingertips, rub into the flour until the mixture resembles fine crumbs. Add the egg and 2 tbsp of cold water, and bring together to form a dough. Knead lightly, wrap and chill.

2 To make the filling, put the lemon and orange juice, orange zest, butter, sugar and eggs in a heavy-based pan and heat gently, stirring continuously, until thickened. Stir in the ground almonds, orange liqueur and food colouring, if using, and put to one side.

3 Preheat the oven to 200°C (180°C fan oven) mark 6. Roll out the pastry on a floured surface and use to line a 23cm (9in) tart tin. Prick the bottom with a fork and chill for 10 minutes. Line the pastry case with greaseproof paper, and fill with baking beans. Bake blind for 15 minutes, then remove the paper and beans and bake for a further 5 minutes. Reduce the oven temperature to 180°C (160°C fan oven) mark 4.

4 Pour the orange filling into the pastry case, put back in the oven and continue to bake for 20 minutes, until just firm. Leave to cool.

5 For the decoration, put 50g (2oz) of the sugar in a pan with 300ml (½ pint) of water. Heat to dissolve the sugar and add the orange slivers. Simmer for 10–15 minutes until the liquid has reduced and the peel is tender. Drain.

6 Preheat the grill. Sprinkle the rest of the sugar over the tart and flash under the grill to caramelise, or use a blowtorch. Cool and spoon the peel around the edge.

(Illustrated)

JUNE

The longest day of the year this month heralds midsummer and, while the sun makes us relax, the abundance of fresh food available makes cooking easier

JUNE KEEPS UP THE GOOD WORK that May began — but in even greater abundance. Asparagus remains the star vegetable, with prices probably lower and quality every bit as good. The latter part of the month is the end of the season, so make the most of it. And experiment with new ways of cooking asparagus, especially if you're getting just the tiniest bit jaded. The Asparagus, Broad Bean and Parmesan Frittata on page 147 is a perfect June dish, and some people think that roasted asparagus — around 10–15 minutes in a hot oven — is even better than boiled or steamed. Some also like to grill it, either indoors or on the barbecue. On the rare evenings when asparagus just doesn't appeal in any form, broad beans continue to thrive; they're likely to be larger, so skinning them is an even better idea than it was in May. Jersey Royals will also be ending their season soon, so take advantage of them. The average size will be larger for them too, as it is for broad beans; try to stick to smaller and medium sizes for best texture.

Other vegetables

New UK veg of the month include courgettes and mangetouts, which should get steadily more plentiful as the month goes on. Think about cooking courgettes on the barbecue, halved lengthways and brushed with oil. Salads, too, are starting to come into their own, with good cos and Little Gem lettuce, cucumbers, and even the first of the UK tomatoes. Supermarkets have made great efforts in the last couple of years, along with growers, to develop tasty tomatoes early in the season. Cherry tomatoes, if well and truly ripe, make a great snack as well as an essential salad ingredient. Summer cabbages are also in their peak season, tender enough for a quick stir-fry.

Left: Chocolate and Cinnamon Sorbet (see page 154)

INGREDIENTS OF THE MONTH

FISH
Brill
Cod
Crab
Haddock
Hake
Halibut
Mackerel
Plaice
Red mullet
Sardines
Skate
Sole
Squid
Trout

VEGETABLES AND HERBS
Asparagus
Broad beans

Cauliflower
Globe artichokes
Lettuce
New potatoes
Peas
Radishes
Spinach
Summer cabbage
Turnips

FRUIT
Apricots
Cherries
Gooseberries
Lemons
Melons
Peaches
Rhubarb
Strawberries

Fruit

For fruit, June is the month when apricots are starting to ripen properly, getting the orange hue that indicates good texture and flavour. Always give each fruit a little squeeze before buying, if possible, as a little bit of 'give' is usually a sign of superior texture. If in doubt, buy just one and taste it the moment you leave the store. If it's good, go back for more. If not, look around or wait a while — all stone fruits get better as summer progresses.

Gooseberries are also coming along by now, with the best fruit arriving after the middle of the month. Among imports there should be melons of real quality coming from Spain, honeydew, Galia, and cantaloupe — try the refreshing Mango and Melon Ginger Salad on page 150, and possibly good peaches and nectarines from Spain and Italy. Cherries are another June speciality, with the first supplies coming from abroad, to be followed later by good fruit from English orchards; among the imports, fruit from the Mediterranean is usually better than what we get from the USA.

But the star among fruits, of course, is the strawberry. With the barbecue season with us we've an unusual way to enjoy them — skewered with brownies and cooked over hot coals (page 154). See the box opposite for more information on selecting and use.

Fish

June is still the month to take advantage of wild salmon, sea trout and crabs, though the advent of the barbecue season means that oily fish like mackerel and sardines also come into their own. Red mullet, often to be found nowadays and with many devoted followers, is another excellent fish for outdoor cooking: its firm, meaty flesh holds up very well over high heat from burning coals. So is trout, though you may prefer the approach taken in the Salt-crusted Trout with Tarragon and Garlic on page 140.

This is a good time for squid also, which can be cooked over coals if it's small or just treated in the usual ways indoors, as in the Moroccan Squid on page 132. And speaking of barbecues, thick steaks cut from salmon or sea trout respond well to that treatment. If you're worried about damaging the fish, the Barbecued Fish Wrapped in Vine Leaves on page 142 offers a delicious and convenient solution.

And another two for the barbecue are the Saffron and Lime Prawns (page 140) and the Chargrilled Lemon Tuna (page 142), both of which can also be cooked under the grill.

STRAWBERRIES

This is the quintessential summer fruit, forever associated with the season of Wimbledon, Glyndebourne, and a million lunches eaten in the garden. Breeders have spent many years and much money trying to find varieties that extend the season, and some may start appearing as early as late May. But there is more to strawberries than a bright red colour, a nice plump size, and a spoonful of double cream. Some of the modern varieties are grown more for their resistance to disease and damage, and for long shelf life, than for flavour and texture. All can be grown to look good, but with strawberries as with any fruit, the proof is in the tasting. And the season progresses so fast that even the same variety can taste sharp one week and glorious the next. Look for berries that are red from crown to tip, and, as always, rely on taste rather than looks alone. But remember: even a strawberry that's a little on the sharp side can be improved no end with a little sugar, or by maceration in balsamic vinegar for serving as a salad. Or in the Eton Mess on page 150.

MOROCCAN SQUID

PREPARATION TIME: 15 minutes,
plus at least 4 hours soaking and marinating
COOKING TIME: 3–4 minutes
PER SERVING: 90cals, 4g fat, trace carbohydrate

SERVES 8

5 level tbsp each freshly chopped coriander and
   flat-leafed parsley

1 level tsp sweet paprika

½ level tsp ground coriander

½ level tsp ground cumin

½ level tsp cayenne pepper

4 garlic cloves, crushed

Juice of ½ lemon

2tbsp olive oil

8 medium squid, slit down one side of each tube

1 Put the coriander and parsley in a mini food processor. Add the paprika, ground coriander, cumin, cayenne, garlic, lemon juice and oil and season well with salt and freshly ground black pepper. Whiz to make a smooth paste, then put into a shallow plastic container.

2 Open out each piece of squid, spread flat and slash one side of each. Add to the paste and stir to coat well. Cover and chill for at least 4 hours or up to 24 hours.

3 Half an hour before cooking, soak 16 bamboo skewers in warm water for 30 minutes, to stop them burning when cooking. To skewer the squid, take two soaked bamboo skewers and push one through one side of the squid and one through the other side. Repeat with the other skewers and remaining squid. Cook under a preheated grill or on the barbecue for 3–4 minutes, turning occasionally.

(Illustrated)

DEVILLED PRAWNS

PREPARATION TIME: 2 minutes
COOKING TIME: 10 minutes
PER SERVING: 200cals, 14g fat, 3g carbohydrate

SERVES 6

1tbsp olive oil

½ onion, finely chopped

2 garlic cloves, crushed

¼ level tsp freshly ground black pepper

¼ level tsp salt

½ level tsp dried oregano

½ level tsp dried thyme

1 level tbsp paprika

4tbsp dry sherry

142ml carton double cream

400g (14oz) cooked, peeled large prawns

Paprika and freshly ground black pepper to serve

1 Heat the oil in a frying pan and lightly fry the onion and the garlic for 3–4 minutes.

2 Add the pepper, salt, oregano, thyme, paprika and sherry. Cook, stirring, for 1 minute.

3 Pour in the cream and bubble to reduce the sauce slightly.

4 Add the prawns then bring back to boiling point. Sprinkle with paprika and grind over some black pepper. Serve immediately.

CRAB CAKES WITH HAZELNUT DRESSING

PREPARATION TIME: 25 minutes,
plus 30 minutes standing and 2–3 hours chilling
COOKING TIME: 15 minutes
PER SERVING: 360cals, 25g fat, 14g carbohydrate

SERVES 6

150ml (¼ pint) each milk and single cream
1 slice each onion, carrot, celery
1 small bay leaf
3 black peppercorns
25g (1oz) butter plus extra for cooling
25g (1oz) flour
2 medium eggs, beaten
25g (1oz) Parmesan cheese, coarsely grated
Finely grated zest of ½ lemon
450g (1lb) white crabmeat, in large chunks
125g (4oz) ciabatta breadcrumbs
Clarified butter for frying (see Cook's Tip)
Salad leaves and lime wedges to serve

FOR THE HAZELNUT DRESSING

2tbsp white wine vinegar
2tsp runny honey
4tbsp olive oil
2tbsp hazelnut oil

1 Put the milk, cream, vegetable slices, bay leaf and peppercorns in a pan and slowly bring to the boil. Remove from the heat, cover and put to one side to infuse for 30 minutes. Strain, reserving the milk. Melt the butter in a pan, stir in the flour and cook gently for 1 minute, stirring. Remove from the heat and gradually stir in the flavoured milk. Bring to the boil and continue to cook, stirring, until the sauce thickens. Remove from the heat, season with salt and ground white pepper and smear the top with a little extra butter to prevent a skin forming. Allow to cool.

2 Mix the eggs, cheese and lemon zest into the cold sauce until well combined. Very lightly mix in the chunks of crabmeat, taking care not to break them up. Chill for at least 1 hour.

3 Gently coat one large serving spoon of crabmeat mixture with the breadcrumbs. Scoop the breadcrumbs over and around the crabmeat to help shape the cakes. Only mould the cakes sufficiently to make the crumbs stick. Repeat the process with the remaining crabmeat mixture. Put on a baking sheet and chill, uncovered, for 2–3 hours.

4 Heat the clarified butter in a frying pan. Fry the crabcakes, turning after 1–2 minutes, until golden on each side. Take care not to overcook.

5 To make the dressing, shake all the ingredients together in a screw-topped jar. Serve the crab cakes with salad leaves tossed in dressing and the lime wedges.

COOK'S TIP To clarify butter, heat unsalted butter until melted and the bubbling stops. Remove from the heat and leave to stand until the sediment has sunk to the bottom. Gently pour off the fat, straining it through muslin if necessary. Chill and use as required.

(Illustrated)

MARINATED TROUT FILLETS

PREPARATION TIME: 2 minutes,
plus overnight marinating
COOKING TIME: 6 minutes
PER SERVING: 250cals, 20g fat, 2g carbohydrate

SERVES 6

4tbsp white wine vinegar
8tbsp olive oil
½ onion, finely sliced
50g (2oz) carrot, peeled and cut into matchsticks
350g (12oz) fresh trout fillet

1 Gently heat the vinegar and oil together. Add the onion and carrot and simmer for 5 minutes.

2 Meanwhile, lay the trout on a rack over a frying pan of simmering water and cover with foil. Steam for 4–5 minutes or until just cooked. Cool.

3 Flake the cooled trout, combine with the warm vinegar mixture and season with salt and freshly ground black pepper. Cool and chill for several hours, even better overnight, spooning the liquid over occasionally. Serve at room temperature.

CHEESE BITES

PREPARATION TIME: 5 minutes

COOKING TIME: 10–15 minutes

PER BITE: 80cals, 6g fat, 4g carbohydrate

MAKES ABOUT 24

225g (8oz) puff pastry

Butter to grease

50g (2oz) olives, pitted and halved or quartered

125g (4oz) firm buttery cheese, such as Jarlsberg or
 Emmenthal, or a soft cheese such as mozzarella, cut
 into small dice

50g (2oz) sun-dried tomatoes in oil, drained and roughly
 chopped

50g (2oz) capers, roughly chopped

50g can anchovy fillets, roughly chopped

50g (2oz) pesto sauce

1 Preheat the oven to 200°C (180°C fan oven) mark 6. Roll out the pastry to 3mm (⅛in), then, using a 5cm (2in) round cutter, stamp out 24 circles. Put on a buttered baking sheet.

2 Arrange the olives, cheese, sun-dried tomatoes, capers and anchovies on each pastry circle. Spoon over a little pesto sauce and season with salt and freshly ground black pepper.

3 Cook for 10–15 minutes, until well risen and crisp. Serve immediately.

PEA AND LETTUCE SOUP WITH LEMON CREAM

PREPARATION TIME: 15 minutes
COOKING TIME: 30 minutes
PER SERVING: 340cals, 27g fat, 17g carbohydrate

MAKES 1.7 LITRES (3 PINTS); SERVES 6

FOR THE SOUP
100g (3½oz) unsalted butter
Peeled rind of 1 unwaxed lemon plus 2tbsp juice
1 bay leaf
75g (3oz) onion, finely chopped
750g (1lb 10oz) frozen peas (see Cook's Tips)
150g (5oz) lettuce, washed, dried and finely shredded
½ level tsp golden caster sugar
1 level tsp salt and freshly ground black pepper

FOR THE LEMON CREAM
142ml carton double cream
200g (7oz) frozen peas, cooked for 1 minute in boiling
    water and drained
Finely grated zest of 1 unwaxed lemon plus 1tbsp juice
Thin strips of unwaxed lemon zest to garnish

1 To make the soup, melt the butter in a large pan. Tie together the lemon rind and the bay leaf and add to the melted butter with the onion. Cook over a low heat for 10 minutes or until the onion is soft and golden. Add the frozen peas, lettuce, sugar, salt and pepper, and stir until coated with the butter.

2 Pour in 900ml (1½ pints) of boiling water, return the mixture to the boil and simmer for 10 minutes or until the peas are very soft. Remove from the heat, take out the lemon rind bundle and discard. Allow the soup to cool a little, then pour into a blender and liquidise until smooth. Add the lemon juice.

3 To make the lemon cream, heat the double cream in a small pan and allow to bubble for 5 minutes. Add the frozen peas and grated lemon zest, season to taste and cook for 2 minutes. Add the lemon juice and stir through.

4 Reheat the soup, check the seasoning and adjust if necessary. Ladle the soup into individual bowls and drizzle the lemon cream over each one. Garnish with the lemon zest strips and serve. (See Cook's Tips.)

TO PREPARE AHEAD Complete the recipe to the end of step 3 up to two days ahead. Cool, cover and chill separately.
TO USE Reheat the soup and lemon cream separately and complete the recipe.
COOK'S TIPS Instead of peas, you could use frozen petits pois.
• You can serve this soup either hot or chilled. If you decide to serve it chilled, it might be too thick for your liking, so add some water or light stock to thin it down a little.

(Illustrated)

CHORIZO PUFFS

PREPARATION TIME: 10 minutes
COOKING TIME: 10–15 minutes
PER PUFF: 70cals, 5g fat, 4g carbohydrate

MAKES ABOUT 18

225g (8oz) puff pastry
1 large egg
125g (4oz) spicy chorizo or pepperoni sausage,
    finely diced
1 small bunch fresh basil – around 15g (½oz) – roughly
    torn
Butter to grease
Poppy seeds or sesame seeds
Fresh basil leaves to garnish

1 Preheat the oven to 200°C (180°C fan oven) mark 6. Roll out the pastry 3mm (⅛in) thick and, using a 7.5cm (3in) round cutter, stamp out about 18 circles.

2 Beat the egg with a pinch of salt in a bowl and use to brush each pastry circle. Put 1 level tsp of the sausage and some torn basil in the centre of each circle, fold over to form a crescent shape and pinch the edges together.

3 Put on a greased baking sheet, brush with egg and sprinkle with poppy seeds. Cook for 10–15 minutes, then serve immediately garnished with the basil leaves.

SPANISH MEATBALLS WITH ALMOND SAFFRON SAUCE

PREPARATION TIME: 15 minutes

COOKING TIME: 40 minutes

PER MEATBALL WITHOUT SAUCE: 40cals, 2g fat, 1g carbohydrate

MAKES ABOUT 30

50g (2oz) sliced white or brown bread, crusts removed

3tbsp milk

175g (6oz) onion, finely chopped

450g (1lb) minced beef or lamb

1 garlic clove, crushed

1 level tbsp dried thyme

2tbsp freshly chopped parsley

1 level tsp freshly grated nutmeg

1 large egg, beaten

Flour to dust

2tbsp olive oil

1 quantity Almond Saffron Sauce (see below)

Lemon juice to taste

1. Soak the bread in the milk for 5 minutes. Squeeze out the liquid then, in a food processor, whiz the bread with the onion, mince, garlic, thyme, parsley, nutmeg and egg and season with salt and freshly ground black pepper. Shape into 30 balls and dust with flour.
2. Heat the oil then fry the meatballs in batches for 4–5 minutes until cooked.
3. Prepare the Almond Saffron Sauce to the end of step 3, adding an extra 150ml (¼ pint) of stock and using the meatballs pan.
4. Add the meatballs, simmer for 25 minutes or until they are tender, stirring occasionally. Squeeze lemon juice over to taste just before serving.

ALMOND SAFFRON SAUCE

PREPARATION TIME: 5 minutes

COOKING TIME: 30 minutes

PER SERVING: 180cals, 16g fat, 3g carbohydrate

SERVES 6

2tbsp olive oil

125g (4oz) whole blanched almonds

25g (1oz) bread, cut into pieces

2 garlic cloves, crushed

Pinch of ground saffron

Pinch of ground cloves

150ml (¼ pint) white wine

300ml (½ pint) chicken stock

Juice of 1 lemon (optional)

1. Heat the oil in a frying pan and cook the almonds and bread over a low heat until golden, stirring frequently.
2. Stir in the garlic, saffron, cloves and wine and season with salt and freshly ground black pepper. Allow to bubble for 1–2 minutes.
3. Put the almond mixture into a food processor, add half the stock and whiz until very smooth. Put back in the pan with the remaining stock and bring back to the boil.
4. Add the lemon juice, cover the sauce and simmer for 25 minutes, stirring occasionally.

CHICKEN PINCHITOS

PREPARATION TIME: 10 minutes,

plus at least 2 hours marinating

COOKING TIME: 15 minutes

PER SERVING: 130cals, 8g fat, trace carbohydrate

SERVES 6

1½ level tsp medium curry powder

1½ level tsp ground cumin

1 level tsp ground coriander

½ level tsp ground turmeric

Pinch of ground cinnamon

Pinch of cayenne pepper

450g (1lb) chicken breast fillets or boned thighs, cut into
  bite-sized pieces

2 level tbsp freshly chopped parsley

Juice of 1 lemon

2tbsp olive oil

5 spring onions, roughly chopped

Saffron Aïoli to serve (see below)

1 Combine the spices in a bowl. Mix in the chicken, parsley and lemon juice, cover and chill for at least 2 hours or overnight.
2 Heat the oil and fry the chicken in batches for 4–5 minutes or until tender, stirring frequently. Add the spring onions and season with salt and freshly ground black pepper. Serve hot with the Saffron Aïoli.

SAFFRON AÏOLI

PREPARATION TIME: 2 minutes

COOKING TIME: 2 minutes

PER 1 LEVEL TBSP: 100cals, 11g fat,

0g carbohydrate

SERVES 6

2tbsp white wine vinegar

Pinch of saffron strands

2 large egg yolks

1 garlic clove, crushed

300ml (½ pint) olive oil

1 Heat the vinegar in a small pan and bubble for 2 minutes, then add the saffron.
2 Put the egg yolks in a food processor with the saffron vinegar and garlic. Whiz for 4–5 seconds with the motor running, then slowly add the oil as for mayonnaise.
3 When the mixture is the consistency of lightly whipped cream, season well with salt and freshly ground black pepper. Chill for up to three days until needed.

SALT-CRUSTED TROUT WITH TARRAGON AND GARLIC

PREPARATION TIME: 10 minutes

COOKING TIME: 20 minutes

PER SERVING: 270cals, 9g fat, 0g carbohydrate

SERVES 6

Around 900g (2lb) sea salt

6 level tbsp freshly chopped tarragon

6–8 unpeeled garlic cloves

6 trout, heads and tails removed, if you like

Lemon wedges to garnish

Tarragon Sauce to serve (see below)

TARRAGON SAUCE

PREPARATION TIME: 3 minutes

COOKING TIME (OPTIONAL): 10 minutes

PER SERVING: 320cals, 33g fat, 2g carbohydrate

SERVES 6

500ml (17fl oz) crème fraîche

1 level tsp Dijon mustard

1 garlic clove, crushed

2 level tbsp freshly chopped tarragon

1 Preheat the oven to 220°C (200°C fan oven) mark 7. Line a roasting tin with foil and add enough salt to make a 1cm (½in) layer. Scatter about half the tarragon over the salt and add the garlic. Press the trout down into the salt, scatter over the remaining tarragon, then cover completely with salt.

2 Cook for about 20 minutes. Remove from the oven, crack the salt open, carefully lift the trout out of the jacket and serve. You can either skin the trout before serving or let your guests do it themselves. (See Cook's Tip.) Garnish the fish with the lemon wedges and serve with Tarragon Sauce (see below).

COOK'S TIP You can serve the trout cold, but remove all the salt and skin before chilling, otherwise it will be too salty.

1 Mix all the ingredients together and season with freshly ground black pepper. To serve the sauce warm, put the crème fraîche in a small pan, add the mustard and garlic, bring to the boil and simmer for 10 minutes. Add the tarragon and serve.

(Illustrated)

SAFFRON AND LIME PRAWNS

PREPARATION TIME: 10 minutes, plus at least 1 hour soaking and marinating

COOKING TIME: 4 minutes

PER SERVING: 160cals, 9g fat, 1g carbohydrate

SERVES 8

Finely grated zest and juice of 1 lime

Good pinch of saffron strands

1 garlic clove, crushed

2 small red chillies, deseeded and very finely chopped

75ml (3fl oz) extra-virgin olive oil

32 raw tiger prawns, shelled

1 Pour the lime zest and juice into a small pan and heat gently. Add the saffron and leave to soak for 5 minutes. Stir in the garlic and chillies and add the oil. Pour into a screwtop jar, secure the lid tightly and shake well.

2 Put the prawns in a shallow dish, add the marinade, cover and leave for at least 1 hour. Soak eight bamboo skewers in water for 30 minutes to stop them burning when cooking.

3 Thread four prawns on to each skewer. Put the skewers under a hot grill or on a barbecue and cook for about 2 minutes on each side until they've just turned pink. Serve hot or cold.

CHARGRILLED LEMON TUNA

PREPARATION TIME: 10 minutes,
plus 30 minutes soaking and marinating
COOKING TIME: 4–6 minutes
PER SERVING: 250cals, 15g fat, 0g carbohydrate

SERVES 8

3 large lemons
2 garlic cloves, crushed
100ml (3½fl oz) extra-virgin olive oil
900g (2lb) fresh tuna in one piece, cut in half lengthways,
 then cut into eight long strips about 2cm (¾in) thick
Fresh flat-leafed parsley

1 Soak eight bamboo skewers in water for 30 minutes to stop them burning when cooking.
2 Take two of the lemons, finely grate the zest from one of them and squeeze the juice from them both. Mix with the garlic and oil and season well with freshly ground black pepper.
3 Lay the tuna strips in a shallow dish, pour the marinade over them and turn the fish to coat. Cover and leave for at least 30 minutes or overnight.
4 Starting at the thinner end of each strip, roll up the tuna and thread on to a skewer, securing the ends (don't worry if any strips break – roll them up separately and thread on to the same skewer). Cut the remaining lemon into eight wedges and push one on to each skewer. Put in a container, pour over the remaining marinade, sprinkle with the parsley and chill until needed.
5 Put the skewers under a hot grill or on a barbecue and cook for 2–3 minutes on each side, brushing with the marinade. Serve hot.

BARBECUED FISH WRAPPED IN VINE LEAVES

PREPARATION TIME: 30 minutes
COOKING TIME: 14 minutes
PER SERVING: 200cals, 8g fat, trace carbohydrate

SERVES 6

6 whole fish, such as red snapper, tilapia or rainbow
 trout, gutted – around 175–225g (6–8oz) each (see
 Cook's Tips)
2 lemons, sliced
Olive oil to brush
227g packet vine leaves (see Cook's Tips)
Lemon wedges to serve

1 Rinse the fish, pat dry and season inside with salt and freshly ground black pepper. Put two or three halved lemon slices in each cavity, then brush the fish with oil. Wrap each fish in vine leaves, tie with wet string (see Cook's Tips) and brush again with oil.
2 Cook the fish on a hot barbecue for 5–7 minutes on each side, depending on thickness. Serve with lemon wedges.

COOK'S TIPS Red snapper and tilapia are from the Caribbean and can be found on the fish counter of most supermarkets.
• Vine leaves are sold in Middle Eastern shops and larger supermarkets.
• Soak the string in water to prevent it from burning on the barbecue.
BARBECUE TIPS Barbecues need a draught to get going, so choose a spot that's neither too exposed nor too sheltered.
• Line the ash tray with foil, shiny side up, to reflect heat and make cleaning easier afterwards.
• Light the fire an hour in advance to allow the flames to die down to ash before you begin cooking. The food will burn on the outside before cooking inside if the barbecue is too hot.
• Use flavoured wood chips and rosemary or thyme sprigs to add extra flavour.
• Open barbecues are fine for cooking foods that require under 30 minutes of cooking, but covered barbecues are better for larger cuts of meat, jacket potatoes and vegetables that require longer or lower temperatures.

POACHED SALMON WITH SAFFRON SAUCE

PREPARATION TIME: 15 minutes

COOKING TIME: 35–45 minutes

PER SERVING USING ESCALOPES: 600cals, 55g fat, 6g carbohydrate

PER SERVING USING FILLETS: 750cals, 65g fat, 6g carbohydrate

SERVES 4

50g (2oz) butter

125g (4oz) shallots, blanched in boiling water, peeled and finely chopped

450ml (¾ pint) medium white wine, such as riesling or Gewürztraminer

300ml (½ pint) fish stock

284ml carton double cream

Saffron strands

1 lemon (optional)

175g (6oz) young spinach, well washed and drained, any tough stalks removed, and roughly chopped

75g (3oz) watercress, washed and roughly chopped

225g (8oz) salmon escalopes or 550g (1¼ lb) salmon fillets

Oil for brushing

Freshly chopped chives to garnish

1 Heat 25g (1oz) of the butter in a large frying pan, add the shallots and cook for 5 minutes, stirring. Add the wine, bring to the boil and reduce by two-thirds. Stir in the stock, cream and a small pinch of saffron, bring to the boil and simmer for 15 minutes or until syrupy. Season with salt and freshly ground black pepper and add a squeeze of lemon if you like.

2 Preheat the oven to 200°C (180°C fan oven) mark 6. Toss the spinach and watercress together and put in four piles on a baking sheet. Dot the remaining butter over each pile. Put an escalope on top, season and brush with oil. Cover with foil and cook for 5–7 minutes or until just cooked. (If using fillets, increase the cooking time by 10–13 minutes.)

3 Put a portion of spinach and salmon on each plate, spoon the sauce around and garnish with the chives.

(Illustrated)

BARBECUED HERB SAUSAGES WITH MUSTARD DIP

PREPARATION TIME: 10 minutes
COOKING TIME: 11 minutes
PER SERVING FOR 4: 880cals, 77g fat,
16g carbohydrate
PER SERVING FOR 6: 590cals, 51g fat,
10g carbohydrate

SERVES 4–6

12 good-quality sausages (see Cook's Tips)
12 rashers smoked streaky bacon
2 level tbsp fresh thyme leaves (see Cook's Tips)
4 level tbsp grainy mustard
8 level tbsp mayonnaise

1 Put the sausages in a pan of boiling water, bring back to the boil and simmer gently for 3 minutes, then drain and leave to cool. Wrap each cold sausage in a rasher of stretched bacon sprinkled with thyme leaves (so the thyme sits next to the sausage) and spear with a wet cocktail stick to secure.

2 Mix together the mustard and mayonnaise and season to taste with salt and freshly ground black pepper.

3 Barbecue or grill the sausages for 7–8 minutes or until well browned. Cook the tomatoes for about 1 minute or until the skins begin to blister and burst.

4 Remove the cocktail sticks from the sausages and serve with the mustard dip.

TO PREPARE AHEAD Complete the recipe to the end of step 2 up to 24 hours ahead. Cover and chill the sausages and the mustard dip separately.
TO USE Complete the recipe.
COOK'S TIPS When buying sausages, check the ingredients list for a high meat percentage (eg 97%) and as few additives as possible.
● You could use any sturdy fresh aromatic herb – oregano or rosemary would make good alternatives to thyme.
● See Barbecue Tips on page 142.

(Illustrated)

MOROCCAN LAMB KEBABS

PREPARATION TIME: 40 minutes,
plus 30 minutes soaking
COOKING TIME: 8–10 minutes
PER SERVING: 300cals, 17g fat, 2g carbohydrate

SERVES 6

3 garlic cloves, roughly chopped
1 medium onion, roughly chopped
½ level tsp each ground coriander, cumin, sweet paprika
   and ginger
1kg (2¼lb) minced lamb
3 level tbsp each freshly chopped mint and coriander
12 large vine leaves
Olive oil
Toasted pitta bread, tzatziki, hummus and a tomato salad
   to serve

1 Soak six long wooden skewers in water for 30 minutes to stop them burning when cooking.

2 Put the garlic, onion and spices in a processor and whiz to form a paste. Add the lamb and herbs and pulse again until mixed. Season with salt and freshly ground black pepper.

3 Divide the mixture into twelve and, with damp hands, roll into long sausage shapes. Rinse and dry the vine leaves on kitchen paper. Wrap each sausage in a leaf and skewer lengthways through the middle, putting two kebabs on each skewer. Brush generously with oil and place side by side across the grill rack.

4 Grill or barbecue on medium heat for 4–5 minutes on each side. Serve with the pitta bread, tzatziki, hummus and salad.

SALMON AND HERB PASTIES

PREPARATION TIME: 40 minutes,

plus 1 hour chilling

COOKING TIME: 35 minutes

PER PASTY: 730cals, 51g fat, 46g carbohydrate

MAKES 6 PASTIES

350g (12oz) plain flour

½ level tsp salt

275g (10oz) butter, frozen (see Cook's Tips)

450g (1lb) salmon fillet, skinned and cubed

25g (1oz) freshly chopped flat-leafed parsley

1 tbsp fresh mint, finely chopped

1 large garlic clove, crushed

100g (3½oz) cooked peeled prawns (optional; see
   Cook's Tips)

Zest of 2 lemons

125g (4oz) trimmed leeks, well washed and finely sliced

Flour to dust

1 large egg, lightly beaten

2 level tbsp mascarpone cheese

Dried crushed chillies or coarse sea salt flakes to garnish

1 Sift the flour into a shallow bowl, add the salt and season with freshly ground black pepper. Coarsely grate 250g (9oz) of the frozen butter into the flour, mixing slightly. Using a fork, stir in 150ml (¼ pint) of cold water, bringing the mixture together until it just forms a ball. Wrap and chill for 30 minutes.

2 Put the salmon, herbs, garlic and prawns, if using, in a bowl. Add the lemon zest to the salmon mixture. Melt the remaining butter in a frying pan, add the leeks and cook briskly for 10 minutes until just golden. Cool.

3 When the cooked leeks are cool, add them to the salmon, herbs and lemon mixture and mix together. Season again, then put to one side. Divide the chilled pastry into 12 equal pieces.

4 Roll out six pieces of pastry on a floured surface and cut into 12.5cm (5in) diameter circles. Roll out the remainder and cut into six 15cm (6in) diameter circles (see Cook's Tips).

5 Brush the edges of the smaller circles with the beaten egg and put two heaped tablespoons of filling in the centre of each one. Put the larger circles on top, press the edges together and decorate. Make a cross in the middle of each pasty and fold back the tips of each cross. Transfer the pasties to a non-stick baking sheet. Spoon 1 level tsp of the mascarpone into each opening and chill for 30 minutes.

6 Preheat the oven to 200°C (180°C fan oven) mark 6 and put a baking sheet in for 5 minutes to warm up. Brush the pasties with beaten egg and sprinkle with crushed chillies or sea salt. Loosely cover with foil, put on the hot baking sheet and cook for 20 minutes. Remove the foil and cook for a further 5 minutes or until golden. Garnish with the chillies and salt flakes and serve.

TO PREPARE AHEAD Complete the recipe to the end of step 5 up to one day ahead. Cover and chill.
TO USE Complete the recipe.
TO FREEZE Complete the recipe to the end of step 5. Cool, pack and freeze.
TO USE Complete the recipe, cooking the pasties from frozen. Cover them with foil for the first 20 minutes of the cooking time, then cook uncovered for a further 10 minutes or until the pastry is golden brown on top.
COOK'S TIPS Freeze the butter for 1 hour just before using.
● Most prawns available in the shops have been frozen, so omit them if you plan to freeze the pasties as prawns should never be refrozen.
● If you've got saucers that are the correct size, they make good templates for pastry circles.

ASPARAGUS, BROAD BEAN AND PARMESAN FRITTATA

PREPARATION TIME: 35 minutes
COOKING TIME: 15–20 minutes
PER SERVING: 350cals, 24g fat, 12g carbohydrate

SERVES 6

225g (8oz) small new potatoes

275g (10oz) asparagus, trimmed and woody stems
 removed

275g (10oz) cooked broad beans

8 large eggs

75g (3oz) freshly grated Parmesan cheese

4tbsp freshly chopped herbs, such as parsley, oregano
 and thyme

75g (3oz) butter

1 Cook the potatoes in boiling salted water for 15–20 minutes until they are tender. Leave to cool, then slice thickly.

2 Steam the asparagus for 12 minutes until tender, then plunge into cold water to set the colour and cool completely.

3 Slip the broad beans out of their waxy skins by pinching one end of the skin to squeeze out the bean. Drain the asparagus, pat dry, then cut into short lengths. Mix with the broad beans.

4 Put the eggs in a bowl with a pinch of salt, plenty of freshly ground black pepper and half the Parmesan. Beat thoroughly until evenly blended then stir in the asparagus, broad beans and chopped herbs.

5 Melt 50g (2oz) of the butter in a 25cm (10in) non-stick heavy-based frying pan. When foaming, pour in the egg mixture. Turn down the heat as low as possible and cook for about 15 minutes, until the frittata is set and the top is still a little runny.

6 Preheat the grill. Scatter the cooked sliced potatoes over the frittata and sprinkle with the remaining Parmesan. Dot with the rest of the butter.

7 Put under the hot grill to brown the cheese lightly and just set the top; don't allow it to brown too much or it will dry out. Slide the frittata on to a warmed dish and cut into wedges to serve.

VARIATION Lay 6 slices of prosciutto over the top of the lightly set frittata and grill for 2–3 minutes until crisp.

FRENCH BEANS WITH BLACK MUSTARD SEEDS

PREPARATION TIME: 5 minutes
COOKING TIME: 5–7 minutes
PER SERVING: 40cals, 3g fat, 2g carbohydrate

SERVES 6

1 tbsp olive oil
1 garlic clove, crushed
1 level tbsp black mustard seeds
450g (1lb) French beans, trimmed

1 Heat the oil in a large frying pan or wok for 30 seconds. Add the garlic and mustard seeds and cook for 30 seconds.
2 Add the beans to the pan and stir-fry for 5–7 minutes until just tender, yet still bright green. Season with salt and serve.

GREEN BEANS WITH ALMONDS

PREPARATION TIME: 10 minutes
COOKING TIME: 4 minutes
PER SERVING FOR 6: 70cals, 6g fat, 3g carbohydrate
PER SERVING FOR 8: 50cals, 5g fat, 2g carbohydrate

SERVES 6–8

450g (1lb) green beans, trimmed
25g (1oz) butter
25g (1oz) flaked almonds
2 tbsp balsamic vinegar

1 Blanch the beans in boiling salted water for 2 minutes, then drain and refresh in cold water.
2 Melt the butter in a pan and cook the almonds until golden, then add the beans. Season with salt and freshly ground black pepper and drizzle with vinegar just before serving.

ASPARAGUS, SPINACH AND POTATO SALAD

PREPARATION TIME: 5 minutes
COOKING TIME: 20–30 minutes, plus 10 minutes marinating
PER SERVING: 270cals, 20g fat, 16g carbohydrate

SERVES 6

450g (1lb) small potatoes
125ml (4fl oz) extra-virgin olive oil
2 shallots, peeled and finely chopped
4 tbsp white wine vinegar
900g (2lb) asparagus, trimmed and woody stems removed
225g (8oz) young spinach leaves, well washed and drained, any tough stalks removed

1 Preheat the oven to 220°C (200°C fan oven) mark 7. Put the potatoes in a roasting tin, drizzle with 1 tbsp of the oil and season with salt and freshly ground black pepper. Roast for 20–30 minutes or until just soft to the centre, then cool.
2 Meanwhile, in a small bowl, whisk together some salt, freshly ground black pepper, the shallots, vinegar and remaining oil. Slice the potatoes thickly, put into a large bowl, pour the dressing over and marinate for 10 minutes.
3 Cook the asparagus in boiling salted water for 3–4 minutes – the thick end of the stalks should be just tender with some bite. Drain carefully and put into a bowl of ice-cold water to retain the colour and stop the spears cooking further. Drain again, then add to the potatoes with the spinach. Toss together carefully and serve.

POTATO AND CELERY SALAD

PREPARATION TIME: 20 minutes
COOKING TIME: 20 minutes
PER SERVING: 360cals, 28g fat, 20g carbohydrate

SERVES 6

2tbsp olive oil

2tbsp white wine vinegar

700g (1½lb) waxy new potatoes, scrubbed

2 celery sticks – around 50g (2oz) total weight – roughly
  chopped

¼ mild Spanish onion, finely chopped

2 large eggs, hard-boiled and roughly chopped

150ml (¼ pint) mayonnaise

150ml (¼ pint) Greek yogurt

1 level tbsp fresh flat-leafed parsley, roughly chopped,
  and a pinch of chilli powder to garnish

1 Mix the oil and vinegar together. Cook the potatoes in boiling salted water for 15–20 minutes or until tender. Drain well, then immediately toss in the oil and vinegar mixture. Leave to cool, then combine with the celery, onion and eggs.

2 Mix the mayonnaise and yogurt together, season well with salt and freshly ground black pepper, then fold into the potatoes.

3 Just before serving, sprinkle the salad with the parsley and chilli powder to garnish.

TO PREPARE AHEAD Complete the recipe to the end of step 2 up to one day ahead. Cover and chill.
TO USE Complete the recipe.

ROASTED POTATOES WITH SHALLOTS AND ROSEMARY

PREPARATION TIME: 10 minutes
COOKING TIME: 1 hour
PER SERVING: 190cals, 9g fat, 26g carbohydrate

SERVES 6

900g (2lb) potatoes, peeled and cut into 2.5cm (1in)
  pieces

1 sprig fresh rosemary

4 tbsp olive oil

150g (5oz) shallots, blanched in boiling water, peeled
  and quartered

2 garlic cloves, finely sliced

1 Preheat the oven to 200°C (180°C fan oven) mark 6. Cook the potatoes in a pan of boiling salted water until just tender. Meanwhile, strip the fresh rosemary off the stem.

2 Heat the oil in a roasting tin and add the drained hot potatoes and the rosemary. Cook in the oven for about 35 minutes, turning occasionally.

3 Add the shallots and garlic and cook for a further 10–15 minutes or until golden. Season and serve sprinkled with sea salt.

ETON MESS

PREPARATION TIME: 10 minutes,
plus 50 minutes chilling
PER SERVING: 270cals, 14g fat, 30g carbohydrate

SERVES 6

142ml carton double cream, lightly whipped

200g pot thick Greek yogurt

500g (1lb 2oz) hulled strawberries

2tbsp crème de cassis

5 ready-made meringue nests

1 Fold the cream into the yogurt and chill for 30 minutes.
2 Put 250g (9oz) of the strawberries in a food processor, whiz to a purée, then stir in the crème de cassis. Measure out 6tbsp of the purée and put to one side. Slice the remaining strawberries into a bowl, reserving six for decoration, then pour the purée over. Chill for 20 minutes.
3 Break up the meringue nests and carefully fold into the cream mixture with the strawberry mixture. Divide between six glass bowls, then drizzle 1tbsp of the reserved purée over each. Decorate with a halved strawberry.

(Illustrated)

FRESH FRUIT WITH FETA CHEESE

PREPARATION TIME: 5 minutes
PER SERVING: 220cals, 11g fat, 18g carbohydrate

SERVES 4

1 melon, peeled and sliced

450g (1lb) strawberries, washed and hulled

225g (8oz) feta or goat's cheese

Put all the fruit into a bowl and mix gently together. Serve with the feta or goat's cheese.

MANGO AND MELON GINGER SALAD

PREPARATION TIME: 20 minutes
PER SERVING: 340cals, 28g fat, 12g carbohydrate

SERVES 4

2 ripe avocados, peeled, stoned and flesh cut into slices

1 ripe mango, peeled and cut into slices

1 ripe cantaloupe or ogen melon – around 450g (1lb)
   total weight – peeled and cut into slices

Grated zest and juice of 2 limes

125g (4oz) Stilton cheese, crumbled

2 level tbsp finely chopped stem ginger

2 passion fruit, halved

Fresh coriander sprigs to garnish

Arrange the slices of avocado, mango and melon decoratively on a serving plate. Sprinkle the fruit with the lime zest and juice, Stilton and stem ginger. Spoon the passion fruit over the salad, garnish with fresh coriander sprigs and serve.

ICED HONEY AND LEMON MOUSSE

PREPARATION TIME: 55 minutes

FREEZING TIME: 6 hours

PER SERVING: 80cals, 0g fat, 19g carbohydrate

SERVES 4

4½ large unwaxed lemons
1 medium egg white
6tbsp acacia blossom runny honey

1 Trim the stalk end from four of the lemons so they stand up. Cut off the tops and put to one side. Using a grapefruit knife and a teaspoon, score around the insides of the lemons and scrape out the flesh. Put into a blender and whiz until smooth, then strain into a jug. Put the hollowed lemon skins and tops on a small tray and freeze.

2 Finely grate the zest of the half lemon and set aside. In a clean grease-free medium bowl, whisk the egg white until stiff peaks form. Gradually whisk in the honey until the mixture is thick and shiny. Slowly whisk in 75ml (3fl oz) of the lemon juice and fold in the zest. Put the rest of the juice aside for future use.

3 Put the mousse mixture into an ice-cream machine and churn until almost frozen (this will take about 45 minutes). Spoon into a piping bag fitted with a 5mm (¼in) plain nozzle and pipe into the frozen lemon skins. Add the tops and freeze until ready to serve.

(Illustrated)

LEMON GATEAU

PREPARATION TIME: 50 minutes
COOKING TIME: 20–25 minutes,
plus 5 hours chilling
PER SERVING: 270cals, 13g fat, 34g carbohydrate

SERVES 8

Butter to grease
2 large eggs, separated
65g (2½ oz) golden caster sugar
Grated zest of 1 lemon
1 level tbsp ground almonds
2 level tbsp fine semolina
2 level tbsp plain flour
1 tbsp lemon juice

FOR THE MOUSSE

Grated zest and juice of 2 lemons
2 level tsp powdered gelatine
3 large eggs, separated
125g (4oz) golden caster sugar
142ml carton double cream
Icing sugar to dust
Raspberries to serve

1 Preheat the oven to 180°C (160°C fan oven) mark 4. Grease and base-line a 20cm (8in) springform cake tin with non-stick baking parchment. Whisk the egg yolks and sugar with the lemon zest in a bowl over a pan of simmering water until thick, pale and mousse-like in texture. Fold in the ground almonds, semolina and flour with the lemon juice.

2 Whisk the egg whites in a clean grease-free bowl until soft peaks form. Stir a small spoonful of egg white into the yolk mixture to lighten it, then fold in the remainder. Spoon into the cake tin. Bake for about 20–25 minutes or until golden, firm, and beginning to shrink slightly from the sides of the tin.

3 Turn on to a wire rack lined with non-stick baking parchment and cool. Carefully slice into two thin rounds. Rinse and dry the tin, then line the base and sides with non-stick parchment, dabbing melted butter around the edge to attach the paper. Put one half of the cake in the base of the tin.

4 To make the mousse, put 3tbsp of the lemon juice in a small bowl with 1tbsp of water. Sprinkle on the gelatine and leave to soak until sponge-like in texture. Meanwhile, in a bowl, whisk together the egg yolks, sugar and lemon zest until thick and mousse-like. Gradually whisk in the remaining lemon juice.

5 Dissolve the gelatine by placing the bowl over a pan of simmering water, then whisk into the egg yolk mixture. Whip the cream until it just holds its shape, then fold into the egg mixture.

6 Whisk the egg whites in a clean grease-free bowl until soft peaks form. Stir a small spoonful of egg white into the mousse to lighten the mixture, then gently fold in the remainder.

7 Pour the mousse over the cake in the tin and level the surface if necessary. Cover and chill until lightly set, about 45 minutes. Carefully put the second cake layer on top of the mousse and re-cover. Chill until set for at least 4 hours, or even better overnight.

8 Remove the sides of the tin and carefully peel away the paper. Put a flat plate on top of the gâteau and quickly invert. Ease off the bottom of the tin. Dust the gâteau generously with sifted icing sugar and serve with raspberries.

BARBECUED SWEET KEBABS

PREPARATION TIME: 3 minutes
COOKING TIME: 3 minutes
PER SERVING: 140cals, 4g fat, 24g carbohydrate

SERVES 6

12 chunks chocolate brownie
12 large strawberries
Whipped cream to serve

Spear the chocolate brownie and strawberries on to skewers and barbecue or grill for 3 minutes, turning occasionally. Serve with whipped cream.

CHOCOLATE AND CINNAMON SORBET

PREPARATION TIME: 5 minutes
COOKING TIME: 15 minutes,
plus 1 hour chilling
FREEZING TIME: 4 hours
PER SERVING: 170cals, 2g fat, 37g carbohydrate

SERVES 6

200g (7oz) golden granulated sugar
50g (2oz) cocoa powder
Pinch of salt
1 level tsp instant espresso coffee powder
1 cinnamon stick
6tsp creme de cacao (chocolate liqueur) to serve

1 Put the sugar, cocoa, salt, coffee powder and cinnamon stick into a large pan with 600ml (1 pint) of water. Bring slowly to the boil, stirring, until the sugar has completely dissolved. Boil for 5 minutes, then remove from the heat. Leave to cool, remove the cinnamon stick, then chill for 1 hour.

2 Pour into a freezerproof container, and put in the coldest part of the freezer until firmly frozen. Remove from the freezer, put the frozen mixture into a blender or food processor and whiz until smooth. Working quickly, return the mixture to the container and put back in the freezer.

3 Freeze for at least 1 hour. Alternatively, put the mixture into an ice-cream maker and blend for about 2 hours until firm. Put into the freezer until needed.

4 Use a spoon to scoop the sorbet and put into little bowls, then pour 1tsp liqueur over each one and serve immediately.

(Illustrated on page 128)

RHUBARB, GINGER AND ALLSPICE CHUTNEY

PREPARATION TIME: 15 minutes,
plus 12 hours standing
COOKING TIME: 1 hour 15 minutes
PER 1 LEVEL TBSP: 30cals, 0g fat,
8g carbohydrate

MAKES ABOUT 1.6KG (3½lb) CHUTNEY

1kg (2¼lb) thick rhubarb stems, trimmed and cut into
   5cm (2in) pieces
4 level tsp salt
225g (8oz) red onions, cut into thick slices
700g (1½lb) dark muscovado sugar
450ml (¾ pint) white wine vinegar
25g (1oz) fresh root ginger, peeled and coarsely grated
¼ level tsp ground allspice
125g (4oz) raisins

1 Put the rhubarb in a non-metallic bowl, mix with 1 level tsp of the salt, then cover and leave in a cool place for 12 hours.
2 Drain and rinse the rhubarb, then put in a preserving pan with all the other ingredients except the raisins. Cook over a gentle heat until the sugar has dissolved, then increase the heat and bubble for 45 minutes–1 hour or until well reduced and pulpy. Add the raisins and bubble for 5 minutes. Pot hot into warm jars, then cover and label the jars (see page 54).

UNCOOKED FREEZER JAM

PREPARATION TIME: 15 minutes,
plus 1 hour macerating and 24 hours standing
PER 1 LEVEL TSP: 35cals, 0g fat,
9g carbohydrate

MAKES ABOUT 3.25KG (7lb) JAM

1.4kg (3lb) raspberries or strawberries, hulled
1.8kg (4lb) golden caster sugar
4tbsp lemon juice
227ml bottle commercial pectin

1 Put the fruit in a large bowl and very lightly crush with a fork.
2 Stir in the sugar and lemon juice and leave at room temperature, stirring occasionally, for about 1 hour until the sugar has dissolved. Gently stir in the pectin and continue stirring for a further 2 minutes.
3 Pour the jam into small plastic containers, leaving a little space at the top to allow for expansion. Cover and leave at room temperature for a further 24 hours. Label and freeze. To serve, thaw at room temperature for about 1 hour.

JULY

Summer is well advanced, the garden beckons and we're
spoilt for choice with the luscious array of colourful
vegetables and soft fruits on offer

W E'RE NOW IN HEAVEN, as far as fruit and vegetables are concerned.
Summer fruits should be at their best, with mountains of berries
and stone fruits, and whole mountain ranges of tomatoes, courgettes, sweetcorn and other quintessential summer veg on the shelves. Any
doubts about the quality of June strawberries should largely be dispelled, with
the English crop now fully ripening under the summer sun. And the summer's
first crop of raspberries should also be with us, far better than any out-of-
season import for that lovely combination of acidity and sweetness. This is also
the time to use them, whether for jam-making, baking, fruit salads or just eating on their own. Make the most of it! It doesn't last for long. The Raspberry
and Peach Cake on page 175 takes full advantage of their abundance. The
cheapest way to buy, important for jam-makers, is by going to a Pick Your
Own farm. Next best is a farmers' market, where the quality will be good and
the prices reasonable – and they're more likely to let you have a taste before
you buy. The jams on page 180 combine, in one, strawberries with redcurrants, while the other teams up raspberries with cinnamon.

Vegetables

Tomatoes are not one of the UK's great crops: we just don't have the sun, most
of the time. But those grown under plastic can give Mediterranean tomatoes
a run for their money if the weather is good. And if it isn't, imports from Italy
and the south of France will make up for the deficit. Beef tomatoes are good
for salads and for cooking, and so are cherry tomatoes – look out for cherry
varieties developed to do well in the UK climate. If it's just cooking you need

Left: Raspberry and Cinnamon Jam (see page 180)

INGREDIENTS OF THE MONTH

FISH
Cod
Crab
Haddock
Hake
Halibut
Herring
Lobster
Mackerel
Monkfish
Plaice
Prawns
Salmon
Scallops
Skate
Sole
Whiting

VEGETABLES
Beans
Beetroot
Celery
Courgettes

Garlic
Lettuce
Mangetout
Peas
Peppers
Radishes
Runner beans
Spring onions
Tomatoes

FRUIT
Cherries
Nectarines
Peaches
Raspberries
Strawberries

BEST BUY
Peas
Corn on the cob
Tomatoes
Raspberries
Strawberries

to do, then plum tomatoes are a prime choice: too tough for eating raw, but with solid flesh and good flavour that make them perfect for sauces. And this is certainly the season to be cooking with fresh tomatoes in new and interesting ways, as in the Roasted Tomato and Pepper Soup with Vodka (page 165) or Roasted Tomato and Tabbouleh Salad (page 160).

Summer is also salad season, and July is one of the peak months for all the ingredients: lettuces, cucumbers and spring onions as well as tomatoes. All these should be of UK origin, and there is no excuse for any greengrocer or supermarket to be selling anything less than the best. An exception to the rule is cucumbers, which keep well and therefore come in good condition from the Mediterranean: Cyprus is a particularly good source. If you think no salad is complete without garlic in the dressing, this is a time when really fresh heads will be arriving from France and Italy.

The two other vegetable stars of July are sweetcorn and peas, two vegetables that are categorically not worth buying fresh at any time other than summer. See the box opposite for the reasons why, and do make the most of these summery specials.

Fruit

For fruit, apart from our own peerless berries, much of the best comes from more southerly climates. Melons are still showing strongly, and peaches and nectarines should be doing the same. Here you have to choose carefully, as these fruits are picked while under-ripe to help them withstand their long journey. Sometimes they ripen after you've taken them home and stored them – unrefrigerated – in a paper bag. Sometimes they do not. Supermarkets have started selling ripe-picked stone fruit at a premium price, and sometimes they deserve the premium. But again, sometimes they do not. Less-than-perfect fruit can be used for cooking in puddings like the already mentioned Raspberry and Peach Cake on page 175. And don't forget mangoes, available all year round but often at their best in summer when they come from Pakistan or India. If you live near an Asian food shop, they may have boxes of mangoes from a special source and at a much lower price than you'll find in supermarkets.

Fish

Summer is a good time to eat fish, both because it's a light alternative to meat and because the quality of several species is at its peak. Plaice is one such fish – try the Grilled Plaice with Red Pepper Salsa on page 169, mackerel is another. Salmon and sea trout are continuing their high season, and shellfish are tops.

PEAS AND SWEETCORN

Both these vegetables, when picked, are packed full of the sugar that can make them addictively sweet. But that sugar doesn't last for long. Sweetcorn and peas both continue to act as if they were still alive even after they are picked, using their sugar as a food source for cells or converting it into starch. At room temperature, sugar loss can be as high and as rapid as 40 per cent in 6 hours – which means a drastic drop in sweetness. The obvious solution is to buy from a farm where the vegetables are picked several times a day, or to pick them yourself if possible, and then cook them as soon as possible after you get them home. If you're not cooking immediately, storing in the fridge will slow the rate of sugar loss.

ROASTED TOMATO AND TABBOULEH SALAD

PREPARATION TIME: 15 minutes,
plus 30 minutes soaking
COOKING TIME: 15 minutes
PER SERVING: 290cals, 18g fat, 27g carbohydrate

SERVES 6

175g (6oz) bulgur wheat

700g (1½lb) cherry tomatoes or baby plum tomatoes

8tbsp extra-virgin olive oil

A handful each fresh mint and basil, roughly chopped,
    plus basil sprigs to garnish

3–4tbsp balsamic vinegar

1 bunch spring onions, sliced

1 Put the bulgur wheat in a bowl and add boiling water to cover by 1cm (½in). Leave to soak for 30 minutes.
2 Preheat the oven to 220°C (200°C fan oven) mark 7. Put the tomatoes in a small roasting tin, drizzle with half the oil and add half the mint. Season with salt and freshly ground black pepper. Roast for 10–15 minutes or until beginning to soften.
3 Put the remaining oil and the balsamic vinegar into a large bowl. Add the warm pan juices from the roasted tomatoes and the soaked bulgur wheat.
4 Stir in the remaining chopped herbs and the spring onions and check the seasoning. (You may need a little more balsamic vinegar depending on the sweetness of the tomatoes.)
5 Carefully toss in the tomatoes and serve garnished with basil sprigs.

COOK'S TIP You could throw in olives, chopped cucumber or capers as well if you have them.

(Illustrated)

CRAB, MELON AND CUCUMBER SALAD

PREPARATION TIME: 20 minutes
PER SERVING: 360cals, 33g fat, 4g carbohydrate

SERVES 4

2tbsp white wine vinegar

150ml (¼ pint) olive oil

2 level tbsp pickled ginger, chopped

2.5cm (1in) piece fresh root ginger, peeled and grated

225g (8oz) fresh white crabmeat, flaked, with claws if
    available

1 large head chicory, trimmed and leaves separated

½ cucumber – around 275g (10oz) – pared into ribbons
    with a peeler

1 charentais melon, peeled and cut into quarters – each
    around 175g (6oz)

Pickled ginger and chives to garnish

1 Mix together the vinegar and oil and season with salt and freshly ground black pepper. Put the pickled ginger and root ginger in a bowl. Toss the crabmeat in half the dressing.
2 On each plate, arrange a few chicory leaves, cucumber ribbons and a melon quarter. Spoon over the crabmeat and remaining dressing and garnish with pickled ginger and chives to serve.

MIXED LEAVES WITH AVOCADO AND CHERRY TOMATOES

PREPARATION TIME: 10 minutes
PER SERVING: 150cals, 14g fat, 3g carbohydrate

SERVES 6

1 level tbsp cider or white wine vinegar
1 level tsp golden caster sugar
4tbsp walnut oil
1 ripe avocado, peeled and flesh diced
150g (5oz) cherry tomatoes
Around 200g (7oz) mixed salad leaves

1 In a large bowl, whisk together the vinegar, sugar and oil and season with salt and freshly ground black pepper.
2 Toss the avocado in the dressing with the tomatoes and salad leaves. Serve at once with chunks of French bread.

BAGNA CAUDA WITH FRESH VEGETABLE CRUDITES

PREPARATION TIME: 10 minutes
COOKING TIME: 2–3 minutes
PER SERVING: 490cals, 49g fat, 5g carbohydrate

SERVES 4

142ml carton thick double cream
4tbsp olive oil
2 garlic cloves
50g can anchovy fillets
125g (4oz) walnut pieces
Selection of fresh vegetable crudités (see Cook's Tips)

1 Pour the cream into a food processor. Add the oil, garlic, anchovy fillets and walnuts and whiz until quite smooth.
2 Pour into a pan and warm through very gently, stirring continuously. Season to taste with salt and freshly ground black pepper and pour into a serving dish (see Cook's Tips).
3 Serve warm with the vegetable crudités.

COOKS' TIPS Serve this warm dip in a dish that will retain the heat.
● Buy ready-prepared crudités or pick a colour theme such as red and green for vegetables that need little preparation, such as radishes, celery, peppers, carrots, cucumber.

ITALIAN BREAD WITH MELTED-CHEESE FILLING

PREPARATION TIME: 25 minutes,
plus at least 4 hours chilling
COOKING TIME: 35 minutes
PER SERVING: 580cals, 28g fat, 56g carbohydrate

SERVES 6

50g (2oz) pecorino or Parmesan cheese, grated
2 x 150g packets mozzarella cheese, drained and cut into small dice
2 round focaccia breads – each around 350g (12oz) – sliced in half horizontally
2tbsp olive oil
75g (3oz) shallots or spring onions, peeled and finely diced
1 red pepper, deseeded and finely diced
225g (8oz) courgettes, finely diced
Fresh rosemary sprigs and sea salt to garnish

1 Combine the grated and diced cheese in a bowl and season generously with freshly ground black pepper.
2 Make a cut in the bottom piece of each focaccia half about 1cm (½in) in from the edge of the bread and about 2.5cm (1in) deep all the way round the edge, then hollow out the centre.
3 Heat the oil in a large pan, then add the shallots or spring onions, red pepper and courgettes. Fry gently for about 10 minutes or until soft and golden. Leave to cool.
4 Stir the cooled vegetables into the cheese mixture and divide between the two hollowed-out focaccia bases. Place the focaccia 'lids' on top and wrap in foil. Chill for at least 4 hours or overnight.
5 Preheat the oven to 200°C (180°C fan oven) mark 6. Cook the foil parcels for 35–40 minutes or until the filling is heated through. Remove the foil and cut each loaf into six wedges. Garnish with the rosemary and salt and serve.

SMOKED MACKEREL SALAD

PREPARATION TIME: 20 minutes
COOKING TIME: 10 minutes
PER SERVING: 290cals, 22g fat, 14g carbohydrate

SERVES 6

450g (1lb) new potatoes, halved lengthways
4tbsp extra-virgin olive oil
3 smoked mackerel fillets, skinned and broken into strips
250g (9oz) cherry tomatoes, halved
½ cucumber, diced
85g bag watercress
2 level tsp creamed horseradish sauce
2tbsp white wine vinegar

1 Put the potatoes in a pan of cold water, cover and bring to the boil. Cook for 10 minutes or until tender.
2 Drain the potatoes well, tip back into the pan and add 1tbsp of the olive oil. Season well with salt and freshly ground black pepper. Cover the pan and shake to mix everything together.
3 Spoon the potatoes into a large bowl. Add the fish, tomatoes and cucumber, top with the watercress and season.
4 Put the horseradish, remaining oil and the wine vinegar in a bowl and season well. Mix together, then pour over the salad. Toss and serve.

SPINACH AND RATATOUILLE TERRINE WITH BASIL SAUCE

PREPARATION TIME: 1 hour 30 minutes

COOKING TIME: 1 hour 15 minutes,
plus overnight chilling

PER SERVING OF TERRINE: 120cals, 9g fat,
5g carbohydrate

SERVES 12

5 red peppers

8tbsp vegetable or olive oil

225g (8oz) onions, roughly chopped

2 garlic cloves, crushed

2 level tbsp tomato purée

125g (4oz) ripe tomatoes, roughly chopped

3 level tbsp fresh basil leaves

150ml (¼ pint) white wine

4 level tsp powdered gelatine

1 aubergine, thinly sliced lengthways

2 courgettes, thinly sliced lengthways, or halve small
   courgettes lengthways

175g (6oz) spinach, well washed and drained

Fresh basil sprigs to garnish

Basil sauce to serve (see below)

1. Roughly chop three of the red peppers. To make the tomato sauce, heat 2tbsp of the oil in a large pan, add the onions and garlic and cook gently for 7–10 minutes until soft. Add the tomato purée and cook for 1 minute. Add the chopped peppers, tomatoes and basil and cook for a further 4–5 minutes. Add the wine, bring to the boil and reduce by half.

2. Add 300ml (½ pint) of water, bring to the boil and simmer gently for 15–20 minutes, uncovered until the vegetables are soft. Purée the mixture in a liquidiser, then sieve to a smooth consistency. Season well with salt and freshly ground black pepper then leave to cool.

3. Pour 4tbsp of cold water into a small bowl, sprinkle over the powdered gelatine and leave to soak for 2–3 minutes. Place the bowl over a pan of gently simmering water for 2–3 minutes to melt the gelatine, then stir into the tomato sauce. Preheat the oven to 220°C (200°C fan oven) mark 7.

4. Brush all the remaining whole peppers and the aubergine strips with the remaining oil. Put on baking sheets and cook for 20–30 minutes or until the peppers are blackened and blistering and the aubergines are golden. Cool, peel and deseed the peppers.

5. Bring a large pan of salted water to the boil and cook the courgettes for 3 minutes only, then drain and plunge into iced water. Drain again. Put the spinach in a colander and pour over boiling hot water to wilt the spinach lightly. Pour over ice-cold water and drain well.

6. To assemble the terrine, line a 1.4 litre (2½ pint) terrine with clingfilm, then with the spinach leaves, making sure there are no gaps. Cover the base of the terrine with 8tbsp of the tomato sauce mixture. Cover with a layer of yellow pepper, trimmed to fit the terrine, then spoon over enough tomato sauce to cover.

7. Continue layering the vegetables with a little tomato sauce in between, finishing with a layer of tomato sauce. Season well between the layers. Cover with spinach leaves, wrap in clingfilm and chill overnight to set.

8. To serve, carefully turn the terrine out on to a board, remove the clingfilm and slice. Put one slice on each plate, garnish with basil sprigs and serve with the Basil Sauce.

BASIL SAUCE

PREPARATION TIME: 10 minutes

PER SERVING: 220cals, 24g fat, 1g carbohydrate

SERVES 12

4 level tbsp fresh basil leaves

300ml (½ pint) mayonnaise

150ml (¼ pint) crème fraîche

1. Purée the basil, mayonnaise and crème fraîche in a food processor until smooth. Sieve, if you like, for a smoother texture then season well with salt and freshly ground black pepper.

2. Cover and chill until required.

ROASTED TOMATO AND PEPPER SOUP WITH VODKA

PREPARATION TIME: 20 minutes
COOKING TIME: 1 hour–1 hour 10 minutes
PER SERVING: 240cals, 17g fat, 14g carbohydrate

SERVES 6

1.1kg (2½lb) tomatoes
300g (11oz) pack on-the-vine tomatoes
2 red peppers, deseeded and chopped
4 garlic cloves, crushed
3 small onions, thinly sliced
20g packet fresh thyme
4tbsp olive oil
4tbsp Worcestershire sauce
4tbsp vodka
6tbsp double cream

1 Preheat the oven to 200°C (180°C fan oven) mark 6. Remove any green stalk heads from the tomatoes and discard. Put all the tomatoes into a large roasting tin with the peppers, garlic and onions. Sprinkle six sprigs of thyme over the top, drizzle with the oil and roast for 25 minutes. Turn the vegetables over and roast for a further 30–40 minutes until tender and slightly charred.

2 Put one third of the vegetables into a liquidiser or food processor with 300ml (½ pint) of boiled water. Add the Worcestershire sauce and vodka, plus plenty of salt and freshly ground black pepper. Whiz until smooth, then pour through a metal sieve into a pan. Whiz the remaining vegetables with 450ml (¾ pint) of boiled water, then sieve and add to the pan. If preparing ahead, pour into a sealable container and chill.

3 To serve, warm the soup thoroughly, stirring occasionally. Pour into warmed bowls, add 1tbsp of double cream to each, then drag a cocktail stick through the cream to create a swirl. Scatter a few fresh thyme leaves over the top and serve.

TO FREEZE Complete the recipe to the end of step 2. Cool and pour into an airtight container. Freeze for up to three months.
TO USE Thaw at cool room temperature for 3–4 hours. Put in a pan, cover and bring to the boil, then simmer for 10 minutes. Complete the recipe as in step 3.

GARLIC AND NUT BUTTER CHICKEN

PREPARATION TIME: 5 minutes,
plus 30 minutes chilling
COOKING TIME: 40 minutes
PER SERVING WITH PASTRY: 620cals, 51g fat,
9g carbohydrate
PER SERVING WITHOUT PASTRY: 550cals, 47g fat,
2g carbohydrate

SERVES 12

225g (8oz) roasted, salted mixed nuts, roughly chopped

5 large garlic cloves, roughly chopped

450g (1lb) unsalted butter, softened

4 level tbsp freshly chopped parsley

2 lemons

225g (8oz) puff pastry (optional)

1 large egg, beaten

1 level tbsp each poppy or sesame seeds and caraway
   seeds

12 small chicken breast fillets

900ml (1½ pints) hot chicken stock

Fresh chervil sprigs and chives to garnish

1 Combine the nuts and garlic with the butter, parsley and 2tbsp of lemon juice and season well with freshly ground black pepper. Cover and chill.
2 Roll out the puff pastry thinly, if using. Prick well and leave to rest for 30 minutes. Preheat the oven to 200°C (180°C fan oven) mark 6. Brush the pastry with beaten egg and, using a small cutter, stamp out shapes. Sprinkle with the seeds and cook for 10 minutes. Cool and store in an airtight container.
3 Arrange the chicken breasts in a roasting tin and half cover with the hot stock. Cover with foil and cook at 200°C (180°C fan oven) mark 6 for 30 minutes or until cooked through.
4 To serve, melt the prepared butter. Drain the cooked chicken breasts from the stock and put on a heated serving dish. Spoon the melted butter over and garnish with fresh chervil sprigs, chives and the pastry shapes, if using.

(Illustrated)

HONEY CHICKEN WITH CASHEWS

PREPARATION TIME: 25 minutes
PER SERVING: 620cals, 50g fat, 5g carbohydrate

SERVES 6

2 warm, ready-roasted chickens or a 2.3kg (5lb)
   home-cooked chicken (see Cook's Tip)

100g (3½oz) roasted, salted cashew nuts, roughly
   chopped

175ml (6fl oz) Vinaigrette Dressing (see page 197)

1tsp runny honey

2.5cm (1in) piece fresh root ginger, peeled and finely
   grated

2 garlic cloves, crushed

½ level tsp ground turmeric

Pinch of garam masala

Freshly chopped flat-leafed parsley to garnish

1 Divide the chicken into large pieces — there's no need to be too neat about this as the warm flesh will tear quite naturally. Put on a serving plate and sprinkle over the cashew nuts.
2 Whisk the vinaigrette dressing together with the honey, ginger, garlic, turmeric and garam masala and pour over the warm chicken.
3 Serve immediately or cover and leave in a cool place for up to two hours. Sprinkle with parsley just before serving.

COOK'S TIP Most supermarkets and good butchers sell small ready-roasted chickens, which make salads like this really simple. If you want to cook your own, pop a 2.3kg (5lb) chicken in a roasting tin and drizzle with olive oil. Season with salt and freshly ground black pepper and roast at 200°C (180°C fan oven) mark 6 for 2 hours or until cooked right through.

STIR-FRIED PORK WITH EGG NOODLES

PREPARATION TIME: 10 minutes

COOKING TIME: 20 minutes

PER SERVING FOR 4: 800cals, 57g fat, 36g carbohydrate

PER SERVING FOR 6: 530cals, 38g fat, 24g carbohydrate

SERVES 4 AS A MAIN COURSE, 6 AS A STARTER

150g (5oz) egg noodles

150g (5oz) creamed coconut, roughly chopped

450g (1lb) pork escalope, cut into thin strips

2tsp soy sauce

Around 6tbsp sunflower oil

125g (4oz) carrots, peeled and cut into thin strips

225g (8oz) broccoli, divided into thin florets

150g (5oz) sugar-snap peas, halved diagonally

1 bunch spring onions, thinly sliced

125g (4oz) mushrooms, thickly sliced

3 level tbsp green Thai curry paste

150ml (¼ pint) hot chicken stock

Fish sauce to taste

1 Cook the noodles according to the packet instructions. Drain, then plunge into cold water. Pour 300ml (½ pint) of boiling water over the coconut, leave for 1 minute, then stir until melted.

2 Season the pork with salt, freshly ground black pepper and the soy sauce. Heat 1tbsp of the oil in a wok or large frying pan and fry the pork in batches over a high heat for 2–3 minutes or until lightly browned, adding extra oil if necessary. Remove and put to one side.

3 Heat 3tbsp of the oil in the pan and stir-fry the carrots, broccoli and sugar-snap peas for 2–3 minutes. Add the spring onion and mushrooms and cook for 1–2 minutes. Remove and put to one side.

4 Add the curry paste, coconut and chicken stock, bring to the boil and simmer for 5 minutes. Drain the noodles, add to the pan with the pork and vegetables. Stir well, bring to the boil and simmer for 1–2 minutes. Season and add the fish sauce, if you like, then serve.

(Illustrated)

GRILLED PLAICE WITH RED PEPPER SALSA

PREPARATION TIME: 10 minutes
COOKING TIME: 40–45 minutes
PER SERVING: 340cals, 9g fat, 31g carbohydrate

SERVES 4

125g (4oz) split yellow peas, rinsed under cold
    running water
1 onion, finely chopped
2 garlic cloves, crushed
1 bay leaf
6 fresh thyme sprigs
2tbsp plain flour
3tbsp finely chopped fresh parsley
4 plaice fillets
1–2tbsp olive oil

FOR THE SALSA

1 red pepper
1 plum tomato, finely diced
½ red onion, finely chopped
½ tsp mustard seeds
Pinch of golden caster sugar
Watercress sprigs to garnish

1 Put the split yellow peas in a pan. Add the onion, garlic, bay leaf and thyme and season with salt and freshly ground black pepper. Pour on 450ml (¾ pint) of cold water, bring to the boil, then simmer for 35–40 minutes, until mushy. Drain then remove the herb sprigs. Check the seasoning and beat to form a rough purée.

2 To make the salsa, grill the pepper under a preheated hot grill, turning until blackened. Cover with a damp clean tea towel; when cool enough to handle, remove the skin. Halve the pepper, remove the core and seeds and finely dice the flesh. Mix the pepper, tomato and onion with the mustard seeds and sugar. Stir well and put to one side.

3 Preheat the grill to medium. Season the flour and mix in the parsley. Dip the flesh side of each plaice fillet in the mixture to coat, then lay them, skin-side down, on the grill rack. Drizzle each fillet with about ¼tsp of oil. Grill for about 5 minutes or until the flesh turns white and is just firm to the touch.

4 To serve, put a spoonful of the split pea mixture on each warmed serving plate. Lay a fish fillet on top and spoon over 2–3tsp of the salsa. Garnish with watercress.

SPAGHETTI WITH COURGETTES

PREPARATION TIME: 10 minutes
COOKING TIME: 25 minutes
PER SERVING: 650cals, 30g fat, 76g carbohydrate

SERVES 2

200g (7oz) spaghetti
3tbsp Italian olive oil
2 courgettes, finely sliced – each slice should be around
    2mm thick
50g (2oz) freshly grated Parmesan cheese

1 Bring a large pan of salted water to the boil and cook the spaghetti according to the instructions on the pack.

2 Heat 1tbsp of the oil in a large frying pan and fry the courgettes in batches until golden, adding more oil when necessary.

3 Drain the spaghetti well, add ½ tbsp of the oil and season generously with salt and freshly ground black pepper. Toss the courgettes with the pasta, then divide between two warmed bowls. Sprinkle with the Parmesan just before serving.

MONKFISH WITH CHILLI OIL

PREPARATION TIME: 40 minutes

COOKING TIME: About 1 hour

PER SERVING WITHOUT MAYONAISE: 600cals,
39g fat, 17g carbohydrate

SERVES 6

2 x 700g (1½lb) monkfish tails, filleted (see Cook's Tips)

2 level tbsp freshly chopped parsley

1 level tbsp freshly chopped thyme

1 level tsp freshly chopped rosemary

350g (12oz) rindless, streaky bacon or thin slices of
    pancetta

3 garlic cloves, crushed

Dried chilli flakes

6tbsp olive oil

2 red peppers, halved, deseeded and cut into strips

450g (1lb) courgettes, sliced

450g (1lb) new potatoes, halved or quartered

Lemon juice

250g (9oz) French beans

Extra-virgin olive oil to drizzle

Garlic mayonnaise to serve

Lemon wedges to garnish

1 Lay two of the monkfish fillets cut-side up and sprinkle with the parsley, 1 level tsp of the chopped thyme and ½ level tsp of the rosemary. Season with salt and freshly ground black pepper. Put the other two fillets on top and wrap in the bacon or pancetta (see Cook's Tips). Put in a shallow container just large enough to hold the monkfish with the garlic, a large pinch of chilli flakes and 4tbsp of the oil. Cover and put to one side in a cool place.

2 Preheat the oven to 220°C (200°C fan oven) mark 7. Put the vegetables in a large roasting tin with ¼ level tsp of the chilli flakes, toss in the remaining oil and season well.

3 Roast the vegetables for 20–25 minutes, basting and turning occasionally. Brown the monkfish all over under a preheated grill for approximately 5 minutes. Remove the vegetables from the oven. Put the monkfish on top of the vegetables with any marinating juices and put back in the oven for a further 15–20 minutes.

4 Lift the monkfish and vegetables out of the tin and put to one side. Put the tin on a low heat and stir in the remaining thyme and rosemary and lemon juice to taste, then season well. Bring to the boil and bubble for 2–3 minutes until syrupy.

5 Cook the French beans in boiling salted water until just tender, then drain. Add the beans and roasted vegetables to the pan and toss, adding a little extra-virgin olive oil.

6 To serve, remove the string from the monkfish and cut into thick slices. Spoon a portion of vegetables onto each plate and drizzle with the pan juices. Put the monkfish on top, then garnish each with a dollop of mayonnaise and a lemon wedge.

COOK'S TIPS Ask your fishmonger to fillet the monkfish. When laying fillets on top of each other, put thicker head ends over thinner tail ends to give an even-sized 'roast'. As a cheaper alternative to monkfish, use rolled plaice or sole fillets; roast on the vegetables for 10–12 minutes.

• If using pancetta, tie fine string round the fish several times to keep the pancetta in place.

GRILLED SARDINES
WITH MEDITERRANEAN VEGETABLES

PREPARATION TIME: 15 minutes
COOKING TIME: 20 minutes
PER SERVING: 520cals, 34g fat, 10g carbohydrate

SERVES 4

3tbsp olive oil

2 red onions – around 300g (11oz) – peeled, halved and cut into petals

2 garlic cloves, crushed

2 red peppers – around 375g (13oz) – halved, deseeded and cut into chunks

225g (8oz) courgettes, cut into small chunks

900g (2lb) sardines – around 16 – cleaned

Olive oil and lemon juice to drizzle

Small fresh basil sprigs to garnish

1 Heat the oil in a large frying pan or griddle, add the onion and fry for 2–3 minutes or until almost soft. Add the garlic and peppers and stir-fry for 5 minutes, then add the courgettes and stir-fry for 4–5 minutes or until almost soft. Keep warm.

2 Season the sardines with salt and freshly ground black pepper and cook under a hot grill or on the barbecue for 3–4 minutes on each side or until cooked in the centre.

3 Drizzle the sardines with a little oil and lemon juice. Garnish with basil and serve with the vegetables.

TO PREPARE AHEAD Complete the recipe to the end of step 1 up to 3 hours ahead. Cover and chill.

TO USE Stir-fry the vegetables for 2–3 minutes or until hot. Complete the recipe.

(Illustrated)

SPICY NOODLE SALAD

PREPARATION TIME: 5 minutes
COOKING TIME: 15 minutes
PER SERVING: 110cals, 3g fat, 16g carbohydrate

SERVES 4

250g (9oz) cooked rice noodles
175g (6oz) each blanched broccoli and mangetout
2tsp sesame oil
2tbsp plum sauce
4tbsp dark soy sauce
Sliced spring onions and chopped red chillies to serve

1 Mix the noodles with the broccoli and mangetout, and toss with the sesame oil, plum and soy sauces.
2 Sprinkle with the spring onions and chillies and serve.

PEPPERED LEAF SALAD

PREPARATION TIME: 5 minutes
COOKING TIME: 5 minutes
PER SERVING: 150cals, 10g fat, 14g carbohydrate

SERVES 6

5 thin slices of bread
1 medium radicchio, torn into bite-sized pieces
1 bunch watercress, washed and stalks removed
1 medium fine frisée, tough outer leaves discarded
50g (2oz) baby leaf spinach: wall washed and drained
50g (2oz) rocket
250g (9oz) radishes, halved or quartered
Vinaigrette Dressing (see page 197)

1 Using a heart-shaped cutter, stamp out the bread. Bake or grill until golden on both sides. Cool then store in an airtight container for up to three days.
2 Wash all leaves in cold water, drain and dry. Chill the leaves and radishes in polythene bags for up to a day.
3 About 1 hour before serving, refresh the croutons in a hot oven then cool. Toss all the ingredients with a little Vinaigrette Dressing to coat.

HOT TOMATO AND HARISSA 'JAM'

PREPARATION TIME: 10 minutes
COOKING TIME: 40 minutes
PER SERVING: 110cals, 8g fat, 10g carbohydrate

SERVES 6

450g (1lb) cherry tomatoes
175g (6oz) onions, finely chopped
2 garlic cloves, crushed
2 level tbsp golden caster sugar
2tbsp olive oil
3–4 level tbsp harissa (chilli paste)
1 level tbsp sun-dried tomato purée

1 Preheat the oven to 200°C (180°C fan oven) mark 6. Put the cherry tomatoes in a large roasting tin with the onions, garlic, sugar, oil and 3tbsp of water.
2 Cook for 45 minutes–1 hour or until the cherry tomatoes are lightly golden, stirring occasionally. Remove from the oven, add the harissa and sun-dried tomato purée and mix well. Serve warm as an accompaniment to spicy roasts.

SIMPLE BEAN SALAD

PREPARATION TIME: 2 minutes
COOKING TIME: 5 minutes,
plus 15 minutes marinating
PER SERVING: 140cals, 9g fat, 9g carbohydrate

SERVES 6

2tbsp olive oil
2 garlic cloves, sliced
2 x 400g cans flageolet beans, drained and rinsed
Extra-virgin olive oil to drizzle
2tbsp fresh pesto sauce
Lemon juice
Small handful of basil leaves

1. Heat the oil in a small pan then fry the garlic until golden. Stir in the flageolet beans then leave to marinate in the oil for 10–15 minutes.
2. When ready to serve, drizzle a little oil over until the beans are generously coated, then add the pesto sauce and lemon juice to taste. Season with salt and freshly ground black pepper, then stir in the bruised basil leaves (see Cook's Tips).

COOK'S TIPS You can add other ingredients of your choice such as some chopped cucumber or raw courgette.
● Bruising the basil saves time as it releases the herb's natural oils into the salad without the need to chop the leaves first – just crush them lightly with your hands before adding to the bowl.

MIXED PEPPER SALAD

PREPARATION TIME: 5 minutes
COOKING TIME: 45 minutes
PER SERVING: 120cals, 10g fat, 7g carbohydrate

SERVES 6

700g (1½lb) red and yellow peppers, halved and
  deseeded
4tbsp olive oil
1 garlic clove, finely chopped
50g (2oz) pitted black olives
A few fresh basil leaves

1. Preheat the oven to 200°C (180°C fan oven) mark 6. Put the peppers in a roasting tin and drizzle with 2tbsp of the oil.
2. Cook for 45 minutes then skin the peppers and cut into thick slices.
3. Mix the garlic with the pepper slices, the remaining oil, the olives and basil. Season with salt and freshly ground black pepper and serve.

FENNEL SALAD

PREPARATION TIME: 5 minutes
PER SERVING: 90cals, 9g fat, 1g carbohydrate

SERVES 6

1 frisée lettuce, washed and dried
1 radicchio
75g (3oz) bag lamb's lettuce, washed and dried
1 fennel bulb, finely sliced
4 tbsp extra-virgin olive oil
2tbsp white wine vinegar
1 level tbsp Dijon mustard

1. Layer all the lettuce leaves in a dish and put the fennel on top.
2. Mix together the oil, vinegar and mustard and season well with salt and freshly ground black pepper. Drizzle the dressing over the salad just before serving.

ANTIPASTI SALAD

PREPARATION TIME: 20 minutes

PER SERVING: 150cals, 9g fat, 13g carbohydrate

SERVES 6

Juice of 1 lime

4 ripe peaches or nectarines, halved, stoned and sliced

50g (2oz) rocket leaves

4–5 small firm round goat's cheeses, thickly sliced

4 grilled red peppers, sliced, or a 285g jar pimientos, drained

2 small red onions, sliced into petals

Handful of black olives

Olive oil to drizzle

1 Squeeze the lime juice over the fruit and add a sprinkling of freshly ground black pepper.

2 Starting in the centre with the rocket, arrange all the ingredients in lines on a large serving plate.

3 Cover with clingfilm and keep in a cool place. Use within 2 hours. Drizzle with oil just before serving.

SUMMER VEGETABLE SALAD

PREPARATION TIME: 25 minutes

COOKING TIME: 1–2 minutes

PER SERVING: 100cals, 9g fat, 2g carbohydrate

SERVES 12

1tbsp cider or white wine vinegar

1 level tsp Dijon mustard

8tbsp olive oil

450g (1lb) baby fennel, trimmed and quartered

450g (1lb) asparagus, trimmed and woody stems removed

175g (6oz) cucumber, peeled, deseeded and thinly sliced

175g (6oz) rocket

1 Whisk together the vinegar, mustard and oil and season with salt and freshly ground black pepper. Put to one side.

2 Cook the fennel and asparagus in boiling salted water for 1 minute. Drain and plunge into cold water. Toss the vegetables and rocket with the dressing and serve.

RASPBERRY AND PEACH CAKE

PREPARATION TIME: 15 minutes

COOKING TIME: 1 hour–1 hour 15 minutes,
plus 10 minutes cooling

PER SERVING: 410cals, 24g fat, 45g carbohydrate

SERVES 8

200g (7oz) unsalted butter, melted, plus extra to grease

250g (9oz) self-raising flour, sifted

100g (3½oz) golden caster sugar

4 medium eggs, beaten

Small punnet – around 125g (4oz) – raspberries

2 large almost-ripe peaches or nectarines, halved, stoned
   and sliced

4 level tbsp apricot jam

Juice of ½ lemon

1 Preheat the oven to 190°C (170°C fan oven) mark 5. Grease and base-line a 20.5cm (8in) springform tin with baking parchment.

2 Put the flour and sugar into a large bowl. Make a well in the centre, add the melted butter and the eggs and mix everything together.

3 Spread half the mixture over the bottom of the cake tin and add half the raspberries and sliced peaches or nectarines. Spoon on the remaining cake mixture, smooth over, then add the remaining raspberries and peaches, pressing them down into the mixture slightly.

4 Bake for 1 hour–1 hour 15 minutes or until risen and golden. A skewer inserted into the centre should come out clean. Cool in the tin for 10 minutes.

5 Warm the jam and the lemon juice together and brush over the top of the cake to glaze.

STRAWBERRY AND MELON CUP

PREPARATION TIME: 30 minutes

FOR THE WHOLE JUG: 750cals, 0g fat,
118g carbohydrate

MAKES 1.7 LITRES (3 PINTS)

300g (11oz) ogen melon, peeled and quartered

350g (12oz) strawberries, hulled and sliced

1.3 litres (2¼ pints) chilled lemonade

450ml (¾ pint) Pimms

Ice cubes and sprigs of fresh borage or mint to serve

1 Put the melon in a food processor or blender and whiz until smooth then sieve.

2 Pour into a jug, add the strawberries and top up with chilled lemonade and Pimms. Add plenty of ice cubes and decorate with sprigs of fresh borage or mint to serve.

SUMMER GRATIN

PREPARATION TIME: 15 minutes
COOKING TIME: 15 minutes
PER SERVING: 180cals , 6g fat, 22g carbohydrate

SERVES 4

3 ripe peaches, halved, stoned and sliced

225g (8oz) wild strawberries or raspberries

3tbsp Kirsch or Eau de Vie de Mirabelle

4 large egg yolks

50g (2oz) golden caster sugar

1 Put the peach slices in a bowl with the strawberries or raspberries and 2tbsp of the Kirsch or Eau de Vie.
2 Put the egg yolks in a bowl with the sugar and the remaining Kirsch, add 2tbsp of water and put over a pan of barely simmering water. Whisk for 5–10 minutes or until the mixture leaves a trail and is warm in the centre. Remove from the heat.
3 Arrange the fruit in four shallow heatproof dishes and spoon the sauce over. Cook under a preheated grill for 1–2 minutes until light golden. Serve immediately.

(Illustrated)

SUMMER FRUITS WITH RICOTTA AND VANILLA DIP

PREPARATION TIME: 5 minutes,
plus 30 minutes chilling
PER SERVING: 430cals, 36g fat, 21g carbohydrate

SERVES 6

250g tub ricotta cheese

250g tub mascarpone cheese

150ml (¼ pint) extra-thick double cream or crème fraîche

A few drops of vanilla extract

Grated zest of 1 lemon

50g (2oz) golden caster sugar

900g (2lb) mixed fresh summer berries

1 Beat the cheeses together with the cream, vanilla extract, lemon zest and sugar (add a little extra for sweetness if you want to). Spoon into a serving dish, cover and chill for at least 30 minutes.
2 Serve with the berries prepared for dipping, or pile the fruit on to a plate and spoon the ricotta and vanilla dip on top.

HAZELNUT PAVLOVA

PREPARATION TIME: 5 minutes
COOKING TIME: 50 minutes,
plus at least 2 hours chilling
PER SERVING: 400cals, 26g fat, 41g carbohydrate

SERVES 6

4 large egg whites

225g (8oz) golden caster sugar

1tsp distilled malt vinegar

284ml carton double cream

50g (2oz) chopped toasted hazelnuts

1 Mix together the egg whites, sugar and vinegar in a clean grease-free heatproof bowl and place over a pan of gently simmering water. Beat with an electric whisk for 10 minutes or until very stiff and shiny.
2 Preheat the oven to 110°C (90°C fan oven) mark low. Line a baking sheet with non-stick baking parchment and spread the meringue mixture into a rectangle, about 30.5x7.5cm (12x3in). Bake for 40 minutes then leave to cool.
3 Whip the cream until it just holds its shape and spread over the cold pavlova. Sprinkle with the nuts and chill for 2–3 hours or overnight. Cut into thick slices to serve.

SORBET WITH RASPBERRY SAUCE

PREPARATION TIME: 20 minutes chilling
FREEZING TIME: 10 minutes
PER SERVING: 140cals, 0g fat, 36g carbohydrate

SERVES 12

500ml (16fl oz) blackcurrant or cassis sorbet
Whitecurrants, raspberries and fresh mint sprigs to
    decorate

FOR THE SAUCE

450g (1lb) fresh or frozen raspberries
225g (8oz) golden caster sugar
2tbsp lemon juice

1 Chill baking sheets in the freezer. Put about 24 scoops of the sorbet in single layers on the sheets, then put back in the freezer for at least 10 minutes to firm up and harden.

2 To make the sauce, purée the raspberries with the sugar in a food processor until the mixture is smooth, then put through a sieve to remove the seeds. Stir in the lemon juice to taste.

3 Flood each serving plate with 2–3tbsp of the Raspberry Sauce and top with scoops of the sorbet. Decorate with fruit and mint sprigs.

COOK'S TIP Serve with a brandy snap basket.

(Illustrated)

GLAZED BERRY PUDDING

PREPARATION TIME: 20 minutes
COOKING TIME: 25 minutes
FREEZING TIME: 7 hours
PER SERVING: 300cals, 12g fat, 45g carbohydrate

SERVES 8

Butter to grease
1 vanilla pod or 1tsp vanilla extract
4 large eggs, separated
50g (2oz) golden caster sugar
25g (1oz) plain flour
142ml carton double cream
150ml (¼ pint) milk
225g (8oz) icing sugar
450g (1lb) mixed red fruits, frozen compote or conserve
    (see Cook's Tip)
Icing sugar to dust
Blueberries and raspberries to decorate

1 Lightly butter eight 150ml (5fl oz) ramekins and put in the freezer to chill. Split the vanilla pod lengthways and scrape the seeds into the bowl with the egg yolks. Combine the yolks and caster sugar and beat until pale then stir in the flour.

2 Bring the cream and milk to the boil in a small pan then pour over the yolks, stirring. Return the mixture to the pan and cook over a gentle heat for 2 minutes, stirring all the time, or until thick and smooth. Turn into a clean bowl, add the vanilla extract, if using, cover and cool.

3 Put the egg whites and icing sugar in a large bowl over a pan of simmering water, whisk for 10 minutes until thick then remove from the heat and whisk until cool.

4 Put 2 level tbsp of the fruits in the bottom of each ramekin. Fold the meringue into the custard and pile on top of the fruits, then put back in the freezer for at least 7 hours or until firm.

5 Preheat the oven to 220°C (200°C fan oven) mark 7. Remove the ramekins from the freezer, put on a baking sheet and dust thickly with icing sugar. Bake for 20 minutes, decorate with the berries and serve immediately.

COOK'S TIP Frozen fruits can be used for this pudding.

RASPBERRY AND CINNAMON JAM

PREPARATION TIME: 10 minutes
(see Jam Tips, page 54)
COOKING TIME: 20 minutes
PER 1 LEVEL TBSP: 60cals, 0g fat,
15g carbohydrate

MAKES ABOUT 1KG (2¼ lb)

900g (2lb) granulated or preserving sugar (see page 54)
900g (2lb) raspberries
Juice of 1 lemon
1 cinnamon stick, crushed and tied in muslin

1 Preheat the oven to 180°C (160°C fan oven) mark 4. Put the sugar in a roasting tin and warm in the oven for 10 minutes. Put the raspberries in a preserving pan and cook over a low heat for 5 minutes or until the juices run. Add the sugar, lemon juice and the cinnamon stick.

2 Bring to the boil then simmer until the sugar has dissolved. Bubble for 15 minutes or until set (see page 54), then remove the cinnamon stick. Pot hot into warm sterilized jars, then cover and label the jars (see page 54).

(Illustrated on page 156)

STRAWBERRY AND REDCURRANT JAM

PREPARATION TIME: 20 minutes
(see Jam Tips, page 54)
COOKING TIME: 30 minutes
PER 1 LEVEL TBSP: 30cals, 0g fat,
9g carbohydrate

MAKES ABOUT 1.4KG (3LB) JAM

700g (1½ lb) granulated or preserving sugar
(see Jam Tips, see page 54)
1kg (2¼ lb) strawberries, hulled and halved if large
225g (8oz) redcurrants, stripped from their stalks
Juice of 1 lemon

1 Preheat the oven to 180°C (160°C fan oven) mark 4. Put the sugar in a roasting tin and warm in the oven for 10 minutes. Put half the strawberries and all the redcurrants in a preserving pan over a low heat and cook until soft and the juice runs.

2 Add the remaining strawberries to the pan and bring to the boil. Add the lemon juice and warmed sugar to the pan, bring to the boil, then simmer until the sugar dissolves. Bubble for 25 minutes or until set (see page 54). Pot hot into warm sterilized jars, then cover and label the jars (see page 54).

APRICOT JAM

PREPARATION TIME: 20 minutes (see Jam Tips, page 54)
COOKING TIME: About 40 minutes
PER 1 LEVEL TBSP: 40cals, trace fat, 10g carbohydrate

MAKES ABOUT 3KG (6½LB)

1.8kg (4lb) apricots, halved and stoned, stones reserved
Juice of 1 lemon
1.8kg (4lb) sugar
Knob of butter

1 Crack a few of the apricot stones with a nutcracker, take out the kernels and blanch them in boiling water for 1 minute then drain.
2 Put the apricots, lemon juice, apricot kernels and 450ml (¾ pint) of water in a preserving pan and simmer for about 15 minutes or until well reduced and the fruit is soft.
3 Off the heat, add the sugar, stirring until dissolved. Add the butter and boil rapidly for 15 minutes or until the setting point is reached (see page 54).
4 Remove any scum with a slotted spoon, then pot and cover in the usual way (see page 54).

BEET RELISH

PREPARATION TIME: 1 hour 30 minutes
COOKING TIME: About 40 minutes
PER 1 LEVEL TBSP: 30cals, trace fat, 7g carbohydrate

MAKES ABOUT 700G (1½LB)

900g (2lb) cooked fresh beetroot, skinned and diced
450g (1lb) white cabbage, finely shredded
75g (3oz) fresh horseradish, grated
1 level tbsp mustard powder
600ml (1 pint) malt vinegar
225g (8oz) sugar
Pinch of cayenne pepper

1 Combine all the ingredients in a large pan. Bring slowly to the boil, then simmer for 30 minutes, stirring occasionally.
2 Spoon into preheated sterilized jars and cover at once with airtight, vinegar-proof tops.
3 Store in a cool, dry, dark place, and leave to mature for 2–3 months before eating.

AUGUST

*A month to make the most of the last
lazy days of summer and its
abundant fresh produce*

THE CROPS MAY BE CHANGING SOMEWHAT, but the picture for August closely resembles the picture in July: this is a month to gladden the hearts of veggie-lovers. There won't be as many good English strawberries around, or any more Jersey Royals or asparagus, but other potatoes will be nearly as good – Maris Piper is a particularly good variety for summer eating in salads. And on the green front, there's so much to get excited about that it's hard to know where to start. Sweetcorn, peas, tomatoes, cucumbers, salad leaves, courgettes – these are all continuing to thrive under the summer sun. Among new arrivals, UK herbs will be popping up in both domestic gardens and on commercial farms; make the most of them while they last as a cheaper and better replacement for expensive imports. They star in the Herb and Lemon Soup on page 186, which is just one idea for getting maximum mileage out of these summer luxuries.

Vegetables

Other new veggie arrivals will be aubergines and peppers grown outdoors in the hot weather of southern France and Italy. These are much better than the year-round imports from Holland, and you should take advantage of them from now through September. These are the best months to make ratatouille, or a more unusual dish like the Aubergine Timbales with Red Pepper Salsa on page 187. Failing that, adding them to the barbecue with courgettes makes a sensational summer vegetable platter. Another true August star is runner beans, always at their best if picked young before they've had a chance to develop the powerful strings and skins that make preparation and eating a bit

Left: Roquefort and Redcurrant Salad (see page 187)

INGREDIENTS OF THE MONTH

GAME
Grouse
Hare
Snipe

FISH
Bass
Brill
Dabs
Halibut
Herring
Mackerel
Prawns
Red mullet
Sardines
Shrimps
Whiting

VEGETABLES
Aubergines
Beetroot
Carrots
Celeriac
Courgettes

Fennel
Globe artichokes
Potatoes
Runner beans
Salad leaves
Tomatoes

FRUIT
Apples
Apricots
Blackcurrants
Cherries
Gooseberries
Nectarines
Peaches
Plums
Redcurrants

BEST BUY
Runner beans
Blackberries

of a chore. Slicing and tossing them with buttery hazelnuts is an unusual way to serve them (see page 197). If you can only find the larger beans, de-stringing, slicing, and long cooking are more or less essential. Or use mangetouts as an easier replacement; they too should be at their best in August.

Don't forget about the new crops of cauliflower, beetroot, carrots and leeks, all of which should be at their youngest and most tender; if there is ever a prime time to eat cauliflower and carrots raw, perhaps in a French plate of crudités with dips or vinaigrette, this is it. Vegetable soups are another obvious area to explore in August. And do pounce on the best of the summer's artichokes from France and Italy. They should have started arriving last month but are even better now. See the box opposite for more information.

Fruit

As for fruit, some summer berries may be going through a dull period after the end of Wimbledon, but not all of them. August is the start of the blackberry season, and with their help you'll be able to put together summer puddings of distinction – unless of course you want to save them for the delicious Blackberry, Apple and Cardamom Jam on page 206. There should also be good English cherries around, for part of the month at any rate, and blackcurrants and blueberries as well. Peaches, nectarines and apricots are at their very best now, literally pouring into the country from all over southern Europe. The same goes for melons, which are never better than they are now.

Fish

Fish for the month include several that are firm barbecue favourites: sardines, herring, prawns, red mullet and sea bass. Why not try ceviche of fish – fillets cut into small pieces and marinated overnight in lime juice? They can be made with sole, bass, whiting, or any other good sea fish including mackerel; while the Mackerel Pâté with Beetroot Salsa on page 189 uses smoked fillets for a tasty starter.

Game

August also sees the official arrival of the game season, with the 'glorious 12th' signalling the beginning of small, costly supplies of grouse and then snipe. In practice, the early birds go to restaurants; most of us are unlikely to see them for a while, and it's better to concentrate on farmed birds. Hare and snipe are the two other August game arrivals, but chicken barbecued with all those glorious summer veg is a much better bet.

ARTICHOKES

Globe artichokes, the flower head of a member of the thistle family, are among the strangest of all vegetables: a good 80 per cent of each piece is inedible. But they're also one of the best, and at their height in summer. Those that come over here are of two types, the small ones (usually from Italy) little bigger than your fist and the large ones (usually from France, especially Brittany) that can equal a grapefruit in size. Care is needed in buying: there should be no sign of browning or shrivelling, and the tips of the leaves should feel soft rather than sharp and spiny. Artichokes harbour a lot of grit, best removed by soaking and then a vigorous shake in the water. To cook, cut off the stem flush with the base of the head and boil them in salted water till a leaf pulls off easily. You'll get more even cooking if you keep the heads submerged by putting a steamer insert on top of them in the water.

HERB AND LEMON SOUP

PREPARATION TIME: 10 minutes

COOKING TIME: 15–20 minutes

PER SERVING: 120cals, 4g fat, 15g carbohydrate

SERVES 6

1.7 litres (3 pints) chicken stock

125g (4oz) orzo or other 'soup' pasta

3 medium eggs

Juice of 1 large lemon

2tbsp finely chopped chives

2tbsp finely chopped chervil

A few very fine slices of lemon to garnish

1 Bring the stock to the boil in a large pan. Add the pasta and cook for 5 minutes or according to the packet instructions.

2 Beat the eggs in a bowl until frothy, then add the lemon juice and 1tbsp of cold water. Slowly stir in two ladles of the hot stock. Return the mixture to the pan, then warm through over a very low heat for 2–3 minutes.

3 Add the herbs and season with salt and freshly ground black pepper. Serve in soup bowls, garnished with lemon slices.

COOK'S TIP Don't boil the soup after adding the eggs – they will curdle.

(Illustrated)

AUBERGINE TIMBALES WITH RED PEPPER SAUCE

PREPARATION TIME: 30 minutes
COOKING TIME: 1 hour 30 minutes
PER SERVING: 480cals, 39g fat, 8g carbohydrate

SERVES 6

2 aubergines – around 275g (10oz) each (preferably
   short, fat shapes) – finely sliced lengthways

6tbsp olive oil

450g (1lb) ricotta cheese

175g (6oz) freshly grated Parmesan cheese

4 large egg yolks

1tsp freshly grated nutmeg

Small handful fresh basil, torn into shreds

2 large red peppers – around 225g (8oz) each –
   deseeded and roughly chopped

4 tomatoes – around 350g (12oz) total weight –
   deseeded and roughly chopped

2 garlic cloves, crushed

2tbsp passata or 1 level tbsp tomato purée

3tbsp pesto sauce to serve

1. Preheat the grill. Put the aubergines on an oiled baking sheet and brush lightly with the oil. Grill one side until well browned then put to one side.

2. To make the filling, put the ricotta and Parmesan cheeses, egg yolks, nutmeg, salt and freshly ground black pepper in a food processor and whiz until smooth. Put 1tbsp of the basil to one side and add the rest to the mixture.

3. Preheat the oven to 190°C (170°C fan oven) mark 5. Line six 150–175ml (5–6fl oz) dariole moulds or ramekins with the aubergine slices, overlapping them with the browned sides facing outwards. Leave a long edge hanging over the outside. Fill each mould with the cheese mixture, pushing it down firmly. Fold the edges of aubergine over the top of the filling to enclose it. Put on a baking sheet and cook for about 15 minutes or until firm.

4. Meanwhile, make the red pepper sauce. Put the peppers and tomatoes in a pan with the garlic, passata or purée and 4tbsp of water. Season well with salt and freshly ground black pepper. Cover and cook over a gentle heat for 10 minutes, then whiz the sauce in a blender until smooth and pass it through a nylon sieve.

5. Stir in the reserved basil and gently reheat the sauce. To serve, pour a pool of sauce on six small plates. Unmould the timbales and put in the centre. Drizzle a little pesto around each timbale.

TO FREEZE Make the red pepper sauce to the end of step 4. Cool, pack and freeze.

TO USE Thaw overnight at cool room temperature and complete recipe.

ROQUEFORT AND REDCURRANT SALAD

PREPARATION TIME: 10 minutes
PER SERVING: 350cals, 32g fat, 5g carbohydrate

SERVES 4

1½tbsp redcurrant jelly

1tbsp white wine vinegar

Pinch of English mustard powder

4tbsp extra-virgin olive oil

A selection of bitter leaves such as curly endive, radicchio
   and chicory

225g (8oz) Roquefort cheese, crumbled

125g (4oz) punnet fresh redcurrants – put four sprays to
   one side to garnish and destalk the rest

1. In a small bowl, whisk together the redcurrant jelly, 1tsp of boiling water, the vinegar, mustard powder and oil. Season with salt and freshly ground black pepper.

2. Arrange the mixed salad leaves and Roquefort on a large plate. Spoon the dressing over the top and sprinkle with the redcurrants. Garnish with redcurrant sprays and serve immediately.

(Illustrated on page 182)

TUNA BEAN SALAD

PREPARATION TIME: 12 minutes

PER SERVING: 130cals, 1g fat, 17g carbohydrate

SERVES 4

FOR THE VINAIGRETTE

2tbsp balsamic vinegar

3tbsp orange juice

Juice of 2 limes

Several dashes of Tabasco sauce

2 garlic cloves, crushed

1 level tbsp caster sugar

FOR THE SALAD

200g can tuna in brine, drained

4 spring onions, trimmed and sliced

2 inner stalks of celery, chopped

410g can cannellini beans, drained and rinsed

1 level tbsp drained capers

2 level tbsp freshly chopped flat-leafed parsley

1 To make the vinaigrette, put all the ingredients in a screw-top jar and shake well to combine.

2 To make the salad, put the tuna in a bowl and flake it with a fork. Toss in the spring onions and celery, then stir in the beans and capers.

3 Pour over the vinaigrette, add the flat-leafed parsley and toss to distribute the dressing evenly. Cover and chill until needed.

(Illustrated)

MACKEREL PATE WITH BEETROOT SALSA

PREPARATION TIME: 15 minutes,
plus cooling and chilling
COOKING TIME: 15–20 minutes
PER SERVING: 490cals, 44g fat, 12g carbohydrate

SERVES 6

FOR THE PÂTÉ

1 tbsp vegetable oil

25g (1oz) butter

1 small onion, finely chopped

225g (8oz) cooking apples, peeled and chopped

4 smoked mackerel fillets, weighing around 300g (11oz)

1 tbsp hot horseradish sauce

6 tbsp mayonnaise

1 tbsp lemon juice

FOR THE SALSA

6 tbsp walnut oil

3 tbsp lemon juice

175g (6oz) cooked beetroot (not in vinegar), diced

2 level tbsp chopped chives

2 small green eating apples, cored and diced

Granary bread, toasted, crusts removed, then sliced into
  fingers to serve

1 To make the pâté, heat the oil and butter in a pan and cook the onion until soft. Add the chopped apple, then cover and cook for about 10–15 minutes until the apple has softened. Leave to cool.

2 Remove the skin from the mackerel, then flake the flesh into a bowl. Add the apple mixture, horseradish, mayonnaise and lemon juice. Mix together and season with salt and freshly ground black pepper. Put into six small bowls, grind over coarse black pepper and chill.

3 To make the salsa, whisk together the walnut oil and lemon juice, then season. Put the beetroot in a bowl and add the chives and diced apple. Add the dressing and mix well. Serve the pâté with the salsa and toast fingers.

TOMATO TARTS WITH FETA CHEESE

PREPARATION TIME: 5 minutes
COOKING TIME: 15–20 minutes
PER SERVING: 280cals, 20g fat, 18g carbohydrate

SERVES 4

150g (5oz) sheet ready-rolled puff pastry

300g (11oz) plum tomatoes, thinly sliced

Pinch of golden caster sugar

150g (5oz) feta cheese, crumbled

1 level tbsp freshly chopped thyme

1 tbsp extra-virgin olive oil

1 Preheat the oven to 200°C (180°C fan oven) mark 6. Cut the puff pastry into four rectangles. Arrange the tomatoes on top, sprinkle over the caster sugar and season well with salt and freshly ground black pepper. Sprinkle the feta and thyme on top and drizzle with the olive oil.

2 Bake the tarts for 15–20 minutes or until the pastry is golden brown and risen.

COOK'S TIP If you have time, it's a good idea to sprinkle the sliced tomatoes with a little salt and leave for 30 minutes to draw out some of the juice before draining and using them, as the pastry will then be crisper.

PRAWN AND PAK CHOI STIR-FRY

PREPARATION TIME: 10 minutes
COOKING TIME: 5 minutes, plus 4 minutes standing
PER SERVING: 340cals, 6g fat, 50g carbohydrate

SERVES 4

250g pack medium egg noodles

1tbsp stir-fry oil or sesame oil

1 garlic clove, sliced

1 level tsp freshly grated ginger

1 bunch spring onions, trimmed and cut into four

250g (7oz) raw peeled tiger prawns

200g bag pak choi, leaves removed and the white base
    cut into thick slices

160g jar Chinese yellow bean stir-fry sauce

1 Put the noodles in a bowl, pour over 2 litres (3½ pints) of boiling water and leave to soak for 4 minutes. Drain and put to one side.

2 Heat the oil in a wok, add the garlic and grated ginger and stir-fry for 30 seconds. Add the spring onions and prawns and cook for 2 minutes.

3 Add the chopped white part of the pak choi and the jar of sauce. Fill the empty sauce jar with boiling water from the kettle and pour this into the wok.

4 Add the noodles to the wok and continue to cook for 1 minute, tossing every now and then to heat through. Finally, stir in the green pak choi leaves and serve.

(Illustrated)

AUBERGINE CANNELLONI

PREPARATION TIME: 45 minutes
COOKING TIME: 45 minutes
PER SERVING: 490cals, 43g fat, 8g carbohydrate

SERVES 6

FOR THE SAUCE

2tbsp olive oil

2 shallots, peeled and chopped

900g (2lb) ripe tomatoes, skinned, deseeded and
    chopped, or 2 x 400g cans chopped tomatoes

2 garlic cloves, crushed

300ml (½ pint) vegetable stock

1tbsp tomato purée

½tsp golden caster sugar

2tbsp dry white wine

FOR THE CANNELLONI

150ml (¼ pint) olive oil

4 aubergines – each around 250g (9oz) – cut lengthways
    into thin slices (you'll need 24 slices), ends and side
    pieces discarded

450g (1lb) ricotta or curd cheese

125g (4oz) freshly grated Parmesan cheese

2tbsp finely shredded fresh basil

Fresh Parmesan shavings and basil sprigs to serve

1 To make the sauce, heat the oil in a heavy-based pan, add the shallots and cook gently for 5–7 minutes, stirring. Add the fresh tomatoes and garlic, cover and cook gently for 10 minutes, stirring occasionally. Add the stock, tomato purée, canned tomatoes, if using, and the sugar and season with salt and freshly ground black pepper. Half cover, then simmer for 30 minutes. Sieve the mixture, add the wine and put to one side.

2 To make the cannelloni, heat 2–3tbsp of the oil in a large non-stick frying pan and fry the aubergine slices in a single layer in batches until lightly golden on both sides. Add a little more oil between batches as necessary. Drain the slices on absorbent kitchen paper.

3 Mix the ricotta or curd and Parmesan cheeses with the basil, season and beat well. Lay the aubergine slices on a clean surface – if small, overlap two slices so that they will roll up as one. Spoon the cheese mixture along the aubergine slices.

4 Preheat the oven to190°C (170°C fan oven) mark 5. Roll up the aubergine slices to enclose the filling and place, seam-side down in a single layer, in an ovenproof dish. Cook for 10–15 minutes until hot. Reheat the tomato sauce and spoon over the cannelloni. Sprinkle lightly with Parmesan shavings and garnish with basil to serve.

PISSALADIERE

PREPARATION TIME: 25 minutes,
plus 30 minutes rising
COOKING TIME: 40 minutes
PER SERVING: 340cals, 13g fat, 46g carbohydrate

SERVES 6

290g packet pizza base mix

100g jar anchovy fillets in olive oil

3tbsp olive oil plus extra to grease

1kg (2¼ lb) onions, finely sliced

16–20 black olives – around 40g (1½oz) – pitted

1 Put the pizza base mix into a bowl, add 200ml (7fl oz) of warm water and make up according to the packet instructions. Knead the dough on a clean surface for 5–10 minutes until soft, smooth and pliable.

2 Put the dough in a lightly oiled bowl, then cover with clingfilm and a clean tea towel. Leave for 30 minutes in a warm, draught-free place until doubled in size.

3 Pour 3tbsp of oil from the anchovy jar into a pan. Add the olive oil and the onions. Cover the pan and cook gently until the onions are soft. Remove the lid, increase the heat and cook for 20 minutes until caramelised. Season well with salt and freshly ground black pepper.

4 Preheat the oven to 230°C (210°C fan oven) mark 9. Knead the dough for 2–3 minutes, then roll it into a rectangle measuring about 28x35.5cm (11x14in). Put the dough on a lightly oiled baking sheet, then spread the onions over the top. Cut the anchovies in half and arrange on top in a lattice pattern. Put an olive inside each diamond, then bake for 15–20 minutes until lightly browned. Serve warm.

PEPPERED FETTUCINE

PREPARATION TIME: 15 minutes
COOKING TIME: 15 minutes
PER SERVING: 870cals, 53g fat, 74g carbohydrate

SERVES 4

350g (12oz) dried pasta noodles

25g (1oz) butter

125g (4oz) each shallots and brown-cap mushrooms,
    sliced

275g (10oz) peppered salami, cut into strips

125g (4oz) soft cheese with garlic and herbs

142ml carton single cream

4tbsp milk

Parmesan cheese, freshly grated, to serve

1 Cook the pasta in boiling salted water according to the packet instructions.

2 Meanwhile, melt the butter in a frying pan and fry the shallots until golden. Add the mushrooms and fry for about 5 minutes or until beginning to soften. Add the salami and fry, stirring, for 1–2 minutes. Lower the heat and stir in the soft cheese, cream and milk. Simmer, stirring, for about 2 minutes until piping hot.

3 Drain the pasta, put back in the pan and stir in the sauce. Serve immediately with a little Parmesan sprinkled over if you like.

CHICKEN, AVOCADO AND PEANUT SALAD

PREPARATION TIME: 15 minutes, plus chilling

PER SERVING: 400cals, 34g fat, 2g carbohydrate

SERVES 4

2tbsp cider vinegar

1tsp English ready-made mustard

5tbsp groundnut oil

1 large ripe avocado, peeled and thickly sliced

2 roasted chicken breasts – around 250g (9oz) total
    weight – skin discarded and meat sliced

75g (3oz) bag watercress

50g (2oz) roasted salted peanuts, roughly chopped

1 Put the vinegar, mustard and oil in a bowl, season with salt and freshly ground black pepper and whisk until well emulsified. Add the avocado and gently toss in the dressing, making sure each slice of avocado is well covered.

2 Arrange the sliced chicken breasts on top of the watercress, cover with clingfilm and chill.

3 Just before serving, spoon the avocado and dressing over the chicken and watercress. Sprinkle with the chopped peanuts and serve immediately.

MIXED MUSHROOM PARCELS

PREPARATION TIME: 20 minutes

COOKING TIME: Around 1 hour

PER PARCEL: 180cals, 9g fat, 22g carbohydrate

MAKES 20

50g (2oz) wild or brown rice

50g (2oz) butter, plus extra, melted, for brushing

175g (6oz) each onion, carrot and celery, chopped

2 garlic cloves, crushed

700g (1½lb) mixed brown and white cap mushrooms,
    chopped

225g (8oz) jar mixed wild mushrooms, drained

75g (3oz) hazelnuts, toasted and chopped

75g (3oz) no-soak dried apricots, chopped

Around 600g (1¼lb) filo pastry

1 level tbsp sesame seeds

4 level tbsp freshly chopped chives, plus extra to
    garnish (optional)

200g (7oz) crème fraîche

1 Cook the rice according to the packet instructions in boiling salted water until tender. Drain, then set aside.

2 Melt 25g (1oz) butter in a frying pan and cook the onion and garlic for 10 minutes or until soft and brown. Add the carrot and celery and fry for 3–4 minutes.

3 Add a further 25g (1oz) butter and the fresh mushrooms to the vegetables. Cook uncovered, stirring, until the excess moisture has evaporated and the mixture is quite dry – about 15 minutes. Add the wild mushrooms and cook for a further 5 minutes then remove from the heat and put to one side. Season with salt and freshly ground black pepper.

4 Stir the wild rice, nuts and apricots into the mushroom mixture.

5 Cut the pastry into about 40 squares, each 18–20.5cm (7–8in) (see Cook's Tip). Divide into two or three stacks and wrap in clingfilm while preparing the parcels. Butter one square of pastry, top with a second piece of pastry and butter again. Spoon about one-twentieth of the mushroom mixture into the centre and gather up the sides to form a parcel. Press gently to seal. Continue with the remaining pastry and mushroom mixture. Brush with melted butter and sprinkle with sesame seeds.

6 Preheat the oven to 190°C (170°C fan oven) mark 5 and put a baking sheet in to warm up. Put the parcels on the heated baking sheet and cook for 25–30 minutes.

7 Stir the chives into the crème fraîche and season. Serve the parcels with a spoonful of crème fraîche mixture, garnished with chives, if you like. Serve the remaining crème fraîche separately.

COOK'S TIP Filo pastry comes in several sizes. Cut squares accurately to waste as little pastry as possible.

ROASTED ORIENTAL SALMON

PREPARATION TIME: 20 minutes,
plus minimum 8 hours marinating
COOKING TIME: 40 minutes,
plus minimum 2 hours cooling
PER SERVING: 300cals, 20g fat, 1g carbohydrate

SERVES 12

2.5kg (5½lb) whole salmon, cleaned and
    scaled (see Cook's Tips)
3 limes, quartered, to serve

FOR THE MARINADE

175ml (6fl oz) dark soy sauce
175ml (6fl oz) rice wine vinegar or dry sherry
6 garlic cloves, cut into wafer-thin slices
7.5cm (3in) piece fresh root ginger, grated
3tbsp runny honey
4 whole star anise, lightly crushed

1 Rinse the salmon well under cold running water. Make three to four diagonal slashes on either side of the fish and put it in a non-metallic dish.
2 To make the marinade, combine all the ingredients in a blender. Coat the salmon with the marinade. Cover and chill for at least 8 hours or overnight, turning occasionally.
3 Preheat the oven to 200°C (180°C fan oven) mark 6. Put the salmon on a large piece of foil in a roasting tin, spoon a little of the marinade over the top and loosely wrap the foil around the fish. Cook for 35–40 minutes or until the salmon is just cooked through (see Cook's Tips).
4 Open the foil and put the fish under a hot grill for 6–8 minutes or until golden. Cool and chill the salmon until required.
5 To serve, arrange the chilled salmon on a large serving dish and garnish with lime quarters.

TO PREPARE AHEAD Complete the recipe to the end of step 4 up to two days ahead. Cool, cover and chill.
TO USE Arrange on a serving plate, garnish and serve.
COOK'S TIPS Ask your fishmonger to scale the salmon. If you do it yourself, remove the scales by gripping the tail with one hand and scraping the scales off by pushing a knife in the opposite direction, from tail to head.
● The cooking time will depend on the thickness of the fish rather than its weight – a fatter-fleshed fish will take more time than a lean one, even if they weigh the same.

ITALIAN PORK ESCALOPES

PREPARATION TIME: 20 minutes
COOKING TIME: 6–8 minutes
PER SERVING: 410cals, 37g fat, 1g carbohydrate

SERVES 4

4tbsp olive oil
4 garlic cloves, finely sliced
Small bunch of fresh sage leaves
4 pork escalopes – around 225g (8oz) total weight (see
    Cook's Tip)
4 slices of Parma ham – around 50g (2oz)
4 level tbsp grated Gruyère cheese
Flour to dust
150ml (¼ pint) crème fraîche
40g (1½oz) spring onions, chopped
1tbsp white wine vinegar
Salad leaves to serve

1 Heat 3tbsp of the oil in a frying pan. Fry the garlic and sage leaves until golden brown. Remove and drain on absorbent paper. Cool, reserving some for the garnish.
2 Put each escalope between two pieces of clingfilm and beat with a rolling pin until very thin.
3 Put a slice of ham, 1 level tbsp of the grated cheese and some of the garlic and sage leaves on each escalope. Season with salt and freshly grated black pepper. Fold the pork in half and season again. Flatten the open edges with a knife to seal. Dust lightly with flour.
4 Heat the remaining oil and cook the pork over a medium heat for 3–4 minutes each side. Mix the crème fraîche, spring onions and vinegar together and serve with the pork and salad leaves, garnished with garlic, sage and pepper.

COOK'S TIP This recipe also works well with chicken fillets, and try varying the cheese, too – Parmesan or a blue cheese would be good alternatives.

SPICED SALAD

PREPARATION TIME: 5 minutes
PER SERVING: 200cals, 17g fat, 9g carbohydrate

SERVES 4

4tbsp olive oil

4tsp lime juice

Large pinch of golden caster sugar

50g (2oz) chorizo sausage, thinly shredded

2 mild red chillies, chopped

2 red peppers, deseeded and sliced

2 shallots, peeled and chopped

4 tomatoes, chopped

Large bag mixed crisp lettuce leaves

Wholemeal rolls or rye bread to serve

1 Put the oil, lime juice, sugar, some salt and crushed black peppercorns into a bowl and stir to combine.

2 Add the chorizo sausage, chillies, red peppers, shallots, tomatoes and lettuce leaves and turn in the dressing. Serve with wholemeal rolls or slices of rye bread.

GOLDEN-TOPPED FENNEL

PREPARATION TIME: 20 minutes
COOKING TIME: 20 minutes
PER SERVING: 340cals, 15g fat, 41g carbohydrate

SERVES 4

4 fennel bulbs – around 225g (8oz) each – halved lengthways, central core discarded

125g (4oz) mixed white and wild rice

2tsp olive or vegetable oil

125g (4oz) onions, roughly chopped

275g (10oz) small brown-cap mushrooms, sliced

1 small bunch watercress, washed and roughly chopped

2tbsp soy sauce

FOR THE PARMESAN SAUCE

25g (1oz) butter

2 level tbsp plain flour

300ml (½ pint) milk

40g (1½oz) freshly grated Parmesan cheese

Grilled cherry tomato halves and watercress to garnish

1 Cook the fennel in boiling salted water for about 15 minutes until just tender, then drain well. Cook the rice according to the packet instructions in boiling salted water until just tender then drain well.

2 Heat the oil in a frying pan and sauté the onion for 2 minutes. Add the mushrooms and cook, stirring, for 4–5 minutes or until all excess moisture is driven off. Add the rice, watercress and soy sauce and season with salt and freshly ground black pepper.

3 Meanwhile, make the Parmesan sauce. Melt the butter in a small pan, then stir in the flour, followed by the milk. Bring slowly to the boil, stirring continuously, until the sauce thickens. Whisk until smooth then simmer gently for 1–2 minutes. Stir in 25g (1oz) of the cheese and season. Keep warm over a low heat.

4 Arrange the fennel halves in a shallow ovenproof dish. Pile the mushroom mixture on to each one, spoon the sauce over, sprinkle with the remaining Parmesan and grill until golden brown. To serve, garnish with the tomatoes and watercress.

BABY COURGETTES WITH PINENUTS

PREPARATION TIME: 10 minutes
COOKING TIME: 5–10 minutes
PER SERVING FOR 4: 120cals, 11g fat,
2g carbohydrate
PER SERVING FOR 6: 80cals, 8g fat,
2g carbohydrate

SERVES 4–6

25g (1oz) pinenuts
1 level tsp cumin seeds
2tbsp extra-virgin olive oil
450g (1lb) baby courgettes, halved
1 garlic clove, crushed
Juice of ½ lemon

1 Heat a non-stick wok or frying pan and dry-fry the pinenuts until golden. Add the cumin and heat until you can smell the cumin cooking. Tip into a bowl to cool.
2 Heat the oil in the same pan and add the courgettes and garlic. Stir-fry for 3–5 minutes or until golden. Add the lemon juice, cumin and pinenuts and serve.

GRILLED PEPPER SALAD

PREPARATION TIME: 15 minutes
COOKING TIME: 15 minutes
PER SERVING FOR 8: 210cals, 19g fat,
8g carbohydrate
PER SERVING FOR 10: 170cals,
15g fat, 6g carbohydrate

SERVES 8–10

4 red peppers, halved and deseeded
1 large red onion, thinly sliced
2tbsp sunflower oil
1 chicory, thinly sliced
1 radicchio, shredded
150g (5oz) watercress, washed, large stalks removed
   and leaves roughly chopped
200g (7oz) mushrooms, thinly sliced
125g (4oz) pitted black olives, sliced

FOR THE SHALLOT DRESSING
8tbsp sunflower oil
2tsp walnut oil
2tbsp red wine vinegar
2 small shallots, peeled and very finely chopped
2 level tsp golden caster sugar

1 Put the red peppers on a baking sheet and cook under a hot grill until the skins are black and well charred. Put into a covered bowl or plastic bag to cool. Remove the skins, roughly slice the flesh and put to one side.
2 Brush the onion slices with the oil, grill until tinged brown, then cool. Make the dressing by whisking all the ingredients together in a bowl.
3 Just before serving, toss the chicory, radicchio, watercress, mushrooms, olives, peppers and onion with the dressing and arrange in a serving dish.

COOK'S TIP This salad can be made more substantial by adding crumbled Stilton, chunks of Brie or freshly grated Parmesan cheese. The red peppers can be made up to five days ahead and will keep in olive oil in the fridge.

RUNNER BEANS WITH HAZELNUT BUTTER

PREPARATION TIME: 15 minutes
COOKING TIME: 10 minutes
PER SERVING FOR 4: 180cals, 16g fat,
6g carbohydrate
PER SERVING FOR 6: 120cals, 10g fat,
4g carbohydrate

SERVES 4–6

Around 700g (1½lb) runner beans, trimmed and thinly
    sliced on the diagonal
50g (2oz) butter
50g (2oz) whole hazelnuts, preferably with skin on,
    chopped
Lemon juice

1 Bring a pan of water to the boil, add salt and then the beans. Boil for
3–4 minutes or until just tender. Drain and pour cold water over the
beans then put to one side.

2 Melt the butter, add the nuts and cook until golden. Toss with the beans
and season with salt and freshly ground black pepper. Add lemon juice
to serve.

GRILLED ARTICHOKE SALAD

PREPARATION TIME: 2 minutes
COOKING TIME: 5 minutes
PER SERVING WITHOUT DRESSING: 40cals,
4g fat, 2g carbohydrate

SERVES 4

400g can artichoke hearts, drained and halved
Olive oil
3 Little Gem lettuces
Vinaigrette dressing (see below)

1 Preheat the grill. Season the artichoke hearts with salt and freshly ground
black pepper and brush with the oil, then grill until charred.

2 Toss the lettuces in the dressing with the artichokes and serve.

VINAIGRETTE DRESSING

PREPARATION TIME: 5 minutes
PER 1 LEVEL TSP: 27cals, 3g fat,
trace carbohydrate

MAKES ABOUT 600ML (1 PINT)

200ml (7fl oz) extra-virgin olive oil
200ml (7fl oz) grapeseed oil
125ml (4fl oz) white wine vinegar
A pinch each sugar and mustard powder
2 garlic cloves, crushed (optional)

Put the oils, vinegar, sugar, mustard powder and garlic, if using, into a
large screw-top jar. Shake well, season to taste with salt and freshly
ground black pepper and store in a cool place.

SUMMER GARDEN SALAD

PREPARATION TIME: 45 minutes

COOKING TIME: 5 minutes, plus 15 minutes cooling

PER SERVING: 110cals, 9g fat, 4g carbohydrate

SERVES 12

FOR THE DRESSING

Juice of 1 lemon

1 level tsp Dijon mustard

1 level tsp golden caster sugar

125ml (4fl oz) olive oil

FOR THE SALAD

175g (6oz) French beans, trimmed and thickly sliced on
the diagonal

175g (6oz) sugar-snap peas, halved on the diagonal

1 cucumber, peeled, halved, deseeded and sliced on the
diagonal

300g (11oz) rocket

1 fennel bulb, quartered and thinly sliced

225g (8oz) red or yellow cherry tomatoes, halved

175g (6oz) red onions, quartered and finely sliced

Lemon zest to garnish

1 To make the dressing, mix together the lemon juice, mustard, sugar and oil and season with salt and freshly ground black pepper.

3 To make the salad, cook the French beans and sugar-snap peas in boiling salted water for 1 minute. Drain and refresh in cold water, then drain again.

4 Put the beans, sugar-snap peas, cucumber, rocket, fennel, tomatoes and red onions in a large bowl. Just before serving, toss in the dressing and garnish with lemon zest.

TO PREPARE AHEAD Complete the recipe to the end of step 3 (do not slice the onions) up to one day ahead. Cover and chill the dressing and vegetables separately.

TO USE Slice the onions and complete the recipe.

PEACHES IN SAUTERNES SYRUP WITH RICOTTA CHEESE

PREPARATION TIME: 5 minutes

COOKING TIME: 25–30 minutes

PER SERVING: 270cals, 7g fat, 43g carbohydrate

SERVES 6

175g (6oz) golden granulated sugar

3 vanilla pods, halved lengthways

200ml (7fl oz) Sauternes or sweet dessert wine

6–8 ripe peaches, halved and stoned

250g tub ricotta cheese

25g (1oz) flaked almonds, toasted

1 Put the sugar in a pan, add the vanilla pods and 300ml (½ pint) of water and heat gently to dissolve the sugar. Bring to the boil.

2 Add the Sauternes and the peach halves and bring back to a simmer, then cover and cook for 15–20 minutes or until the peaches are tender.

3 Remove the fruit from the pan and put to one side. Boil the liquid for around 3 minutes until reduced and syrupy.

4 The peaches can be served warm or chilled. Divide between six plates, top with a dollop of ricotta cheese, sprinkle with the toasted almonds and drizzle the syrup over.

(*Illustrated*)

GLAZED NECTARINE TART

PREPARATION TIME: 10 minutes
COOKING TIME: 15 minutes
PER SERVING: 180cals, 10g fat, 21g carbohydrate

SERVES 6

175g (6oz) puff pastry

25g (1oz) butter, melted

550g (1¼ lb) ripe nectarines or peaches, quartered, stoned and sliced

2 level tbsp apricot jam

1 Preheat the oven to 230°C (210°C fan oven) mark 8. Roll out the pastry thinly to a 28cm (11in) round. Put on a non-stick baking sheet and prick well all over. Bake for 8–10 minutes or until well browned and cooked through.

2 Brush some of the melted butter over the pastry and arrange the fruit slices over, right to the edges of the pastry. Drizzle with the remaining butter and grill for 5 minutes or until the fruit is just tinged with colour. Cool slightly.

3 Warm the apricot jam with a little water and brush over the fruit to glaze. Serve warm.

(Illustrated)

CHERRY CLAFOUTIS

PREPARATION TIME: 10 minutes,
plus 1 hour marinating
COOKING TIME: 50–60 minutes
PER SERVING: 340cals, 17g fat, 39g carbohydrate

SERVES 6

350g (12oz) stoned cherries

3tbsp kirsch

140g (4½oz) golden caster sugar plus extra to dust

4 large eggs

25g (1oz) flour

150ml (¼ pint) milk

150ml (¼ pint) double cream

1tsp vanilla extract

Golden icing sugar, to dust

1 Put the cherries in a bowl with the kirsch and 1tbsp of the caster sugar. Mix together, then cover and put to one side for 1 hour.

2 Meanwhile, whisk the eggs with the remaining caster sugar and the flour.

3 Pour the milk and cream into a pan and bring to the boil, then pour on to the egg mixture and whisk until combined. Add the vanilla extract and strain into a bowl, then cover and put to one side for 30 minutes.

4 Preheat the oven to 180°C (160°C fan oven) mark 4. Lightly butter a 1.7 litre (3 pint) shallow ovenproof dish and dust with caster sugar. Spoon the cherries into the dish, whisk the batter and pour over. Bake for 50–60 minutes or until golden and just set. Dust with icing sugar and serve warm with cream.

CREMA CATALANA WITH BERRIES IN CASSIS

PREPARATION TIME: 10 minutes,
plus 30 minutes infusing and overnight chilling
COOKING TIME: 10 minutes
PER SERVING: 460cals, 25g fat, 52g carbohydrate

SERVES 6

450ml (¾ pint) full-fat milk

200ml (7fl oz) double cream

Zest of 1 lemon

1 level tsp fennel seeds, crushed

6 large egg yolks

175g (6oz) golden caster sugar

2 level tbsp cornflour

¼ level tsp ground cinnamon

FOR THE BERRIES IN CASSIS

450g (1lb) strawberries, hulled, halved or quartered

200g (7oz) mixture of blueberries and wild strawberries,
   halved or quartered

4 level tsp golden caster sugar

4tbsp crème de cassis

Juice of ½ lemon

1 Put the milk, cream, lemon zest and fennel seeds in a heavy-based pan. Heat to boiling point and set aside for 30 minutes to infuse.

2 In a small bowl, beat together the egg yolks, 125g (4oz) of the sugar and the cornflour until the mixture is light and fluffy.

3 Strain the infused milk on to the egg yolk mixture, a little at a time, stirring constantly. Pour the mixture back into the clean pan. Cook over a low heat, stirring, until the cream just comes to the boil and is thick and leaves a trail. This will take 6–8 minutes.

4 Pour into six 150ml (¼ pint) ramekins or heatproof pots. Cool, then cover loosely with foil. Chill overnight to set.

5 To make the berries in cassis, put the strawberries, blueberries and wild strawberries in a bowl. Sprinkle the 4tsp sugar, the cassis and lemon juice over, toss together, then cover and chill.

6 Preheat the grill until very hot. Mix the remaining 50g (2oz) of sugar with the cinnamon and sprinkle evenly over each of the custards. Put under the hot grill until the sugar has caramelised. (It's a good idea to put the custard in the freezer for 30 minutes before grilling to prevent the set custard curdling.) Allow to stand for at least 20 minutes before serving with the macerated fruit.

TO PREPARE AHEAD Complete the recipe to the end of step 4 up to one day ahead. Cover and chill for up to one day.
Make the fruit mixture as in step 5; cover and chill for up to 4 hours.
TO USE Remove the macerated berries from the fridge 1 hour before serving. Complete the recipe.
TO FREEZE Complete the recipe to the end of step 4, then wrap and freeze.
TO USE Thaw at cool room temperature for 3–4 hours. Complete the recipe.

(Illustrated)

COCONUT TART

PREPARATION TIME: 20 minutes,
plus 30 minutes chilling
COOKING TIME: 50 minutes
PER SERVING: 490cals, 32g fat, 46g carbohydrate

SERVES 8

FOR THE PASTRY

200g (7oz) plain flour, sifted, plus extra to dust

2 level tbsp golden icing sugar

75g (3oz) unsalted butter, diced

1 medium egg, beaten

FOR THE FILLING

75g (3oz) unsalted butter, softened

75g (3oz) golden caster sugar

2 x 125g pots coconut yogurt

2 medium eggs, beaten

225g (8oz) sweetened and tenderised coconut
 plus extra to decorate

2 level tbsp plain flour, sifted

Fresh fruit to accompany

1 To make the pastry, put the flour, icing sugar and a large pinch of salt in a food processor, add the butter and whiz until the mixture looks like crumbs. Add the egg and whiz to form a dough. Bring together on a lightly floured surface, wrap in clingfilm and chill for 30 minutes.

2 Preheat the oven to 200°C (180°C fan oven) mark 6 and put a baking sheet in the oven to heat. Dust the worksurface with flour, roll out the pastry and use to line a 20.5cm (8in) loose-bottomed sandwich tin. Prick the base all over with a fork. Line the pastry case with greaseproof paper and fill with baking beans. Put the tin on the hot baking sheet and bake blind for 15 minutes. Carefully remove the paper and baking beans and bake for a further 5 minutes or until the pastry is dry.

3 To make the filling, put the butter, sugar, yogurt and eggs in a large bowl and combine with an electric hand mixer. Mix in the coconut and flour.

4 Spoon into the pastry case, level the surface and bake for 30 minutes or until set and golden (cover the pastry edge with foil if it starts to go brown). Allow to cool for 10 minutes, then remove from the tin and leave to cool on a wire rack.

5 Put on a serving plate and sprinkle the tart with extra coconut. Serve with a selection of fruit, such as raspberries, blueberries and strawberries.

(Illustrated)

BLUEBERRY TRIFLE

PREPARATION TIME: 15 minutes,
plus 1 hour or overnight chilling
PER SERVING: 540cals, 34g fat, 52g carbohydrate

SERVES 6

1 ready-made all-butter Madeira cake, cut into cubes
6tbsp white wine
4tbsp elderflower cordial
3 level tbsp blueberry conserve
500g carton fresh custard
284ml carton double cream
125g (4oz) blueberries
1 level tbsp pistachio nuts, roughly chopped

1 Put the cake into a 2.3 litre (4 pint) glass serving bowl. Mix the wine with 2tbsp of the cordial, then pour over the cake.
2 Dot the blueberry conserve over the cake, then pour the custard on top. Whip the cream into soft peaks, then fold in the remaining cordial and half the blueberries. Add to the trifle.
3 Cover and chill for at least 1 hour but preferably overnight.
4 Just before serving, scatter the remaining blueberries and the nuts over the top.

COOK'S TIP This trifle tastes better the day after making it, so save time and prepare it ahead.

GOOSEBERRY AND ELDERFLOWER JAM

PREPARATION TIME: 15 minutes
COOKING TIME: 35 minutes
PER 1 LEVEL TBSP: 45cals, 0g fat, 12g carbohydrate

MAKES ABOUT 1.6KG (3½lb) JAM

900g (2lb) green gooseberries, topped and tailed
900g (2lb) granulated or preserving sugar (see Jam Tips, page 54)
Juice of 1 lemon
300ml (½ pint) elderflower cordial

1 Preheat the oven to 180°C (160°C fan oven) mark 4. Put the gooseberries in a preserving pan with 150ml (¼ pint) of water, then cook over a low heat until the gooseberries are very soft. Meanwhile, put the sugar in a large roasting tin and warm in the oven for 10 minutes.
2 Add the lemon juice, elderflower cordial and warmed sugar to the gooseberries, bring to the boil and simmer gently until the sugar has dissolved. Increase the heat and bubble for 25–30 minutes or until the jam is set (see page 54). Cool, pot, then cover and label the jars (see page 54).

BLACKBERRY, APPLE AND CARDAMOM JAM

PREPARATION TIME: 10 minutes
(see Jam Tips, page 54)
COOKING TIME: 35 minutes
PER 1 LEVEL TBSP: 30cals, 0g fat,
9g carbohydrate

MAKES ABOUT 1.4KG (3LB) JAM

700g (1½lb) granulated or preserving sugar (see Jam
  Tips, page 54)
350g (12oz) green cooking apples, peeled and cut into
  chunks
900g (2lb) blackberries
3 cardamom pods, seeds removed and lightly crushed,
  tied in muslin
Juice of ½ lemon

1 Preheat the oven to 180°C (160°C fan oven) mark 4. Put the sugar in a roasting tin and warm in the oven for 10 minutes. Meanwhile, put the apples and 150ml (¼ pint) of water in a preserving pan, bring to the boil and simmer very gently for 15 minutes or until the apples are soft.

2 Add the blackberries and cook for about 5 minutes or until soft and the juices run. Add the sugar, crushed cardamom seeds and lemon juice. Bring to the boil and bubble for 20 minutes or until the jam is set (see page 54). Remove the cardamom seeds and pot hot in warm sterilized jars, then cover and label the jars (see page 54).

(Illustrated)

SPICED PEPPER CHUTNEY

PREPARATION TIME: 20 minutes
COOKING TIME: 1 hour 45 minutes
PER 1 LEVEL TSP: 15cals, trace fat,
4g carbohydrate

MAKES ABOUT 1.6KG (3½LB) JAM

3 red peppers, washed, deseeded and finely chopped
3 green peppers, washed, deseeded and finely chopped
450g (1lb) onions, sliced
450g (1lb) tomatoes, skinned and chopped
450g (1lb) apples, peeled, cored and chopped
225g (8oz) demerara sugar
1 level tsp ground allspice
450ml (¾ pint) malt vinegar
1 level tsp peppercorns
1 level tsp mustard seeds

1 Put the peppers in a preserving pan with the onions, tomatoes, apples, sugar, allspice and vinegar. Tie the peppercorns and mustard seeds in a piece of muslin and add to the pan.

2 Bring to the boil and simmer over a medium heat for about 1½ hours until soft, pulpy and well reduced.

3 Remove the muslin bag, spoon the hot chutney into warm sterilized jars and cover at once with airtight, vinegar-proof tops.

SEPTEMBER

*A fickle month, with misty mornings,
glorious days, cool breezes and the russet tones
of approaching autumn*

SEPTEMBER SEES THE BEGINNING in earnest of one of the great glories of the British cookery year: the game season. Grouse, hare and snipe began last month, but September is when all the rest of our furred and feathered game starts to appear on the scene: partridge, pheasant, wild duck, wild geese, teal, woodcock. The first three are those that most home cooks will stand a good chance of spotting in local suppliers, and perfect for the warming casseroles that we'll need increasingly as the weather cools. Prices may be at their highest when the season gets underway but should drop after a few weeks, as supplies increase. Pheasant is the most economical of the game birds, followed by wild duck. Partridge, though one of the priciest, is a treat you should allow yourself at least once a season.

Fruit

September is also, where fruit and some vegetables are concerned, the end of summer rather than the beginning of autumn. Remember, it's still quite hot in southern Europe even if the weather might be turning a bit nippy up here. This is a prime month for tomatoes, with UK farms producing their long-ripened best and often selling them at their cheapest because of the end-of-summer glut as the imports keep flooding in. If you like making tomato sauce or pickles for long storage, this is the time to buy. Local markets and farmers' markets may have stacks of them, sometimes in imperfect cosmetic condition but still perfectly good for cooking. And don't forget that small cherry tomatoes are ideal for sauce-making because the skins give good colour. They're also good roasted, for a hot tomato salad (see page 218). Consider

Left: Mussels with Linguine and Saffron (see page 224)

INGREDIENTS
OF THE MONTH

GAME

Grouse

Hare

Partridge

Snipe

Wild duck

Wild goose

Woodcock

Leeks

Marrow

Parsnips

Pumpkin

Squash

Tomatoes

Turnips

Wild mushrooms

FISH

Clams

Dover sole

Halibut

Lobster

Mussels

Oysters

Plaice

Scallops

Sea bass

Skate

FRUIT

Apples

Blackberries

Damsons

Figs

Greengages

Pears

Plums

Scottish raspberries

Walnuts

Hazelnuts

Cobnuts

VEGETABLES

Beetroot

Cabbages

Carrots

Chard

Corn on the cob

Fennel

BEST BUY

Tomatoes

Pears

Plums

Nectarines

Peaches

making ketchup as well, if you have access to very large supplies at a low cost.

The same end-of-summer abundance makes this a time to eat and cook all the soft fruits you can lay your hands on, especially peaches, nectarines and plums. Peaches and nectarines should still be sugar-sweet, whether from France or Italy, and very ripe. Ripeness brings dangers, however: the fruits will be soft and need both careful handling and quick eating. For UK fruit there is nothing better than Scottish raspberries, considered by many to be the finest in the world, or than British plums – damsons, greengages and Victorias.

There should also be the first UK pears at some point, and the first Cox's as well. Until they arrive, native fruits are supplemented by wonderful imports from Europe: great melons, figs and grapes and all that superb stone fruit. And if you're hungry for apples, the Cox's season is preceded by other excellent native varieties: the short-lived Discoveries and such relative rarities as Worcester Pearmain and James Grieve. Farmers' markets are the best place to look; some supermarkets are making an effort with them, but small growers don't usually reach the big multiples. Make the most of this popular fruit in the Apple, Almond and Cinnamon Cake on page 228.

Vegetables

The summery theme continues in vegetables, certainly through the first half of the month. Courgettes and marrow, peppers, beetroot, aubergines, fennel, good garlic, the last of the sweetcorn, more good carrots – there is no shortage of good things to cook in September. We'll also get the first arrivals of beautiful squash in all its entrancingly colourful variety. Experiment with them in soups and stews, roasting with olive oil or try the Butternut Squash with Beetroot and Goat's Cheese (page 216). Don't forget the last of the summer beans, either, or more new-season leeks. And most of all, don't forget a group of edibles that are not only world-class but free: wild mushrooms. See the box below for more on collecting and preparing these seasonal splendours.

Fish

September is, finally, another very good month for fish of just about every kind, whether white fish, oily fish, or shellfish. One that hasn't been mentioned until now is clams, more popular on the continent than they are here – partly because they're not always easy to find, and partly because they are expensive. They're particularly good this month, and worth looking out for. Best as a starter if you get the large Venus or razor clams, or in a tomato sauce for pasta if they're smaller.

WILD MUSHROOMS

The season is dependent on weather conditions, but the message is clear: you should eat wild mushrooms every chance you get. Some supermarkets are selling them at high prices and with quality that varies greatly. The much better option by far is to collect them yourself, and they may be closer to your home than you realise. There are too many varieties to go into detail about their preferred habitats, but in general you'll be looking for woodland. One exception: common field mushrooms, which can grow in open grass. If you want to go mushrooming, you must buy a reliable guide for proper identification: remember, some mushrooms can cause illness and occasionally death. The best known varieties found here are ceps (penny buns), chanterelles (which usually begin earlier than other types), and oyster mushrooms. But you may find dozens of other varieties. And once you get the fungi-foraging bug, it tends to be a lifelong vocation.

GRILLED CORN AND SPROUTING BEAN SALAD

PREPARATION TIME: 30 minutes,
plus 10 minutes marinating
COOKING TIME: 10 minutes
PER SERVING FOR 6: 120cals, 7g fat,
10g carbohydrate
PER SERVING FOR 8: 90cals, 6g fat,
8g carbohydrate

SERVES 6–8

2 corn on the cob
2.5cm (1in) piece fresh root ginger, peeled and finely
   grated
Finely grated zest and juice of 1 orange
4tsp soy sauce
3tbsp olive oil
225g (8oz) beansprouts, washed and drained
2 Little Gem lettuces, washed and dried
Mixed salad leaves, such as baby spinach and frisée
   lettuce, washed and dried

1 Put the corn on the cob under a hot grill and cook until golden brown on all sides. Cool, then carefully cut the kernels from the cob with a sharp knife.
2 Whisk together the grated ginger, orange zest, 3tbsp of the orange juice and the soy sauce and season with salt and freshly ground black pepper, then whisk in the oil.
3 Toss the corn kernels and beansprouts with the ginger dressing and leave to marinate for 10 minutes.
4 Just before serving, toss the dressing mixture into the salad leaves.

COOK'S TIP To serve the salad at a picnic, take the salad leaves and dressing separately. Toss just before serving.

SCALLOPS WITH SWEET AND SOUR CUCUMBER AND PICKLED GINGER

PREPARATION TIME: 20 minutes,
plus 2 hours marinating
PER SERVING: 220cals, 7g fat, 6g carbohydrate

SERVES 6

18 large fresh scallops, without roe, well chilled
Juice of 2 limes
2 level tbsp golden caster sugar
1tbsp white wine vinegar
½ cucumber, deseeded and diced
2tbsp mild extra-virgin olive oil
Pickled ginger
A bunch (around 100g (3½oz) salad, washed, to garnish

1 Trim and discard any hard muscle from the side of each scallop, then slice each very thinly crosswise. Put in a single layer on a large plate and squeeze the juice of 1½ limes over the top. Cover and chill for 2 hours.
2 Put the sugar, a pinch of salt, plenty of freshly ground black pepper and 2tbsp of boiling water into a bowl, then stir to dissolve the sugar. Mix in the vinegar. Add the cucumber, cover the bowl and chill for 1 hour.
3 Put the remaining lime juice into a small bowl, add a pinch of salt and a little freshly ground black pepper and whisk. Then whisk in the oil to make a dressing.
4 Remove the scallops from the lime juice and arrange the slices in pairs on individual plates. Using a slotted spoon, put some drained cucumber in the centre and top with slivers of pickled ginger. Drizzle the dressing over the scallops and arrange sprigs of watercress around them.

GARLIC SOUP WITH THYME CROÛTONS

PREPARATION TIME: 15 minutes

COOKING TIME: 1 hour 30 minutes

PER SERVING WITHOUT CROÛTONS: 260cals, 19g fat, 19g carbohydrate

SERVES 6

4tbsp olive oil

3 large onions – around 700g (1½lb) – chopped

16 garlic cloves, roughly chopped

150ml (¼ pint) white wine or cider

350g (12oz) potatoes, roughly chopped

1.6 litres (2¾ pints) vegetable stock

125ml (4fl oz) whipping cream, plus extra to drizzle

Thyme Croûtons to serve (see below)

THYME CROÛTONS

PREPARATION TIME: 1 minute

COOKING TIME: 10 minutes

PER SERVING: 120cals, 7g fat, 13g carbohydrate

SERVES 6

4 slices of bread, cut into cubes

3–4tbsp olive oil

1 level tsp dried thyme

Fresh thyme sprigs to garnish

1 Heat the oil in a heavy-based pan, add the onions and garlic, then cover and cook over a low heat, stirring occasionally, for 20–30 minutes or until translucent and very soft. Do not allow to colour. Add the wine or cider and bring to the boil. Bubble until the liquid has reduced by half.

2 Add the potatoes and stock, bring to the boil and simmer, uncovered, for 45 minutes or until reduced slightly. Cool a little. Pour the soup into a blender and whiz until smooth. Add the cream, season well with salt and freshly ground black pepper and pour into the pan to reheat.

3 Ladle the soup into bowls, drizzle with a little cream, sprinkle the Thyme Croûtons on top and serve.

TO PREPARE AHEAD Complete the recipe to the end of step 2, but don't add the cream or reheat, up to two days ahead. Cool, cover and chill. **TO USE** Bring the soup back to the boil, add the cream and simmer for 1–2 minutes. Complete the recipe. **TO FREEZE** Complete the recipe to the end of step 2, but don't add the cream and don't reheat. Cool and freeze. **TO USE** Thaw at cool room temperature overnight. Bring the soup to the boil, add the cream and simmer for 1–2 minutes. Complete the recipe.

1 Preheat the oven to 200°C (180°C fan oven) mark 6. Put the bread cubes in a bowl with the oil and dried thyme.

2 Place on a baking tray and cook for 10 minutes or until golden. Sprinkle with salt and fresh thyme sprigs and serve warm.

(Illustrated)

THAI CRAB BALLS WITH SWEET CHILLI SAUCE

PREPARATION TIME: 30 minutes, plus 20 minutes chilling
COOKING TIME: 20 minutes
PER BALL WITH SAUCE: 110cals, 4g fat, 11g carbohydrate

MAKES 18 BALLS

FOR THE SWEET CHILLI SAUCE

2tsp sesame oil
½ level tsp chopped red chillies
2 level tbsp finely chopped fresh root ginger
1 garlic clove, crushed
8 level tbsp light muscovado sugar
2tsp fish sauce
2tbsp light soy sauce
Juice of 2 limes

FOR THE CRAB BALLS

1 tbsp oil
4 spring onions, finely chopped
1 garlic clove, crushed
2.5cm (1 in) piece fresh root ginger, peeled and finely grated
1 small red chilli, deseeded and finely chopped
1 lemongrass stalk, outer leaves discarded and remainder finely chopped
350g (12oz) fresh or frozen crab meat
2 level tbsp freshly chopped coriander
1tsp fish sauce
75g (3oz) white breadcrumbs
3 medium eggs
50g (2oz) plain flour
Sunflower oil for deep-frying
Fresh coriander sprigs and shredded red chilli to garnish

1 To make the chilli sauce, put the oil in a pan and heat gently. Add the chillies, ginger and garlic and cook for 1–2 minutes until softened. Add the sugar, fish and soy sauces, then bring to the boil and simmer for 2 minutes. Remove from the heat, then stir in 8tbsp of water and the lime juice. Pour into a serving bowl, cover and put to one side.

2 To make the crab balls, heat the oil in a small pan and add the spring onions, garlic, ginger, chilli and lemongrass. Cook gently for 2–3 minutes or until soft. Transfer to a bowl, cool and stir in the crab meat, coriander, fish sauce, 6 level tbsp of the breadcrumbs and one egg. Mix and season with freshly ground black pepper (see Cook's Tips). Shape tablespoonfuls of the mixture into 18 balls, put on a baking sheet and chill for 20 minutes. (See Cook's Tips.)

3 Coat each ball lightly with flour, roll in the remaining beaten eggs, then in the remaining breadcrumbs. Deep-fry in batches in hot oil for 3–4 minutes or until golden. Drain on absorbent kitchen paper and keep warm while frying the remaining balls. Garnish with coriander and shredded red chilli, and serve with the sweet chilli sauce.

TO PREPARE AHEAD Make the sweet chilli sauce as in step 1 up to five days ahead. Cover and chill. Make and fry the crab balls up to one day ahead. Cool, cover and chill.
TO USE Remove the sweet chilli sauce from the fridge one hour before using. Put the crab balls on a wire rack over a baking sheet and reheat at 200°C (180°C fan oven) mark 6 for 8–10 minutes. Garnish the balls and serve with the sauce.
TO FREEZE Make and fry the crab balls, then pack and freeze.
TO USE Thaw the balls at cool room temperature and reheat on a wire rack over a baking sheet at 190°C (170°C fan oven) mark 5 for 20 minutes. Garnish the balls and serve with the sauce.
COOK'S TIPS Fish sauce is very salty so there's no need to add any extra salt.
● As a variation, flatten the crab balls into cakes with the palm of your hand and shallow-fry in a little oil. Serve as a starter with the sweet chilli sauce drizzled over.

(Illustrated)

BUTTERNUT SQUASH
WITH BEETROOT AND GOAT'S CHEESE

PREPARATION TIME: 20 minutes
COOKING TIME: 35 minutes
PER SERVING: 200cals, 16g fat, 8g carbohydrate

SERVES 4

1 medium butternut squash, peeled, deseeded and cut
    into wedges
4tbsp olive oil
2 raw beetroot, peeled and cut into thin wedges
50g (2oz) rocket
2tbsp balsamic vinegar
150g (5oz) firm goat's cheese, cut in slices

1 Preheat the oven to 220°C (200°C fan oven) mark 7. Put the squash in a roasting tin, drizzle with 2tbsp of the oil and season with salt and freshly ground black pepper. Put the beetroot in another tin, toss in 1tbsp of the oil and season. Cook the vegetables for 25–35 minutes or until slightly charred, swapping shelves halfway through.

2 Put the rocket in a bowl, add the remaining oil and the balsamic vinegar and toss together.

3 Grill the goat's cheese for 1 minute or until the edges melt.

4 Arrange the vegetables on top of the rocket and top with the melted cheese.

(Illustrated)

SOURED CREAM AND ONION TARTS

PREPARATION TIME: 20 minutes,
plus 30 minutes chilling
COOKING TIME: 1 hour 10 minutes
PER SERVING: 570cals, 42g fat, 39g carbohydrate

SERVES 6

700g (1½lb) tomatoes, halved
1 level tbsp freshly chopped thyme, plus extra sprigs
    to garnish
2tbsp olive oil
200g (7oz) chilled butter
175g (6oz) plain flour
6–7 level tbsp soured cream
900g (2lb) onions, finely sliced
125g (4oz) Roquefort cheese

1 Preheat the oven to 170°C (150°C fan oven) mark 3. Put the tomatoes on a baking sheet, season with salt and freshly ground black pepper, sprinkle with the thyme, drizzle with the oil and cook, uncovered, in the oven for 40 minutes until slightly shrivelled.

2 Meanwhile, cut 150g (5oz) of the butter into small dice and put in a food processor with the flour. Pulse until the butter is roughly cut up through the flour (you should still be able to see pieces of butter), then add the soured cream and pulse again for 2–3 seconds until just mixed.

3 On a floured surface, cut the pastry into six and roll each thinly into a 12.5cm (5in) round. Put on two baking sheets, cover and chill for 30 minutes.

4 Melt the remaining butter in a pan, add the onions and cook slowly for about 15 minutes until very soft. Increase the heat and fry the onions for 3–4 minutes or until well browned and caramelised. Cool.

5 Spoon the onions into the centre of the pastries, leaving a 1cm (½in) edge. Crumble the cheese on top and add the tomatoes. Season, then roughly fold up the pastry edge.

6 Increase the oven temperature to 200°C (180°C fan oven) mark 6, and cook the tarts for 30 minutes until golden. Garnish with fresh thyme sprigs and serve immediately.

GRILLED PROSCIUTTO WITH FIGS

PREPARATION TIME: 5 minutes
COOKING TIME: 5–10 minutes
PER SERVING: 140cals, 8g fat, 12g carbohydrate

SERVES 4

8 fresh ripe figs
Extra-virgin olive oil
12 thin slices of Parma ham or other prosciutto
Parmesan cheese to serve

1 Stand each fig upright. Using a sharp knife, cut crosswise, leaving the base of each fig intact. Ease the figs open and brush with some of the oil.
2 Put the figs, cut-side down, under a preheated very hot grill (or on a preheated barbecue) and cook for 5–10 minutes until hot and golden brown, turning once.
3 Meanwhile, put half the Parma ham or other prosciutto under a very hot grill (or on the barbecue) and cook for 2–3 minutes until starting to crisp. Remove and keep warm while cooking the remaining Parma ham.
4 Arrange 3 slices of Parma ham and 2 figs on each warmed plate. Drizzle with the oil and season with plenty of freshly ground black pepper. Serve with a small chunk of fresh Parmesan on each plate.

HOT TOMATO SALAD

PREPARATION TIME: 5 minutes
COOKING TIME: 10–12 minutes
PER SERVING: 310cals, 20g fat, 27g carbohydrate

SERVES 6

700g (1½lb) mixed cherry tomatoes (red and yellow, if possible), halved
2 garlic cloves, sliced
2 level tbsp capers, drained and rinsed
1 level tsp golden caster sugar
125ml (4fl oz) extra-virgin olive oil
1 ready-to-bake olive ciabatta loaf
2tbsp freshly chopped basil
Balsamic or red wine vinegar to taste
Fresh basil sprigs to garnish

1 Preheat the oven to 200°C (180°C fan oven) mark 6. Put the tomatoes, garlic, capers and sugar into a small roasting tin and stir to mix. Season well with sea salt and freshly ground black pepper and pour on the oil.
2 Cook for 10–12 minutes or until the tomatoes are hot and beginning to soften. Pop the bread in the oven to bake alongside.
3 Remove the tomatoes from the oven and stir in the basil with a few drops of vinegar to taste. Slice the hot bread and spoon over the warm tomatoes and juices. Garnish with sprigs of fresh basil and serve immediately.

ROASTED VEGETABLE LASAGNE

PREPARATION TIME: 30 minutes,
plus 15 minutes infusing
COOKING TIME: 1 hour 30 minutes
PER SERVING: 680cals, 40g fat, 53g carbohydrate

MAKES 2 MEALS FOR 4

4 medium red onions, sliced into wedges

3 each small red and yellow peppers, deseeded and cut
    into 5cm (2in) pieces

4 medium courgettes, cut into 5cm (2in) pieces

4 large garlic cloves, chopped

6tbsp olive oil

450g (1lb) cherry tomatoes

2 x 400g cans artichokes, drained and cut into quarters

6 level tbsp tomato purée

75g (3oz) each pitted black and green olives

3 x 125g packs mozzarella cheese, coarsely grated

14–16 sheets 'no pre-cooking required' lasagne

FOR THE SAUCE

1.7 litres (3 pints) full-fat milk

1 bay leaf

Pinch of ground nutmeg

6 peppercorns, crushed

100g (3½oz) butter

100g (3½oz) plain flour

75g (3oz) pecorino cheese, grated

3 level tbsp freshly chopped basil

1 Preheat the oven to 220°C (200°C fan oven) mark 7. Divide the onions, peppers and courgettes between two large roasting tins, sprinkle over the garlic, drizzle each with 3tbsp of the oil, season well with salt and freshly ground black pepper and toss together. Cook for 30 minutes on two shelves, stirring from time to time.

2 Meanwhile, make the sauce: put the milk in a pan with the bay leaf, nutmeg and peppercorns, bring to the boil, turn off the heat, leave to infuse for 15 minutes, then strain. Melt the butter in a separate pan, stir in the flour until smooth and cook for 1 minute. Gradually add the strained milk, whisking until smooth. Bring to the boil, stirring, and cook for 2 minutes until thickened. Stir in the pecorino cheese and basil and season to taste. Cover with a wet disc of greaseproof paper and put to one side.

3 Remove the roasting tins from the oven, then toss the cherry tomatoes and artichokes through the vegetables. Switch the position of the tins in the oven and cook for a further 20 minutes until the vegetables are slightly charred at the edges. Remove from the oven and, into each, stir 3tbsp of the tomato purée and half the olives. Reduce the oven temperature to 200°C (180°C fan oven) mark 6.

4 Layer the vegetables, mozzarella, lasagne and sauce into two 2.6 litre (4½ pint) deep ovenproof dishes, finishing with the sauce and mozzarella.

5 Bake for 35–40 minutes or until bubbling and golden at the edges.

TO FREEZE Complete the recipe to the end of step 4. Cool, wrap and freeze for up to three months.
TO USE Thaw at cool room temperature overnight. Cook at 190°C (170°C fan oven) mark 5 for 45 minutes or until hot to the centre.

DUCK BREASTS WITH CINNAMON PLUM SAUCE

PREPARATION TIME: 45 minutes,

plus at least 1 hour marinating

COOKING TIME: 1 hour 10 minutes

PER SERVING: 560cals, 42g fat, 13g carbohydrate

SERVES 6

Duck breast fillets – around 1kg (2¼lb) total weight
   (see Cook's Tips)

¾ level tsp ground cinnamon

Vegetable oil

300ml (½ pint) red wine

25g (1oz) butter

2 small onions, finely chopped

450g (1lb) red plums, halved, stoned
   and roughly chopped

½ level tsp golden caster sugar

4 level tsp redcurrant jelly

125ml (4fl oz) orange juice

1 tbsp red wine vinegar

300ml (½ pint) chicken stock

Caramelised plum slices (see Cook's Tips) and fresh
   thyme sprigs to garnish

1 Using a sharp knife, remove the silvery membrane from the fleshy side of the duck breasts. Season with salt and freshly ground black pepper and sprinkle with ½ level tsp of the ground cinnamon. Turn the duck breasts over, score the skin side (to release its fat during cooking), rub with a little oil and sprinkle with salt. Put the duck, skin-side up, in a shallow non-metallic dish and pour 150ml (¼ pint) of the wine around. Leave uncovered in the fridge for at least 1 hour to marinate.

2 Heat the butter in a wide pan and cook the onions for 3–4 minutes. Add the plums, sugar, redcurrant jelly (see Cook's Tips), orange juice, red wine vinegar and the remaining ground cinnamon and red wine. Bring to the boil and simmer for 15–20 minutes or until very soft. Cool a little, then pour into a food processor and whiz until smooth. Sieve and put back in the clean pan with the stock. Bring to the boil and bubble for 10–15 minutes, skimming occasionally, until syrupy. Season to taste.

3 Drain the marinade from the duck and add to the plum sauce. Preheat a heavy-based non-stick frying pan and fry the duck breasts, skin-side down, in batches, over a medium heat for 10–15 minutes until the fat runs and the skin is dark brown and crisp. Turn the breasts over and cook for a further 3–4 minutes (see Cook's Tips).

4 Preheat the oven to 170°C (150°C fan oven) mark 3. Using a slotted spoon, transfer the duck breasts, skin-side up, to a warmed serving dish. Cover loosely with foil and leave in the oven for 10 minutes so the flesh becomes evenly 'rosy'. Bring the plum sauce to the boil and bubble for 2–3 minutes.

5 To serve, slice the duck thickly, spoon the Cinnamon Plum Sauce around and garnish with caramelised plum slices and thyme sprigs.

COOK'S TIPS This recipe uses French magret duck breasts, which are meatier than English duck and are widely available. If you can't find magrets, use English duck breasts, each weighing around 175g (6oz).

● To caramelise plums, cut them into thick slices, sprinkle heavily with golden caster sugar and fry immediately in hot butter until golden brown.

● If the plums are sharp or you prefer a sweeter sauce, add more redcurrant jelly to taste.

● If using English duck breasts, brown quickly, skin-side down, in a heavy-based frying pan, then transfer to a roasting tin and cook at 200°C (180°C fan oven) mark 6 for 10 minutes for medium rare. Whether you're using magrets or English duck breasts, allow an extra 5 minutes cooking time if you like your duck breasts cooked medium.

THAI GREEN SHELLFISH CURRY

PREPARATION TIME: 5 minutes

COOKING TIME: 15 minutes

PER SERVING: 230cals, 14g fat, 2g carbohydrate

SERVES 6

1tbsp vegetable oil

1 lemongrass stalk, chopped

2 Thai chillies, deseeded and chopped

2tbsp freshly chopped coriander, plus extra leaves
   to garnish

2 lime leaves, chopped

1–2 level tbsp green Thai curry paste

400ml can coconut milk

450ml (¾ pint) vegetable stock

375g (13oz) queen scallops with corals

250g (9oz) raw tiger prawns, peeled with tails on

1 Heat the vegetable oil in a wok and fry the Thai herbs for 30 seconds. Add the green Thai curry paste and fry for 1 minute.

2 Add the coconut milk and stock and bring to the boil. Simmer for 5–10 minutes until reduced a little. Season well with salt and freshly ground black pepper.

3 Add the scallops and tiger prawns, bring to the boil and simmer gently for 2–3 minutes or until cooked. Spoon into bowls of Thai jasmine rice and garnish with coriander.

COOK'S TIPS Thai green curry paste gives this dish its punchy flavour – always taste the paste before you cook as strengths vary from jar to jar.
● Serve with Thai jasmine rice.

(Illustrated)

ROAST PORK WITH FENNEL, GARLIC AND APPLE

PREPARATION TIME: 40 minutes
COOKING TIME: 1 hour 45 minutes
PER SERVING: 480cals, 31g fat, 14g carbohydrate

SERVES 6

2 level tbsp fennel seeds

7 garlic cloves

½ level tsp salt

2 level tbsp freshly chopped rosemary

3tbsp olive oil plus extra to grease

1.4kg (3lb) boned loin of pork with skin

450g (1lb) Spanish onions, finely sliced

2 sharp apples such as Granny Smith, peeled and finely
    sliced

1 level tbsp light muscovado sugar

600ml (1 pint) dry cider

1 Preheat the oven to 240°C (220°C fan oven) mark 9. Pound the fennel seeds in a pestle and mortar until they're broken down, then crush five garlic cloves and add with the salt and rosemary and pound again until a smooth paste is formed. Mix in the oil.

2 Remove the skin from the loin of pork, leaving behind a thin layer of fat. Score the skin with deep cuts – a clean Stanley knife is really effective for this. Massage a little oil into the skin and set aside. Turn the skinless loin over so that it's sitting on its fatty side, then smear the pork with the fennel seasoning.

3 Wrap the scored skin over the seasoned side. Tie the pork with string to secure the fat. Sprinkle the skin liberally with salt.

4 Peel and finely slice the remaining two garlic cloves and put in a roasting tin with the onions and apples. Sprinkle in the sugar. Put the pork on a rack over the onion mixture and cook for about 30–40 minutes or until the skin blisters. Turn the oven down to 200°C (180°C fan oven) mark 6 and cook for a further 50–60 minutes or until the pork is cooked to the centre. Turn the onion mixture regularly and remove once golden brown. Put to one side.

5 Add the cider to the roasting tin, bring to the boil and bubble until reduced by one third. Return the onion mixture to the roasting tin, bring to the boil and simmer for 2–3 minutes. Season with salt and freshly ground black pepper. Cut away the string from the pork, remove the crackling and cut it into rough strips. Slice the pork and serve with the crackling, onion mixture and the juices.

TO PREPARE AHEAD Complete the recipe to the end of step 3 the night before. Chill, uncovered.
TO USE Take the pork out of the fridge 30 minutes before cooking. Complete the recipe.

(Illustrated)

MUSSELS WITH LINGUINE AND SAFFRON

PREPARATION TIME: 20 minutes
COOKING TIME: 15 minutes
PER SERVING: 680cals, 31g fat, 73g carbohydrate

SERVES 4

350g (12oz) dried linguine pasta
25g (1oz) butter
1tbsp olive oil
2 medium onions, separated into petals
3 garlic cloves, chopped
Pinch of saffron threads
900g (2lb) fresh mussels, prepared as on page 13
125ml (4fl oz) dry white wine
200ml (7fl oz) crème fraîche
Fresh chives to garnish

1 Bring a large pan of salted water to the boil, add the pasta and cook according to the packet instructions, then drain (see Cook's Tip).
2 Meanwhile, heat the butter and oil in a heavy-based pan, add the onion and cook gently for 10 minutes or until softened. Add the garlic and saffron and cook for 1 minute. Increase the heat, add the mussels and wine, cover and cook for 2 minutes or until the shells have opened. Discard any that remain closed. Add the crème fraîche and stir to heat through.
3 Add the pasta to the mussel and cream mixture, toss together and season to taste with salt and freshly ground black pepper. Serve garnished with chives.

COOK'S TIP If the pasta is ready before you've finished making the sauce toss it with a tablespoon of olive oil after cooking to prevent it from sticking together before you're ready to serve the meal.

(Illustrated on page 208)

PARSLEY AND OLIVE OIL MASH

PREPARATION TIME: 20 minutes
COOKING TIME: 25 minutes
PER SERVING: 260cals, 15g fat, 29g carbohydrate

SERVES 6

1.1kg (2½lb) potatoes, peeled and cut into even-sized chunks
100ml (3½fl oz) olive oil
4 level tbsp freshly chopped flat-leafed parsley

1 Cook the potatoes in boiling salted water for 20 minutes or until tender. Drain well, put back in the pan and dry over a low heat until fluffy. Mash until smooth.
2 Beat in the oil, add the parsley and season with salt and freshly ground black pepper.

TO PREPARE AHEAD Complete the recipe up to 24 hours ahead. Cool, cover and chill.
TO USE Warm 6tbsp of olive oil in a heavy-based pan, add the mash and, stirring continuously, reheat over a moderately low heat.

MUSTARD MASH

PREPARATION TIME: 5 minutes
COOKING TIME: 15-20 minutes
PER SERVING: 290cals, 17g fat, 32g carbohydrate

SERVES 6

1.25kg (2¾lb) potatoes, chopped
100ml (3½fl oz) warm milk
100ml (3½fl oz) olive oil, plus extra to drizzle
2 level tbsp Dijon mustard

1 Put the potatoes in a pan of cold salted water, bring to the boil and boil for 15–20 minutes, then drain. Dry over a gentle heat, then mash.
2 Beat in the milk, oil and mustard and season well with salt and freshly ground black pepper. Serve drizzled with the oil.

WILD MUSHROOM RICE

PREPARATION TIME: 20 minutes

COOKING TIME: 25 minutes

PER SERVING: 230cals, 6g fat, 40g carbohydrate

SERVES 12

75g (3oz) butter

450g (1lb) trimmed leeks, well washed, halved
    lengthways and thinly sliced

350g (12oz) wild or flat mushrooms, cleaned and roughly
    chopped

450g (1lb) long-grain rice

125g (4oz) wild rice

Freshly chopped chives to garnish

1 Melt the butter in a large heavy-based pan. Add the leeks and cook, stirring, for 3—4 minutes. Add the mushrooms and cook for a further 2 minutes, season well with salt and freshly ground black pepper and put to one side.

2 Cook the rice according to the packet instructions. Drain well. Reheat the mushroom and leek mixture, stir into the hot rice and garnish with the chives.

SWEET ROASTED FENNEL

PREPARATION TIME: 10 minutes

COOKING TIME: 1 hour

PER SERVING FOR 4: 210cals, 20g fat,
4g carbohydrate

PER SERVING FOR 6: 140cals, 14g fat,
3g carbohydrate

SERVES 4–6

700g (1½lb) fennel bulbs – around 3 bulbs – trimmed
    and quartered

3tbsp olive oil

50g (2oz) butter, melted

1 lemon, halved

1 level tsp golden caster sugar

2 large sprigs of thyme

1 Preheat the oven to 200°C (180°C fan oven) mark 6. Put the fennel in a large roasting tin.

2 Drizzle the oil and melted butter over the fennel and squeeze the lemon juice over. Add the lemon halves to the tin. Sprinkle with the sugar and season generously with salt and freshly ground black pepper. Add the thyme and cover with a damp piece of non-stick baking parchment.

3 Cook for 30 minutes, then remove the baking parchment and cook for 20—30 minutes or until roasted and tender.

SWEET POTATO CHIPS

PREPARATION TIME: 20 minutes
COOKING TIME: 5–10 minutes
PER SERVING: 290cals, 13g fat, 43g carbohydrate

SERVES 6

3 litre bottle vegetable oil
1.5kg (3¼lb) sweet potatoes, peeled and cut into thick chips
2tbsp oil
1 level tbsp each coriander, cumin, sesame and mustard
   seeds

1 Pour the oil into a deep-fat fryer up to the maximum mark and heat to 170°C. Fry the potatoes in batches for a few minutes until soft but not coloured. Drain.
2 Heat the oil to 190°C and fry the chips again, in batches, until golden brown. Put the 2tbsp of oil in a pan and fry the seeds. Toss the seeds with the chips and season with salt.

TOMATO SALAD WITH
CHILLI PEPPERS AND SPRING ONIONS

PREPARATION TIME: 20 minutes
PER SERVING: 110cals, 9g fat, 6g carbohydrate

SERVES 6

900g (2lb) ripe plum tomatoes, skinned and cut into
   rough pieces
3 halved, deseeded and sliced Anaheim chilli peppers
   (see Cook's Tip)
1 bunch spring onions, trimmed and finely chopped
1tbsp balsamic vinegar
4tbsp olive oil
Fresh flat-leafed parsley to garnish

Combine the tomatoes, chillies and spring onions in a bowl. Season with salt and freshly ground black pepper, then toss with the balsamic vinegar and oil. Garnish with flat-leafed parsley to serve.

TO PREPARE AHEAD Complete the salad up to one day ahead. Cover and chill.
TO USE Garnish and serve.
COOK'S TIP Anaheim chillies are available in larger supermarkets. If you are unable to buy them, substitute two green peppers and one large green chilli.

MINT JELLY

PREPARATION TIME: 5 minutes
COOKING TIME: 1 hour 10 minutes
PER 1 LEVEL TBSP: 90cals, 0g fat,
23g carbohydrate

MAKES ABOUT 450G (1LB)

2.3kg (5lb) whole Bramley apples, roughly chopped
A few fresh mint sprigs
1.1 litres (2 pints) white wine vinegar
450g (1lb) granulated sugar for each 600ml (1 pint) of
   juice
8 level tbsp freshly chopped mint

1 Put the apples in a preserving pan with 1.1 litres (2 pints) of water and the mint sprigs. Bring to the boil and simmer gently for 45 minutes or until the apples are soft and pulpy. Add the vinegar and boil for 5 minutes. Spoon into a jelly bag or cloth and leave overnight to strain into a large bowl.
2 Return the juice to the preserving pan with 450g (1lb) granulated sugar for each 600ml (1 pint) of juice. Heat gently until the sugar has dissolved and then boil rapidly for about 10 minutes or until setting point is reached. Remove the scum, stir in the chopped mint, allow to cool and pot in the usual way (see page 54).

COOK'S TIP Baste lamb chops with the jelly while grilling.

FIGS IN CINNAMON SYRUP

PREPARATION TIME: 15 minutes

COOKING TIME: 35 minutes,
plus 30 minutes cooling and overnight chilling

PER SERVING: 230cals, 16g fat, 19g carbohydrate

SERVES 6

1 orange

1 lemon

300ml (½ pint) red wine

50g (2oz) golden caster sugar

1 cinnamon stick

450g (1lb) ready-to-eat dried figs

200g tub mascarpone cheese or vanilla ice cream to serve

1 Pare the rind from the orange and lemon and put in a medium pan. Squeeze and add the orange and lemon juice with the wine, sugar and cinnamon stick. Bring very slowly to the boil, stirring occasionally.

2 Add the figs and simmer very gently for 20 minutes until plump and soft. Remove the figs, rind and cinnamon with a slotted spoon and transfer to a serving bowl.

3 Return the liquid to the boil and bubble until syrupy. Pour over the figs, then cool, cover and chill. The figs can be kept, covered, in the fridge for up to one week. Just stir occasionally.

4 To serve, warm the figs, if you like, in the syrup for 3–4 minutes, then serve with mascarpone or ice cream.

TARTE TATIN

PREPARATION TIME: 15 minutes,
plus 1 hour chilling

COOKING TIME: 45–55 minutes,
plus 55 minutes cooling

PER SERVING: 730cals, 39g fat, 96g carbohydrate

SERVES 6

FOR THE PASTRY

225g (8oz) plain flour

150g (5oz) butter

¼ level tsp salt

50g (2oz) golden icing sugar

1 large egg

Vanilla extract

FOR THE CARAMEL

125g (4oz) butter

200g (7oz) golden caster sugar

1.4–1.5kg (3–3¼lb) eating apples, peeled, cored and quartered

Juice of ½ lemon

Cream, custard or ice cream to serve

1 To make the pastry, sift the flour on to a surface, make a hollow in the centre and add the butter with the salt. Work the butter and salt together using the fingers of one hand until smooth and pliable (do not work in the flour). Add the icing sugar to the butter mixture and mix in the same way. Add the egg and vanilla extract and mix with the butter mixture until it resembles scrambled egg. Cut the flour into the butter mixture with a palette knife. Knead lightly until smooth, then wrap and chill for 1 hour or until firm (see Cook's Tips).

2 To make the caramel, melt the butter in a 28cm (11in) tarte tatin mould (see Cook's Tips) and add the sugar. Pack the apples tightly in the mould, standing them on one end, and cook for 20–25 minutes until well caramelised. Turn apples round two-thirds of the way through cooking time. Add the lemon juice. Allow the apples to cool.

3 Preheat the oven to 220°C (200°C fan oven) mark 7. Roll the pastry out so that it is 2.5cm (1in) larger all round than the top of the mould or pan. Lay on top of the cooked apples. Prick the pastry with the tip of a sharp knife. Bake for 25–30 minutes until the pastry is brown all over.

4 Leave to cool for 10 minutes. Turn out on to a plate and serve at room temperature with cream, custard or ice cream.

COOK'S TIPS To make this pastry in a food processor, whiz the butter, sugar, egg and vanilla extract together for 1 minute. Work in the flour and salt until the mixture just comes together. Knead lightly on a floured surface.

● Tarte tatin moulds are expensive. As an alternative, cook the apples in a non-stick frying pan and transfer to a deep sloping-sided cake tin to bake, or use a shallow flameproof casserole dish. Start cooking the apples on a low heat, increasing the heat as the apples begin to produce juice.

SHORTBREAD WITH PEARS IN ORANGE SYRUP

PREPARATION TIME: 30 minutes,
plus 30 minutes chilling and 30 minutes cooling
COOKING TIME: 40 minutes
PER SERVING: 660cals, 29g fat, 94g carbohydrate

SERVES 6

FOR THE SHORTBREAD

250g (9oz) plain flour

175g (6oz) unsalted butter, cut into pieces

Grated zest of 1 lemon

75g (3oz) golden caster sugar plus sugar to dust

FOR THE PEARS

150ml (¼ pint) white wine

150g (5oz) golden caster sugar

Zest of 1 large orange

1 vanilla pod

6 medium pears, quartered, cored and thickly sliced

175ml (6fl oz) low-fat crème fraîche

1 To make the shortbread, put the flour, butter and lemon zest in a food processor and whiz until the mixture resembles fine crumbs. Add the sugar and 2tsp of water and pulse until the mixture forms a dough. Wrap and chill for 30 minutes.

2 Preheat the oven to 200°C (180°C fan oven) mark 6. Roll out the shortbread on a lightly floured surface to a thickness of 5mm (¼in). Cut out 12 star shapes, approximately 7.5cm (3in) in diameter. Dust with caster sugar and put on baking sheets lined with greaseproof paper. Bake for 10–12 minutes or until pale golden brown. Cool.

3 To cook the pears, put the wine, sugar, orange zest, vanilla pod and pears in a wide pan or frying pan. Cook over a low heat until the sugar dissolves, then increase the heat, cover the pears and simmer for 10–15 minutes or until the pears are just transparent. Lift the pears out of the syrup to cool. Bring the liquid to the boil and bubble for 2–3 minutes or until syrupy. Cool.

4 Just before serving, put one shortbread on each serving plate, arrange the sliced pears on top, add 2tbsp of the crème fraîche to each, then drizzle with orange syrup and top with another shortbread.

TO PREPARE AHEAD Complete the recipe to the end of step 3. Store the shortbread in an airtight container for up to one week. Cool, cover and chill the pears and orange syrup separately for up to two days.
TO USE Complete the recipe.

APPLE, ALMOND AND CINNAMON CAKE

PREPARATION TIME: 45 minutes
COOKING TIME: 1 hour 10 minutes
PER SERVING: 680cals, 42g fat, 71g carbohydrate

SERVES 6

250g (9oz) unsalted butter, softened, plus extra to grease

4 sharp eating apples, peeled, quartered, cored and each quarter cut in half

250g (9oz) golden caster sugar

Grated zest of 1 lemon

3 medium eggs, beaten

150g (5oz) self-raising flour, sifted

1 level tsp ground cinnamon

½ level tsp baking powder

50g (2oz) ground almonds

1 Grease and baseline a 23cm (9in) diameter springform tin. Preheat the oven to 180°C (160°C fan oven) mark 4.

2 Melt 50g (2oz) of the butter in a pan, add the apples and 50g (2oz) of the sugar. Fry until the apples are caramelised, then add the lemon zest, place in the tin and cool.

3 Put the remaining butter and sugar in a bowl and beat until light and fluffy, then gradually beat in the eggs. Fold in the flour, cinnamon, baking powder and almonds. Spoon the mixture on top of the apples and smooth over.

4 Bake for 50–60 minutes or until a skewer inserted comes out clean. Leave to cool in the tin for 15 minutes before turning out.

COOK'S TIP This moist cake improves in flavour and texture if kept – you can store it in an airtight container in a cool place for up to one week. Serve with crème fraîche or yogurt.

PLUM AND CARDAMOM FOOL

PREPARATION TIME: 15 minutes

COOKING TIME: 35 minutes,

plus 30 minutes cooling and 2 hours chilling

PER SERVING: 370cals,11g fat, 64g carbohydrate

SERVES 4

1kg (2¼lb) dessert plums, stoned and sliced

125g (4oz) golden caster sugar

4 cardamom pods, split, seeds removed and crushed

2tbsp lemon juice

150g tub fresh custard

2 x 200g tubs Greek yogurt

Amaretti biscuits to serve

1 Put the plums, sugar, cardamom seeds and lemon juice in a pan. Cover and bring to the boil, then simmer for 20–25 minutes or until plums are soft but still holding their shape. Pour into a cold bowl and leave for 30 minutes. Remove eight slices for decoration and set aside.

2 Lift the plums out of the bowl with a slotted spoon reserving the juices. Purée in a food processor and pour into a bowl. Boil the juices for 3–4 minutes until reduced to 3tbsp, then stir into the plum purée with the custard and one tub of yogurt until smooth. Spoon into four tumblers and chill for up to 2 hours. Decorate with yogurt and plum slices and serve with amaretti biscuits.

(Illustrated)

PEAR AND BLACKBERRY CRUMBLE

PREPARATION TIME: 20 minutes
COOKING TIME: 35–45 minutes
PER SERVING: 530cals, 21g fat, 82g carbohydrate

SERVES 6

450g (1lb) blackberries

450g (1lb) pears, peeled and halved lengthways

Juice of 1 lemon

225g (8oz) golden caster sugar

1 level tsp ground mixed spice

100g (3½oz) butter, chopped, plus extra to grease

225g (8oz) plain flour

75g (3oz) ground almonds

Single cream or ice cream to serve

1 Fill the sink with cold water. Put the blackberries in a colander and lower carefully into the water. Toss the fruit to wash thoroughly. Lift out the colander and leave the blackberries to drain.
2 Halve the pears again and core, then slice each quarter into two or three pieces. Put the pieces in a bowl, add the lemon juice and toss well.
3 Add 100g (3½oz) of the sugar to the sliced pears, along with the ground mixed spice, then add in the blackberries and toss thoroughly to coat with sugar and spice.
4 Preheat the oven to 200°C (180°C fan oven) mark 6. Grease a 1.8 litre (3¼ pint) shallow dish with a little butter, then carefully tip the fruit into the dish in an even layer.
5 Put the butter, flour, ground almonds and the remaining sugar into a food processor and pulse until the mixture begins to look like breadcrumbs. Tip into a bowl and bring parts of it together with your hands to make lumps.
6 Spoon the crumble topping evenly over the fruit, then bake for 35–45 minutes until the fruit is tender and the crumble is golden and bubbling. Serve with cream or a scoop of vanilla ice cream.

(Illustrated)

SUMMER PICKLE

PREPARATION TIME: 10 minutes
COOKING TIME: 8 minutes
PER 1 LEVEL TBSP: 15cals, 1g fat,
2g carbohydrate

MAKES ABOUT 1.4KG (3LB)

225g (8oz) each prepared celery, cucumber, carrot and
    red pepper, trimmed and thickly sliced

225g (8oz) red onion, cut into wedges

125g (4oz) each baby corn, green beans, topped and
    tailed, and mushrooms

600ml (1 pint) distilled malt vinegar

6 each allspice berries and black peppercorns

1 blade of mace

1 bay leaf

2 cloves

Pinch of saffron

2 level tbsp freshly chopped dill

6 level tbsp light muscovado sugar

125g (4oz) cherry tomatoes

6tbsp walnut oil

1 Put all the vegetables in a pan and stir in the vinegar, allspice, black peppercorns, mace, bay leaf, cloves, saffron, dill and sugar. Season well with salt and freshly ground black pepper. Bring to the boil and simmer gently for about 5 minutes.
2 Stir in the cherry tomatoes and walnut oil. Cool overnight. Pack into pickle jars and seal (see page 54).

COOK'S TIP Serve with deep-fried Camembert or Brie.
● Top Welsh rarebit with the pickle before grilling.

OCTOBER

As the days get ever shorter, October reminds us that we're well into autumn — traditionally the month of harvest

OCTOBER IS SOMETIMES VIEWED as a poor relation of September, but the reputation is not quite deserved. It may not be summer, when orchard and vine are exploding with their juicy, sun-filled abundance, but the warm summer months have helped breed new things for autumnal enjoyment and storage, and some are uniquely wonderful. For one thing, this may be an even better month for wild mushrooms (depending again on the weather). The choice of squashes should be even greater, and there are more pumpkins around owing to the increasing popularity of Hallowe'en as a semi-official British holiday. See the box on page 235 for tips on preparing and using them.

Vegetables

There are also veggie stragglers from summer still lurking on the shelves, especially in the early part of the month: beans, courgettes, peppers and aubergines from the continent. Beetroot, sweetcorn, celery, main-crop potatoes, carrots, marrow — all of these should be of top quality. Sweet potatoes are also abundant now, wonderful when baked as you would an ordinary potato, and root vegetables apart from potatoes should be prime: look for salsify, parsnips, celeriac, swedes and turnips. The Oven-Baked Root Vegetable Chips with Tomato Ketchup (page 248) shows a delicious and somewhat unusual way of using these humble delicacies. There are also lovely autumn cabbages coming in, of all the major varieties, and a good selection of onions. If you pickle your own, now's the time. Or make the Sweet Roast-Onion Salad on page 238 as an accompaniment to the game dishes we're all likely to cook this month.

Left: Red Cabbage with Pears (see page 251)

INGREDIENTS
OF THE MONTH

GAME

Grouse

Hare

Partridge

Pheasant

Snipe

Venison

Wild duck

Wild geese

FISH

Bass

Cod

Crab

Dabs

Flounder

Haddock

Hake

Halibut

Herring

Mussels

Oysters

Plaice

Scallops

Shrimp

Skate

Sole

Sprats

Squid

Turbot

Whiting

VEGETABLES

Baking potatoes

Brussels sprouts

Cabbages

Carrots

Cauliflower

Kale

Parsnips

Pumpkin

Salsify

Swede

Turnips

Watercress

Wild mushrooms

FRUIT

Apples

Damsons

Figs

Pears

Quince

Walnuts

BEST BUY

Apples

Pumpkins

Fruit and Nuts

The berries of summer are all gone now, but other fruits make up their much-regretted absence. And none is more special for UK home cooks than the big push of the apple season, crowned by Cox's Orange pippins. And with them will come delicious pears and more damsons – perfect for the Sticky Plum Tart on page 254. Autumn is also the season for nuts, with fresh walnuts leading the charge. They are never better than at this time of year, before the flesh has lost its moist, delicate freshness. Figs are another of October's highlights, pulled from the tree when fully ripe and offering their inimitable sweet flavour for a short time before they go too squishy. They're perfect just cut open and slurped out of the skin, but also take well to quick baking. Quinces are a top choice now, especially for jam makers. And don't neglect pomegranates coming over from the Mediterranean: one of the hardest fruits to eat, but utterly delicious.

Fish

October is also another great month for fish of every kind. The list of choice shellfish is enlarged by mussels, the cheapest type around and one of the best. Look for smaller mussels, which often have the sweetest flavour, and experiment with different ways of flavouring them outside the French standards. Flat fish are also in one of their best seasons: plaice, every type of sole, and turbot are all in prime condition. And don't forget herring and sprats, cheap fish that can be the greatest crowd-pleasers of all; the Marinated Herring, Potato and Dill Salad on page 238 is a classic dish of real excellence. Squid is in the last month of its prime season, and should also be eaten as often as you can find good fresh specimens.

Game

For main courses at this time of year, pride of place has to go to game. We're into the height of the season, and prices should have dropped about as low as they will get. Wild duck is a true delicacy, with a deep, rich flavour quite unlike that of farmed duck. Roast it whole and give each diner half a bird, or bone the breasts out and cook them in a frying pan while making a simple casserole from the legs. Wild duck goes especially well with autumnal fruits, either as the basis for a sauce or cooked in pieces with the legs. And if you like the powerful flavour of wild venison, in rich wine-based sauces, now is the time to cook it, or try the Mustard Venison with Hot Mushroom Dressing on page 243.

PUMPKIN

Americans think of pumpkin as something you put in a pie and serve at Thanksgiving. Europeans know it primarily as a savoury ingredient. In this case, the old world and the new both have it right. Pumpkin is indeed delicious in pies, but it can be put to good use in all manner of savoury dishes as well. The simplest is just cutting the pumpkin into pieces, removing the seeds and strings from the central cavity, and then steaming or baking the pieces for serving plain with a little butter. Some care has to be taken in handling it, however. The flesh becomes extremely fragile once it's cooked, and can break up easily. This doesn't matter so much if you're going to mash the pumpkin, though you then have the problem of getting rid of the high water content. The easiest way of dealing with this is to roast the pieces at a low temperature for a long time, which cooks them while simultaneously evaporating much of the water.

SPINACH, DOLCELATTE CHEESE AND WALNUT SALAD

PREPARATION TIME: 5 minutes
COOKING TIME: 15–20 minutes
PER SERVING: 470cals, 36g fat, 23g carbohydrate

SERVES 6

1 ciabatta or small baguette

9tbsp walnut oil

200g (7oz) baby spinach leaves, washed

250g (9oz) dolcelatte cheese, sliced

1 fennel bulb, washed and sliced

50g (2oz) walnut pieces

2 oranges, peeled, pith removed, segmented and juice
   put to one side

1tbsp Dijon mustard

1 Preheat the oven to 200°C (180°C fan oven) mark 6. Cut the loaf into three slices lengthways, then cut each slice into two. Put on to a baking sheet and drizzle with 3tbsp of the oil. Bake for 15–20 minutes or until crisp and light brown.

2 Arrange the spinach, cheese and fennel in six salad bowls, scatter over the walnut pieces and orange segments and season generously with salt and freshly ground black pepper.

3 Whisk together the orange juice, remaining walnut oil and the Dijon mustard. Drizzle over the salad and serve.

PUMPKIN AND BUTTERNUT SQUASH SOUP

PREPARATION TIME: 15 minutes
COOKING TIME: 40 minutes
PER SERVING: 400cals, 29g fat, 27g carbohydrate

SERVES 4

900g (2lb) pumpkin, peeled and roughly diced

750g (1lb 10oz) butternut squash, peeled and roughly
   diced

125g (4oz) shallots, blanched in boiling water, peeled
   and roughly chopped

1 large garlic clove, chopped

1tsp coriander seeds, crushed

125g (4oz) butter, melted

600ml (1 pint) vegetable stock

600ml (1 pint) warm milk

Fresh basil sprigs and soured cream to garnish

1 Preheat the oven to 220°C (200°C fan oven) mark 7. Put the pumpkin, squash, shallots, garlic and coriander seeds in a large roasting tin and toss with the melted butter. Season the vegetables well with salt and freshly ground black pepper and cook until golden and just cooked through – about 30 minutes.

2 Tip the vegetables into a large pan, then use the vegetable stock to rinse all the remaining bits out of the roasting tin. Add this to the vegetables in the pan, then stir in the milk.

3 Put three-quarters of the soup into a food processor or blender and whiz until smooth. Mash the remaining soup mixture, then stir the two together and reheat. Garnish with basil and swirls of soured cream, then serve with crusty bread.

MUSHROOM AND SAGE FRITTATA

PREPARATION TIME: 10 minutes,
plus 3 minutes standing
COOKING TIME: 27–37 minutes
PER SERVING: 330cals, 23g fat, 8g carbohydrate

SERVES 4

2tbsp olive oil
2 large onions, finely sliced
150g (5oz) baby chestnut mushrooms, sliced
75g (3oz) Pecorino cheese, coarsely grated
6 sage leaves, roughly chopped, plus extra to garnish
6 large eggs, beaten

1 Preheat the oven to 200°C (180°C fan oven) mark 6. Line an 18x28x2.5cm (7x11x1in) tin with baking parchment.

2 Heat the oil in a pan and fry the onions gently for 10–15 minutes or until soft. Increase the heat, add the mushrooms and cook for 2 minutes, then tip into the prepared tin. Sprinkle over the cheese and chopped sage leaves.

3 Season the eggs well, then pour into the tin. Cook in the oven for 15–20 minutes until just firm in the centre and lightly golden. Leave to stand for 2–3 minutes.

4 Loosen the frittata around the edges, turn out on to a chopping board and cut into four wedges. Serve garnished with the remaining sage leaves.

(Illustrated)

MARINATED HERRING, POTATO AND DILL SALAD

PREPARATION TIME: 5 minutes
COOKING TIME: 20–25 minutes
PER SERVING: 640cals, 42g fat, 41g carbohydrate

SERVES 4

1kg (2¼lb) new potatoes
2tbsp soured cream
6tbsp mayonnaise
2 level tbsp freshly chopped dill
8 pickled gherkins, thinly sliced
550g (1¼lb) sweet cured herrings, drained, sliced into
2cm (¾in) strips

1 Put the potatoes in cold water, bring to the boil and cook for 15–20 minutes or until tender. Drain, then cut into wedges.
2 Meanwhile, make the dressing. Mix the soured cream, mayonnaise and dill together in a large bowl. Season well with salt and freshly ground black pepper.
3 To assemble the salad, put the potatoes, gherkins and herrings in a bowl with the dressing and toss together. Check the seasoning and serve.`

(Illustrated)

SWEET ROAST-ONION SALAD

PREPARATION TIME: 3 minutes
COOKING TIME: 1 hour 50 minutes
PER SERVING: 240cals, 22g fat, 9g carbohydrate

SERVES 6

6 even-sized onions – around 700g (1½lb) total weight
50ml (2fl oz) oil

FOR THE DRESSING

3 level tbsp capers, roughly chopped
Zest and juice of 1 large lime
½ level tsp golden caster sugar
150ml (¼ pint) olive oil
2 level tbsp freshly chopped flat-leafed parsley
Salad leaves, such as rocket, to serve

1 Preheat the oven to 200°C (180°C fan oven) mark 6. Peel the onions, if you like, and put in an ovenproof dish (see Cook's Tip). Pour over the oil and cook for 1½ hours or until beginning to colour, then cover with foil and cook for a further 20 minutes or until soft in the centre.
2 To make the dressing, mix together the capers, zest and juice of the lime, the sugar, oil and parsley and season with salt and freshly ground black pepper. Cover and put to one side.
3 To serve, add any cooking juices to the dressing and adjust the seasoning. Halve each onion and put on a bed of salad leaves. Spoon over the dressing and serve.

COOK'S TIP It's best to use an ovenproof dish just large enough to hold the onions, so any cooking juices don't evaporate.

SAUSAGE MEATBALLS AND BOSTON BEANS

PREPARATION TIME: 25 minutes,
plus 20 minutes chilling
COOKING TIME: 1 hour
PER SERVING: 600cals, 34g fat, 50g carbohydrate

SERVES 6

FOR THE MEATBALLS

750g (1lb 10oz) good-quality coarse sausages

4tbsp freshly chopped flat-leafed parsley

2tbsp freshly chopped or 1 level tsp dried oregano

3tbsp oil

FOR THE BOSTON BEANS

2tbsp oil

1 medium onion, chopped

3 level tbsp plain flour

150ml (¼ pint) vegetable stock

2 x 400g cans chopped tomatoes

3tbsp Dijon mustard

3 level tbsp light muscovado sugar

2tbsp treacle

3tbsp Worcestershire sauce

1tbsp white wine vinegar

3 x 420g cans cannellini beans, drained and rinsed

4tbsp soured cream

50g (2oz) Cheddar cheese

Fresh oregano sprigs to garnish

1 To make the meatballs, slit the sausage skins with a small sharp knife and squeeze the meat into a large bowl. With your hands, mix in the herbs and season with salt and freshly ground black pepper. Shape the meat into 18 balls, put on a baking sheet, then cover and chill for 20 minutes.

2 Meanwhile, make the Boston beans. Heat the oil in a pan, add the onion and cook for 5 minutes until softened. Stir in the flour and cook for a further minute. Add the stock, stirring until smooth, then add the tomatoes, mustard, sugar, treacle, Worcestershire sauce, white wine vinegar and beans. Season, then bring slowly to the boil, stirring constantly. Pour into a shallow 2.8 litre (5 pint) ovenproof dish.

3 Heat the oil for the meatballs in a large frying pan and fry them in batches for 2 minutes until lightly browned. Put them on absorbent kitchen paper and keep to one side until all the meatballs are cooked.

4 Preheat the oven to 180°C (160°C fan oven) mark 4. Add the meatballs to the beans, turning to coat in the bean mixture, and cook for 40–45 minutes or until bubbling. Drizzle with the soured cream, sprinkle with the cheese, then grill until golden. Garnish with oregano and serve.

PORK FILLETS WITH FIGS AND TALEGGIO CREAM

PREPARATION TIME: 20 minutes,
plus overnight soaking
COOKING TIME: About 40 minutes
PER SERVING: 750cals, 53g fat, 23g carbohydrate

SERVES 6

12 ready-to-eat dried figs
125ml (4fl oz) white wine
2 large sprigs fresh rosemary
2 pork fillets
225g (8oz) Taleggio, Fontina, Delice de Bourgogne or
    Vignotte Cheese
Around 75g (3oz) Parma ham, sliced
2tbsp olive oil
25g (1oz) butter
284ml carton double cream

1 Soak the figs overnight in the wine with one sprig of the rosemary. (See Cook's Tip.)
2 Drain the figs, reserving the wine, and remove the hard stalk from each one. Split both pork fillets open lengthways like a book, cover with clingfilm and beat with a rolling pin until double their original width. Season with salt and freshly ground black pepper. Cut 25g (1oz) of the cheese into 12 small dice, then push a piece of cheese into each fig. Put the slices of Parma ham down the centre of each fillet, arrange the figs on top and fold over the Parma ham. Reshape the fillets and tie at intervals with fine string.
3 Preheat the oven to 200°C (180°C fan oven) mark 6. Sit the pork fillets on the remaining rosemary sprig in a roasting tin just large enough to hold them and drizzle over the oil. Pour in the reserved wine. Roast the pork for 30–35 minutes or until just tender.
4 Meanwhile, chop the remaining cheese and put in a pan with the butter. Pour in the cream and melt over a low heat until blended. Season lightly.
5 Spoon or brush a little of the cheese sauce over the pork for the last 15 minutes of cooking time. Cover the remainder and keep warm just off the heat.
6 Transfer the cooked fillets to a board ready for carving and cover with foil to keep warm. Scrape down the sediment from the sides of the roasting tin, put the tin on the hob and bring the pan juices to the boil. Bubble for 3–4 minutes until only 3–4tbsp of liquid remains, then stir into the remaining cheese sauce.
7 Carve the pork into thick slices and serve with the sauce.

COOK'S TIP If you forget to soak the figs overnight, put them in a small pan with the wine and rosemary. Bring to the boil, cover and leave to soak for 20 minutes.

VENISON SAUSAGES WITH RED ONION MARMALADE

PREPARATION TIME: 5 minutes
COOKING TIME: 35 minutes
PER SERVING: 320cals, 22g fat, 20g carbohydrate

SERVES 6

12 venison sausages

2tbsp redcurrant jelly

1tsp lemon juice

400g (14oz) red onions, peeled and chopped

2tbsp olive oil

4tbsp red wine vinegar

2 level tbsp demerara sugar

1 level tsp juniper berries, crushed

1 Preheat the oven to 210°C (190°C fan oven) mark 7. Put the sausages into a small roasting tin. Mix together the redcurrant jelly and lemon juice and spoon over the sausages. Roast for 35 minutes, turning once.

2 Gently fry the onions in the oil for 15–20 minutes. Add the vinegar, sugar and juniper berries and continue cooking for 5 minutes or until the onions are really tender. Serve with the sausages.

(Illustrated)

MUSTARD VENISON WITH HOT MUSHROOM DRESSING

PREPARATION TIME: 15 minutes
COOKING TIME: 25 minutes
PER SERVING: 510cals, 39g fat, 8g carbohydrate

SERVES 4

550g (1¼lb) strip-loin venison – 6.5cm (2½in) diameter
1 level tbsp wholegrain mustard
8–10 button onions, thinly sliced
350g (12oz) small shiitake or brown-cap mushrooms
150ml (¼ pint) olive oil
2 level tbsp freshly chopped parsley and thyme
5tsp balsamic vinegar
Lemon juice to taste
Thinly cut potato chips to serve (optional)

1 Preheat the oven to 230°C (210°C fan oven) mark 8. Rub the venison with the mustard and put in a roasting tin. Scatter the onions around the venison with the mushrooms and drizzle over half the oil. Roast for 30–35 minutes for medium-rare (40 minutes for well-done).
2 Roll the hot venison in the freshly chopped herbs (see Cook's Tip) and put on a warmed serving plate with the mushrooms and onions. Cover with foil and keep warm in a low oven while you make the dressing.
3 Add the remaining oil and the vinegar to the roasting tin and warm on the hob, stirring. Season with salt and freshly ground black pepper and add lemon juice to taste.
4 Carve the venison into thick slices and serve with the dressing and the potato chips (if using).

COOK'S TIP For a spicier version, try rolling the hot venison in crushed peppercorns instead of fresh herbs.

CHEESE AND PASTA BEEF BAKE

PREPARATION TIME: 25 minutes,
plus 30 minutes chilling
COOKING TIME: 35 minutes
PER SERVING: 750cals, 44g fat, 35g carbohydrate

SERVES 6

Butter to grease
75g (3oz) peppered salami, finely chopped
450g (1lb) minced beef
3 garlic cloves, crushed
2 level tbsp freshly chopped parsley
225g (8oz) grated Parmesan cheese
50g (2oz) fresh white breadcrumbs
1 large egg, beaten
3tbsp olive oil
250g (9oz) dried pasta
1kg (2¼lb) passata
2 level tbsp freshly chopped basil, parsley, thyme or chives, or 2 level tsp dried mixed Italian herbs
400g (14oz) mozzarella cheese, diced

1 Grease a 3.4 litre (6 pint) ovenproof dish with butter.
2 In a large bowl, combine the salami, beef, garlic, parsley, 75g (3oz) of the Parmesan, the breadcrumbs and plenty of salt and freshly ground black pepper with the egg and 150ml (¼ pint) of water. Mix the ingredients together well with your hands or use a mixer with the flat beater attached. Shape into walnut-sized balls and chill for 30 minutes.
3 Heat the oil in a non-stick frying pan and fry the meatballs in batches until golden brown and cooked through – about 5 minutes.
4 Cook the pasta in plenty of boiling salted water. Drain well then mix with the passata, herbs, half the mozzarella, 50g (2oz) of the Parmesan and the meatballs. Season generously then spoon into the prepared dish and sprinkle with the remaining mozzarella and Parmesan. Preheat the oven to 200°C (180°C fan oven) mark 6.
5 Cook for 30 minutes or until golden brown, then serve hot.

TO PREPARE AHEAD Complete the recipe to the end of step 4 up to 1 day ahead. Cover and chill.
TO USE Continue as step 5. Allow an extra 10 minutes cooking time.

PUMPKIN AND CHEESE BAKE

PREPARATION TIME: 10 minutes
COOKING TIME: 1 hour–1 hour 10 minutes
PER SERVING: 530cals, 32g fat, 30g carbohydrate

SERVES 6

350g (12oz) any leftover cheeses, such as emmenthal,
  Cheddar, mozzarella
450g (1lb) pumpkin, peeled and roughly chopped
4tbsp olive oil
150g (5oz) polenta
4 level tbsp Parmesan cheese, grated
275g (10oz) onions, roughly chopped
2 garlic cloves, crushed
1 level tsp dried thyme
2 x 400g cans chopped tomatoes
2 level tbsp sun-dried tomato purée
200ml (7fl oz) red or white wine (optional) or vegetable
  stock
1 level tsp sugar
175g (6oz) wafer-thin ham
Fresh marjoram sprigs to garnish
Green salad to serve

1 Preheat the oven to 230°C (210°C fan oven) mark 8. Grate any hard cheese; cut soft cheese into small cubes. Put the pumpkin in a roasting tin with 2tbsp of the oil and roast for 25 minutes or until tender and golden.
2 Meanwhile, line a tin approximately 25.5x16cm (10x6½ in) with greaseproof paper. Bring 900ml (1½ pints) of water to the boil in a large pan, and, while still boiling, gradually add the polenta in a thin stream, stirring all the time. Keep stirring over a low heat until the mixture begins to stiffen, about 10 minutes. Season well with salt and freshly ground black pepper and add 3 level tbsp of the Parmesan.
3 Immediately spread the polenta to about 1cm (½ in) thick. Put clingfilm on the surface to prevent a skin forming. When cool, cut into squares or triangles.
4 Heat the remaining oil in a large pan and add the onions, garlic and thyme. Cook for about 10 minutes or until the onions are soft. Add the chopped tomatoes, sun-dried tomato purée, wine, if using, or stock, and 200ml (7fl oz) of water. Bring to the boil and bubble, uncovered, for about 10–15 minutes or until reduced by a third. Add the sugar and season well.
5 Spoon half the quantity of tomato sauce into a large ovenproof dish. Layer half the ham, polenta, pumpkin and cheese over the sauce. Repeat the layers, finishing with a layer of polenta and cheese.
6 Reduce the oven to 200°C (180°C fan oven) mark 6 and cook for 35–45 minutes or until golden and bubbling. Garnish with marjoram sprigs and serve with a green salad.

WILD MUSHROOM TAGLIATELLE

PREPARATION TIME: 5 minutes,
plus 20 minutes soaking
COOKING TIME: 45 minutes
PER SERVING: 790cals, 52g fat, 73g carbohydrate

SERVES 6

40g (12oz) dried cep, porcini or fairy mushrooms
2tbsp olive oil
2 onions, chopped
2 garlic cloves, crushed
2tbsp freshly chopped flat-leafed parsley
1tsp good powdered vegetable stock
568ml carton double cream
1tbsp lemon juice
500g packet tagliatelle
Parmesan cheese shavings to garnish

1 Put the dried mushrooms in a large bowl with 600ml (1 pint) of boiling water and leave to soak for 20 minutes.
2 Heat the oil in a pan and fry the onion for 6–7 minutes until soft but not coloured. Add the garlic and cook for 1 minute then stir in the parsley.
3 Strain the mushrooms, reserving the soaking liquid, then add them to the garlic and onions and cook for 10 minutes.
4 Add the stock powder to the mushroom soaking liquid, then pour into a pan. Bring to the boil and simmer for 10 minutes.
5 Add the cream and bubble to reduce for 5–10 minutes. Stir in the lemon juice and season with salt and freshly ground black pepper.
6 Meanwhile, cook the tagliatelle according to the packet instructions until al dente – tender yet still with a slight bite. Drain.
7 Toss the pasta with the mushroom sauce, garnish with Parmesan shavings and serve immediately.

GUINEA FOWL WITH PUY LENTILS, BACON AND THYME

PREPARATION TIME: 30 minutes, plus minimum 4 hours marinating

COOKING TIME: 1 hour 10 minutes

PER SERVING: 680cals, 46g fat, 22g carbohydrate

SERVES 6

200ml (7fl oz) white wine

4 garlic cloves, crushed

7tbsp olive oil

6 guinea fowl or corn-fed chicken breasts with skin on

4 celery sticks

175g (6oz) Puy lentils

1 medium onion

2 sprigs of thyme

350g (12oz) shallots or button onions, blanched in boiling water, peeled and quartered

225g (8oz) streaky bacon, derinded and cut into 1cm (½in) strips, or lardons

1 level tbsp tomato purée

1 level tbsp freshly chopped thyme

1 tbsp balsamic vinegar

Frisée salad to serve

1 Mix the wine with two of the garlic cloves and 3tbsp of the oil. Lay the guinea fowl or chicken in a non-metallic dish and pour over the wine mixture. Cover and chill for 4 hours or overnight.

2 Cut three of the celery sticks into strips. Put the lentils in a large pan with the remaining celery stick, the onion and thyme sprigs. Cover with cold water, bring to the boil and simmer for 25–30 minutes or until just tender. Drain, reserving 200ml (7fl oz) of the cooking liquor. Discard the celery, onion and thyme.

3 Preheat the oven to 200°C (180°C fan oven) mark 6. Lift the birds from the marinade and pat dry with kitchen paper. Heat 2tbsp of the oil in a large frying pan and brown the birds, skin-side down, for 2–3 minutes. Transfer to a roasting tin and pour the marinade over. Cook for 15–20 minutes.

4 Meanwhile, add the shallots to the frying pan and fry for 4–5 minutes until golden. Add the bacon or lardons and cook until crisp. Add the tomato purée, the remaining garlic and the celery strips and cook for 3–4 minutes. Add the cooked lentils, chopped thyme and vinegar.

5 Lift the birds from the tin and keep warm. Add the pan juices and reserved liquor to the lentils, bring to the boil and simmer for 2–3 minutes. Add the remaining oil and season with salt and freshly ground black pepper. Serve with the guinea fowl or chicken and the frisée salad.

RAVIOLI WITH MUSSEL AND TOMATO SAUCE

PREPARATION TIME: 20 minutes

COOKING TIME: 35 minutes

PER SERVING: 460cals, 18g fat, 46g carbohydrate

SERVES 4

1kg bag of mussels in their shells – to give 100g (3½oz) –
   prepared as on page 13

2–3tbsp olive oil

1 large garlic clove, chopped

1 tiny dried red chilli

250g (9oz) cherry tomatoes

2 x 250g packs spinach and cheese ravioli

1 level tbsp freshly chopped parsley, plus a few sprigs
   to garnish

1 Discard any open mussels. Put the mussels in a large pan, cover and simmer for 2 minutes or until the shells open. Discard any that remain closed. Strain, reserving the cooking liquid, and put to one side.

2 In another pan, heat the oil, add the garlic and crumble in the chilli. Cook for 1–2 minutes until the garlic is golden. Add the tomatoes and mussel liquor and season with freshly ground black pepper. Bring to the boil and cook for 10–15 minutes until thick and pulpy.

3 Cook the ravioli according to the packet instructions. Meanwhile, ease the mussels from their cooled shells and add to the tomato sauce.

4 Cook the tomato sauce for 1–2 minutes and stir in the chopped parsley. Drain the ravioli, toss with the sauce and garnish with parsley sprigs to serve.

(Illustrated)

RED LAMB CURRY WITH PUMPKIN AND COCONUT

PREPARATION TIME: 10 minutes

COOKING TIME: 1 hour 20 minutes

PER SERVING: 530cals, 38g fat, 16g carbohydrate

SERVES 4

550g (1¼ lb) diced leg of lamb (see Cook's Tips)

1tbsp sunflower oil

225g (8oz) red onion, chopped

125g (4oz) block creamed coconut (see Cook's Tips)

2 level tsp red Thai curry paste

2.5cm (1in) piece fresh root ginger, peeled and chopped

225g (8oz) pumpkin, peeled and cut into thin wedges
   (see Cook's Tips)

4 level tbsp mango chutney

Fresh basil leaves and fried red onion rings to garnish

Basmati rice to serve

1 Fry the lamb on a high heat in the oil until deep golden brown. Lower the heat, add the onion and continue to fry, stirring, until the onion is soft and golden. Take a good 10 minutes to do this as it brings out the natural sweetness of the onions and adds to both the flavour and colour of the finished recipe.

2 Meanwhile, pour 600ml (1 pint) of boiling water over the creamed coconut and leave to dissolve.

3 Add the curry paste and ginger to the lamb and fry together for a further 1–2 minutes. Stir in the coconut liquid and bring to the boil. Season with salt, then cover and simmer on a very low heat for 30 minutes.

4 Stir the pumpkin and chutney into the lamb, cover again and continue to cook for a further 30 minutes or until the lamb and pumpkin are tender. Garnish with basil leaves and onion rings, then serve with basmati rice.

COOK'S TIPS Diced leg of lamb is available in most supermarkets but it's still worth spending 2–3 minutes trimming the lamb of any excess fat before frying.

• If you can't find block creamed coconut, you can use canned coconut milk – you'll need 600ml.

• All shapes and sizes of pumpkin and other winter squash are in the shops now. Pick one the size of a small football for this recipe.

OVEN-BAKED ROOT VEGETABLE CHIPS

PREPARATION TIME: 30 minutes

COOKING TIME: 55 minutes

PER SERVING: 200cals, 6g fat, 32g carbohydrate

SERVES 6

700g (1½lb) large Maris Piper potatoes, peeled and cut
  lengthways into 1cm (½in) x 7.5cm (3in) chips

300g (11oz) large carrots, peeled and cut lengthways into
  1cm (½in) x 7.5cm (3in) chips

3 large parsnips – around 700g (1½lb) in total – peeled
  and cut lengthways into 1cm (½in) x 7.5cm (3in) chips

4tbsp olive oil

2 level tsp all-purpose seasoning

½ level tsp sea salt

1 Preheat the oven to 220°C (200°C fan oven) mark 7. Put the vegetables in a bowl and toss with the oil, all-purpose seasoning and the salt, then transfer into two roasting tins.

2 Cook for 50–55 minutes or until the vegetables are tender and golden. Toss frequently and swap the tins over occasionally, so that the vegetables cook evenly.

3 Drain the vegetables on kitchen paper and serve warm with Home-made Tomato Ketchup (see below).

TO PREPARE AHEAD Complete the recipe to the end of step 1, then cover and chill vegetables for up to 4 hours. Alternatively, complete to the end of step 2, put the vegetables in one roasting tin, then cool, cover and chill for up to 24 hours.

TO USE Complete the recipe. Or, to reheat cooked vegetables, uncover, leave at room temperature for 30 minutes, then cook at 180°C (160°C fan oven) mark 4 for 15 minutes until warmed through.

(Illustrated)

HOME-MADE TOMATO KETCHUP

PREPARATION TIME: 5 minutes

COOKING TIME: 10 minutes

PER 1 LEVEL TBSP: 15cals, trace fat,
4g carbohydrate

MAKES ABOUT 300ML (½ PINT)

700g (1½lb) ripe tomatoes, sliced

50g (2oz) golden caster sugar

75ml (3fl oz) malt vinegar

¼ level tsp each cayenne, paprika and salt

1 level tsp sun-dried tomato purée

1 Put the tomatoes in a pan and cook over a high heat until reduced to a thick pulp.

2 Sieve and put back in the pan. Add the sugar, vinegar, cayenne, paprika, salt and sun-dried tomato purée. Continue to cook until the mixture has thickened.

3 Pour the hot ketchup into warm, sterilised screw-top jars (see page 54) and store in the fridge for up to 1 week.

ORANGE-GLAZED CARROTS

PREPARATION TIME: 15 minutes

COOKING TIME: 10–15 minutes

PER SERVING: 120cals, 5g fat, 15g carbohydrate

SERVES 8

700g (1½lb) carrots, peeled and cut into thin matchsticks

50g (2oz) butter

50g (2oz) light muscovado sugar

150ml (¼ pint) each orange juice and dry white wine

2tbsp balsamic vinegar

2 level tbsp freshly chopped flat-leafed parsley

1 Put the carrots, butter, sugar, juice, wine and vinegar into a pan and season with salt and freshly ground black pepper. Bring to the boil, then reduce the heat and simmer, uncovered, for 10–15 minutes or until the carrots are tender and the liquid has evaporated enough to form a glaze.

2 Scatter with parsley just before serving.

LEEK AND PARSNIP MASH

PREPARATION TIME: 10 minutes

COOKING TIME: 30 minutes

PER SERVING: 130cals, 4g fat, 19g carbohydrate

SERVES 6

700g (1½lb) trimmed leeks, well washed and sliced

700g (1½lb) parsnips, peeled and quartered

2 garlic cloves, peeled

200ml (7fl oz) milk

6 level tbsp freshly chopped parsley plus sprigs to garnish

6 level tbsp freshly grated Parmesan cheese

1 Put the leeks, parsnips and garlic in a pan of cold salted water, bring to the boil, then simmer for 15–20 minutes. Drain, return to the pan and dry off over a low heat for 3–4 minutes.

2 Preheat the oven to 140°C (120°C fan oven) mark 1. Heat the milk and put in a food processor with the leeks, garlic, parsnips, parsley, 5 level tbsp of the Parmesan and plenty of freshly ground black pepper. Whiz until just smooth. Put into an ovenproof dish and put in the oven to warm through. To serve, sprinkle with the remaining Parmesan and garnish with the parsley sprigs.

SOUFFLE POTATOES

PREPARATION TIME: 10–15 minutes

COOKING TIME: 50 minutes

PER SERVING: 270cals, 13g fat, 25g carbohydrate

SERVES 6

700g (1½lb) floury potatoes, cut into chunks

Butter to grease

6tbsp finely grated Parmesan

300g carton fresh four-cheese sauce

1tbsp wholegrain mustard

3 medium eggs, separated

1 Put the potatoes in a pan of cold salted water, bring to the boil and cook for 20 minutes or until tender. Drain then put back in the pan and mash over a low heat for 1–2 minutes to dry a little. Put in a bowl and cool for 10 minutes.

2 Preheat the oven to 200°C (180°C fan oven) mark 6. Butter six 225ml (8fl oz) ramekins, sprinkle each with 1tbsp of the Parmesan cheese and put them on a baking sheet.

3 Add the cheese sauce, mustard and egg yolks to the potato, season well with salt and freshly ground black pepper and beat together.

4 Whisk the egg whites in a clean grease-free bowl until they stand in stiff peaks, then fold into the mashed potato. Spoon into the prepared dishes and bake for 30 minutes until well risen. Serve immediately.

RED CABBAGE WITH PEARS

PREPARATION TIME: 10 minutes

COOKING TIME: 50 minutes

PER SERVING: 80cals, 2g fat, 14g carbohydrate

SERVES 8

1 tbsp olive oil

1 red onion, halved and sliced

2 garlic cloves, crushed

1 large red cabbage – around 1kg (2¼lb) – shredded

2 level tbsp light muscovado sugar

2 tbsp red wine vinegar

8 juniper berries

¼ level tsp ground allspice

300ml (½ pint) turkey or vegetable stock

2 pears, cored and sliced

1 Heat the oil in a large pan and fry the onion for 5 minutes to soften. Add the garlic, cabbage, sugar, vinegar, juniper berries, allspice and stock, season with salt and freshly ground black pepper and bring to the boil. Reduce the heat, cover and simmer for 30 minutes.

2 Add the pears to the red cabbage and cook for a further 15 minutes or until nearly all the liquid has evaporated and the cabbage is tender.

(Illustrated on page 232)

CURLY KALE WITH CRISPY BACON

PREPARATION TIME: 5 minutes,

plus 10 minutes cooling and 10 minutes draining

COOKING TIME: 5 minutes

PER SERVING: 190cals, 16g fat, 3g carbohydrate

SERVES 6

1.1kg (2½lb) curly kale or 1.1–1.4kg (2½–3lb) Savoy cabbage, quartered, cored and coarsely shredded

25g (1oz) butter

6 rashers dry cure, rindless streaky bacon, cut into strips

1 Remove and discard any tough or discoloured outer leaves from the curly kale.

2 Blanch the curly kale for 20 seconds in boiling salted water; blanch the cabbage for 1–2 minutes. Drain and immediately plunge into cold water to stop further cooking. Drain again and tip out on to kitchen paper to dry. Put to one side.

3 Melt the butter in a wok or large frying pan. Add the bacon and fry gently for 3–4 minutes or until turning golden brown. Toss in the curly kale or cabbage and stir-fry for 3–4 minutes until coated with butter and heated through. Season well and serve.

BUTTERED SPINACH

PREPARATION TIME: 5 minutes

COOKING TIME: 5 minutes

PER SERVING: 60cals, 3g fat, 2g carbohydrate

SERVES 6

900g (2lb) spinach, well washed and drained

A little butter

Lemon juice

1 Put the spinach in a large pan in just the water that clings to the leaves. Cook for 4–5 minutes.

2 Drain well, then toss in a little butter and lemon juice and season with salt and freshly ground black pepper. Serve hot.

CARAMELISED APPLE TARTS

PREPARATION TIME: 5 minutes,
plus 10 minutes chilling
COOKING TIME: 25 minutes
PER SERVING: 400cals, 23g fat, 44g carbohydrate

SERVES 6

40g (1½oz) butter plus extra to grease
1 sheet pastry from a 375g pack all-butter puff pastry
125g (4oz) white marzipan, chilled and coarsely grated
4 Braeburn apples, quartered, cored and sliced
Juice of 1 large lemon
25g (1oz) demerara sugar
½ level tsp ground mixed spice
Crème fraîche to serve

1 Preheat the oven to 200°C (180°C fan oven) mark 6. Grease the bases of six 7.5cm (3in) individual tartlet tins. Roll out the pastry sheet a little more thinly. Stamp out six 12.5cm (5in) rounds of pastry, using a saucer as a guide. Line the tins and prick the bases twice with a fork. Chill for 10 minutes.

2 Line the pastry with greaseproof paper and baking beans. Bake blind for 10 minutes, remove the paper and beans and cook for a further 10 minutes. Sprinkle in the marzipan and cook for a further 5 minutes or until the marzipan melts and the pastry is cooked.

3 Heat the butter in a large non-stick frying pan. Add the apples, lemon juice, sugar and spice and cook over a high heat for 5 minutes, turning as needed until most of the lemon juice has evaporated and the apples are just tender. Pile into the warm pastry cases, then put back in the oven for 2–3 minutes. Serve with crème fraîche.

(Illustrated)

HAZELNUT MERINGUE CAKE

PREPARATION TIME: 40 minutes,
plus 1 hour cooling
COOKING TIME: About 1 hour 30 minutes
PER SERVING: 440cals, 26g fat, 51g carbohydrate

MAKES 10 SLICES

5 egg whites
375g (13oz) golden caster sugar
½ level tsp ground mixed spice
200g (7oz) hazelnuts, toasted and roughly chopped
75g (3oz) white chocolate, roughly chopped
75g (3oz) plain chocolate, roughly chopped
284ml carton double cream, lightly whipped
Cocoa powder to dust

1 Line 2 baking sheets with non-stick baking parchment. Draw a 23cm (9in) circle on one sheet, using a plate as a guide. On the other sheet draw an 18cm (7in) circle. Turn each piece of paper over. Preheat the oven to 140°C (120°C fan oven) mark 1.

2 To make the meringue, whisk the egg whites in a clean grease-free bowl until stiff but not dry. Gradually whisk in 250g (9oz) of the sugar, a tablespoon at a time, whisking well after each addition until the meringue is stiff and very shiny. Whisk in the spice with the last tablespoon of sugar. Carefully fold in 125g (4oz) of the chopped hazelnuts and the white and plain chocolate.

3 Spoon the meringue on to the baking parchment circles, then spread neatly into rounds. Bake for about 2–2½ hours until dry and the undersides are firm when tapped. Turn the oven off and leave the meringues to cool in the oven.

4 Put the remaining hazelnuts in a small, heavy-based pan with the remaining sugar. Put over a gentle heat until the sugar melts. Continue cooking until the mixture caramelises to a rich golden brown colour, then pour on to an oiled baking sheet. Leave to cool and harden.

5 Put the caramel mixture in a polythene bag and crush with a rolling pin until it forms coarse praline.

6 Spread the double cream evenly over the large meringue and cover with the smaller meringue round.

7 Sprinkle with the praline and dust the top of the cake with cocoa powder before serving.

QUICK GOOEY CHOCOLATE PUDDINGS

PREPARATION TIME: 10 minutes

COOKING TIME: 20 minutes

PER PUDDING: 490cals, 34g fat, 40g carbohydrate

SERVES 4

100g (3½oz) good-quality dark chocolate with 70% cocoa solids

100g (3½oz) butter plus extra to grease

2 large eggs

100g (3½oz) golden caster sugar plus extra to dust

20g (¾oz) plain flour

Icing sugar to dust

1 Preheat the oven to 200°C (180°C fan oven) mark 6. Put the chocolate and butter in a heatproof bowl and melt over a pan of gently simmering water. Allow to cool.

2 Whisk together the eggs, caster sugar and flour. Combine the chocolate and egg mixtures and pour into four buttered and sugared 200ml (7fl oz) ramekins.

3 Put the ramekins on a baking tray and bake for 12–15 minutes or until the puddings are puffed and set on the outside but runny inside. Turn out, dust with icing sugar and serve.

(Illustrated)

STICKY PLUM TART

PREPARATION TIME: 5 minutes, plus 10–15 minutes chilling

COOKING TIME: 1 hour 5 minutes– 1 hour 15 minutes

PER SERVING: 240cals, 12g fat, 33g carbohydrate

SERVES 6

125g (4oz) plain flour

1 level tsp ground cinnamon

75g (3oz) butter

1 egg yolk

450g (1lb) plums, halved, stoned and sliced

2 level tbsp golden caster sugar

3 level tbsp apricot jam or redcurrant jelly

Cinnamon Cream to serve (see below)

1 Sieve the flour into a food processor, add the ground cinnamon, a pinch of salt, the butter and egg yolk. Whiz for 30 seconds or until evenly combined. Add 1tbsp of chilled water and whiz for a further 30 seconds. Knead together lightly and roll out to a circle approximately 25.5cm (10in) in diameter. Put on a baking sheet and chill for 10–15 minutes.

2 Preheat the oven to 200°C (180°C fan oven) mark 6. Prick the pastry all over with a fork. Bake for 20–25 minutes or until golden brown.

3 Arrange the plums over the cooked pastry and sprinkle with the sugar. Put back in the oven for 45–50 minutes or until the plums are tender.

4 Melt the jam or jelly with 2tbsp of water, bring to the boil and bubble for 1 minute. Brush or spoon over the warm tart. Serve warm with Cinnamon Cream.

CINNAMON CREAM

PREPARATION TIME: 5 minutes

PER SERVING: 220cals, 23g fat, 4g carbohydrate

SERVES 6

284ml carton double cream

1 level tbsp sieved golden icing sugar

1 level tsp ground cinnamon

Whip the cream into soft peaks. Fold in the icing sugar and ½tsp of the cinnamon. Sprinkle with the remaining ground cinnamon to decorate and serve with the warm Sticky Plum Tart.

FRANGIPANE-BAKED PEARS

PREPARATION TIME: 15 minutes,
plus minimum 6 hours marinating
COOKING TIME: 1 hour 20 minutes
PER SERVING: 580cals, 28g fat, 75g carbohydrate

SERVES 6

25g (1oz) each raisins, chopped almonds and mixed peel

3tbsp kirsch or rum

75g (3oz) flaked almonds

50g (2oz) plain flour

225g (8oz) golden caster sugar

6 pears, peeled, peel reserved

1 level tbsp apricot jam

125g (4oz) butter

2 large eggs

Few drops of almond extract (optional)

Extra-thick cream to serve

1 Combine the raisins, chopped almonds and mixed peel in a small bowl with the kirsch or rum. Cover and leave to marinate for 6 hours or overnight. Drain the fruits, reserving the marinade.

2 Put the flaked almonds and flour in a food processor and whiz until the nuts are very finely ground (see Cook's Tip) then put to one side.

3 Put 125g (4oz) of the sugar and 900ml (1½ pints) of water in a large pan and bring to the boil, stirring, until the sugar has completely dissolved.

4 Put the pears with the peelings in the simmering syrup. Cover with a disc of greaseproof paper and poach gently for 10–15 minutes or until the pears are tender. Drain the pears, reserving the liquid and discard the peelings. Return the liquid to the pan with the apricot jam and bubble for 30 minutes or until syrupy. Put to one side.

5 Cream together the remaining sugar with the butter until light and fluffy. Add the eggs a little at a time, beating well. Fold in the flour and almond mixture, the kirsch and almond extract, if using.

6 Preheat the oven to 200°C (180°C fan oven) mark 6. Using a teaspoon, scoop out the base of each pear. Combine a spoonful of the creamed mixture with the nuts and fruit and fill the pears. Put in a 900ml (1½ pint) shallow ovenproof dish and spoon round the remaining creamed mixture. Brush the pears with a little of the syrupy glaze.

7 Bake for 55 minutes–1 hour or until the frangipane is golden brown and just firm to touch. Cover with foil if browning too much.

8 Brush with a little more glaze and serve with plenty of extra-thick cream.

TO FREEZE Complete the recipe to the end of step 7. Cool, pack and freeze.
TO USE Thaw overnight at cool room temperature. Cover loosely with foil and reheat at 200°C (180°C fan oven) mark 6 for 30–35 minutes or until heated through.
COOK'S TIP Roughly processed flaked almonds give a rougher texture to the frangipane, but you can use ground almonds if you like.

CARAMELISED PINEAPPLE SLICES

PREPARATION TIME: 20 minutes
COOKING TIME: 20–30 minutes
PER SERVING: 70cals, 0g fat, 17g carbohydrate

SERVES 6

2 level tbsp light muscovado sugar

1 level tsp ground ginger

550–700g (1¼–1½lb) peeled fresh pineapple, cut into
   1cm (½in) thick slices

1 Mix the sugar with the ground ginger and sprinkle over one side of the pineapple.

2 Grill for 10 minutes or until caramelised. Serve with cream or ice cream.

APPLE AND ORANGE CURD

PREPARATION TIME: 20 minutes
COOKING TIME: 20–30 minutes
PER 1 LEVEL TBSP: 40cals , 2g fat,
5g carbohydrate

MAKES 900G (2LB)

1 quantity Apple Sauce (see below)
Grated zest and juice of 2 oranges
Grated zest and juice of 1 lemon
225g (8oz) golden caster sugar
125g (4oz) butter, roughly chopped
4 large egg yolks, beaten

1 Put the apple sauce in a heatproof bowl with the orange and lemon zests and juices, sugar, butter and egg yolks. Put over a pan of simmering water for 20–30 minutes, stirring frequently, or until the mixture will just coat the back of a wooden spoon.
2 Pot the curd in warm jars (see page 54), and store in the fridge for up to one week.

COOK'S TIP Use as a filling for meringues and for sandwich cakes; it's also good served with toasted teacakes.

APPLE SAUCE

PREPARATION TIME: 10 minutes
COOKING TIME: 10 minutes
PER 1 LEVEL TBSP: 20cals, 1g fat,
3g carbohydrate

MAKES 225ML (8FL OZ)

450g (1lb) Bramley apples, roughly chopped
1tbsp lemon juice
15g (½oz) butter
Golden caster sugar (optional)

1 Put the apples in a pan with the lemon juice and 3tbsp of water, cover and simmer for about 10 minutes or until softened.
2 Push through a nylon sieve. Stir in the butter and sweeten to taste, if you like.

COOK'S TIP Excellent with roast pork, this Apple Sauce is also good served with fresh blackberries and crème fraîche, or use with lightly whipped cream, as a filling for sponge cakes.

PLUM JAM

PREPARATION TIME: 15 minutes
(see Jam Tips, page 54)
COOKING TIME: 45 minutes
PER 1 LEVEL TBSP: 40cals, trace fat,
10g carbohydrate

MAKES ABOUT 4.5KG (10LB)

2.7kg (6lb) plums (see Cook's Tip)
2.7kg (6lb) sugar
Knob of butter

1 Put the plums and 900ml (1½ pints) of water in a preserving pan and simmer gently for about 30 minutes, until the fruit is very soft and the contents of the pan are well reduced.
2 Remove the pan from the heat, add the sugar, stirring until dissolved, then add the butter. Bring to the boil and boil rapidly for 10–15 minutes, stirring frequently or until the setting point is reached (see page 54).
3 Take the pan off the heat. Using a slotted spoon, remove the plum stones and skim off any scum from the surface of the jam. Pot and cover in the usual way (see page 54).

COOK'S TIP If dessert plums are used, rather than a cooking variety, add the juice of 1 large lemon.

NOVEMBER

Winter is with us, but party time grows closer and it's a busy time in the kitchen as preparations for Christmas begin with the making of the cake and pudding

OVEMBER IS THE MONTH when summery foods start seeming like a distant memory. But there is also a certain pleasure in getting reacquainted with autumnal foods and rediscovering their particular delights. Cabbages are at the centre of vegetable cookery from now through late winter, and this is the month to explore new ways of using them. Cabbage with Caraway Seeds (page 273) and Braised Red Cabbage (page 272) are two classic approaches. Stir-fries, spicy Indian seasonings, and Chinese-style pickles are others to consider, and if you're patient you can even make delicious sauerkraut using ordinary white cabbage.

Vegetables

This is also another big month for something that's often neglected in favour of 'sexier' vegetables: the lowly onion. See the box on page 261 for tips on their use. Elsewhere it's the root vegetables — swede, turnips, celeriac, sweet potatoes, Jerusalem artichokes and the like — that play a starring role this month. With cold weather making long-cooked comfort food an absolute necessity, these veg are just what we need. Hearty dishes like Mustard Roast Potatoes and Parsnips (page 274) and Celeriac Mash (page 273) are perfect accompaniments for game dishes, and parsnips on their own can be roasted with pheasant or partridge to soak up the flavourful meat juices. The same is true of all the cabbage dishes here, and cabbage cooked with pheasant is another classic that makes an easy one-pot meal. Indeed, November should be regarded as braising month — so many of the best seasonal ingredients seem to lend themselves to that gentle, mellowing treatment.

Left: Cranberry and Red Onion Marmalade (see page 278)

Game

Game is also ideal for braising, and not just the ubiquitous pheasant but hare and wild goose. All furred and feathered game tends to be tougher and chewier than its farmed counter- parts, and braising is the way to soften up those well-exercised muscles. Wild goose is an especially tough old bird that takes well to the casserole, and hare – with its dense, powerfully flavoured, extremely muscular flesh – positively demands it. Hare is almost completely fat-free, a quality that has obvious advantages, but can therefore be on the dry side if not treated carefully. Cook it in a pot with streaky bacon, dried herbs, and lots of red wine. The game birds can be treated in the same way, though with careful attention you can roast them or pan-cook them just to the point where they're cooked through but still tender.

On a completely different note: if you want to buy a spectacular Christmas turkey, goose or ham from one of the increasing number of mail-order specialist retailers, start shopping around now. These excellent suppliers tend to fill their order books very early in the season.

Fish

In November as in October, fish is spectacular. There's just about every variety - take your pick of whatever looks best. Cheaper flat fish such as dabs and flounder should be great now, and cheaper round fish such as grey mullet, gurnard and hake are great for turning out warming stews and curries. If you have access to them at your fishmonger, beg all the bones and heads you can get to make fish soup – a good item to keep in the freezer for weekend lunches or dinner parties. Noble flat fish such as turbot and halibut, both of high quality in November, will make an unforgettable main course. And use this month's excellent wealth of fish to make the soothing Seafood Pie with Leeks and Blue Cheese on page 268.

Fruit and Nuts

Fruit is not in its greatest period as far as variety is concerned, though there will still be UK apples and pears in the market – and they should be very good. Look for Egremont Russets at farmers' markets and some supermarkets – they're one of the best varieties for flavour. Nuts continue to multiply, with new crops of chestnuts, Brazil nuts, hazelnuts, filberts and others joining the walnuts we've already been enjoying. Use them in salads and stir-fries when you're not just cracking and eating straight from the shell. In general, the November fruit markets are dominated by imports of steadily increasing quality. Cranberries from north America and the first citrus from southern Europe are two harbingers of the approaching Christmas season.

ONIONS

No kitchen should ever be without a supply of onions – and not just one bag of yellow onions but red onions, baby pickling onions, mild white onions, shallots. These alliums are all of the same family, but they're all different; their presence can make the difference between an ordinary old dish and a distinguished dish. In all of them, quality is crucial: squeeze all over to check for firmness, and don't even think about buying something that isn't as hard as a cricket ball. Spanish onions, usually very large, are one of the mildest types and good used raw in salads; English onions are superior in flavour, especially if cooking takes away their sharp edge, as well as cheaper. Red onions are good cookers and equally good in salad, where their colour is a plus; look at the Red Onion and Parmesan Tarts (page 265) and Chilli Red Onions with Goat's Cheese (page 274) for two imaginative ways of using them. If you want to use your onions raw, macerating them in salt and vinegar helps take away some of the sting.

POTTED PHEASANT WITH THYME AND GIN

PREPARATION TIME: 25 minutes,
plus 2 hours chilling
COOKING TIME: 3 hours
PER SERVING FOR 8: 470cals, 32g fat,
trace carbohydrate
PER SERVING FOR 10: 380cals, 26g fat,
trace carbohydrate

SERVES 8–10 AS A STARTER

2 pheasants or guinea fowl
250g (9oz) unsalted butter
8 garlic cloves
1 level tsp grated nutmeg
8 black peppercorns
300ml (½ pint) dry white wine
150ml (¼ pint) gin
Handful fresh or 1 level tbsp dried thyme
Extra thyme and cracked black peppercorns
Fresh rocket and pickled walnuts to serve

1 Preheat the oven to 200°C (180°C fan oven) mark 6. Put the pheasants or guinea fowl in a small roasting tin and smear with 75g (3oz) of the butter. Roast, breast-side down, for 1 hour.

2 Reduce the oven temperature to 170°C (150°C fan oven) mark 3. Add the garlic, nutmeg, peppercorns, wine, gin and thyme to the tin, cover with foil and cook for 2 hours. Cool a little.

3 Lift the birds out of the cooking juices. Strip away the skin and bones and coarsely shred the flesh. Season with salt and freshly ground black pepper, then pack tightly into a shallow earthenware 2.3 litre (4 pint) terrine. Skim off the fat from the cooled cooking liquid and put to one side. Strain the juices over the terrine, cover and chill for 1 hour.

4 Melt the remaining butter. Skim off the foam, add the reserved fat, extra thyme and cracked peppercorns. Spoon over to cover the meat and put back in the fridge to set. Serve with the rocket and walnuts.

TO PREPARE AHEAD Complete the recipe up to two days ahead. Cover and chill.
TO USE Serve as above.

CHEESY POTATO SKINS

PREPARATION TIME: 10 minutes
COOKING TIME: 1 hour 30 minutes
PER SERVING: 310cals, 17g fat, 28g carbohydrate

SERVES 4

3 x 300g (11oz) baking potatoes, scored into quarters
1tsp vegetable oil
50g (2oz) lean smoked back bacon, roughly chopped
175g (6oz) brown cap mushrooms, roughly chopped
125g (4oz) low-fat soft cheese with garlic and herbs
50g (2oz) Cheddar cheese, grated
6tbsp milk
1½ level tsp wholegrain mustard
Mixed-leaf salad to serve

1 Preheat the oven to 200°C (180°C fan oven) mark 6. Cook the potatoes for about 1 hour 10 minutes.

2 Heat the oil in a non-stick frying pan and fry the bacon for 2–3 minutes or until cooked. Add the mushrooms and cook until all the excess moisture has evaporated.

3 Blend together the soft cheese, half the Cheddar, the milk and mustard and season with salt and freshly ground black pepper.

4 When the potatoes are cooked, quarter them and scrape out the potato, leaving about 5mm (¼in) on the skin, and put to one side. Put the shells on a baking sheet, season and put back in the oven for a further 5 minutes.

5 Mash the potato and stir into the cheese mixture with the mushrooms and bacon. Adjust the seasoning. Pile the mixture back into the potato shells and sprinkle with the remaining cheese.

6 Put back in the oven for a further 10 minutes, until golden brown. Serve immediately with a mixed-leaf salad.

TO PREPARE AHEAD Complete the recipe to the end of step 5 up to twelve hours ahead. Cool, cover and chill.
TO USE Complete as above, increasing the cooking time to 20 minutes or until piping hot (cover with foil to prevent the potato from drying out).

CLAM CHOWDER

PREPARATION TIME: 45 minutes
COOKING TIME: Approx. 35 minutes
PER SERVING: 360cals, 21g fat, 24g carbohydrate

SERVES 8

1.5kg (3¼lb) fresh clams, washed, tapped and open or
   damaged ones discarded

2tbsp vegetable oil

2 medium onions, chopped

2 medium carrots, peeled and chopped

4 celery sticks, sliced diagonally

3 medium potatoes – around 450g (1lb) – such as Maris
   Piper, diced

25g (1oz) plain flour

75ml (3fl oz) bourbon whiskey

284ml carton double cream

1 level tbsp freshly chopped thyme

2 bay leaves

1 Put the clams in a large pan with 300ml (½ pint) of cold water, cover with a lid and bring to the boil. Steam for 1–2 minutes or until all the shells have opened. Drain, reserving the cooking liquor, then cool a little and remove the clams from the shells, discarding any that remain closed. Chill the clams until needed.

2 Heat the oil in the same pan, add the onions, carrots, celery and potatoes and cook gently for 5 minutes. Stir in the flour and cook for a further 2 minutes.

3 Put the whiskey in a ladle and heat the base directly over a flame until the spirit ignites. Pour over the vegetables. Add the reserved clam cooking liquor, double cream, chopped thyme and bay leaves. Season with salt and freshly ground black pepper and cook gently for 20 minutes or until the vegetables have softened.

4 Add the clams, then cook for 2–3 minutes to heat them through. Pour into bowls and garnish with the reserved shells if you like.

TO FREEZE Complete the recipe to the end of step 3, remove the bay leaves and cool in a freezerproof container. Put the clams in a separate container and freeze both for up to one month.

TO SERVE Thaw at cool room temperature for 3–4 hours. Heat the soup in a covered pan until boiling, then simmer for 2–3 minutes. Add the clams and heat through.

(Illustrated)

SWEET POTATO AND SQUASH SOUP

PREPARATION TIME: 8 minutes

COOKING TIME: 45 minutes

PER SERVING: 330cals, 21g fat, 34g carbohydrate

SERVES 6

6 acorn squash

50g (2oz) butter

1 medium onion, finely chopped

1tsp ground coriander

500g (1lb 2oz) sweet potato, peeled, washed and cubed

900g (2lb) kabocha squash or pumpkin, peeled, deseeded and roughly chopped

1.4 litres (2½ pints) hot vegetable stock

300ml (½ pint) orange juice

200ml tub crème fraîche

Freshly chopped flat-leafed parsley

1 Preheat the oven to 200°C (180°C fan oven) mark 6. Roast the acorn squash for 45 minutes, then, when cool enough to handle, deseed them.

2 Meanwhile, heat the butter in a pan, add the onion and coriander and cook for 4 minutes to soften. Add the sweet potato, chopped squash or pumpkin, stock and orange juice. Season with salt and freshly ground black pepper, bring to the boil and simmer for 25 minutes.

3 Blend in a processor until smooth then stir in half the crème fraîche and warm through gently.

4 Spoon into the roasted acorn squash and sprinkle with parsley. Serve the remaining crème fraîche separately.

(Illustrated)

RED ONION AND PARMESAN TARTS

PREPARATION TIME: 40 minutes,
plus 15 minutes chilling and 10 minutes freezing
COOKING TIME: 30 minutes
PER SERVING: 500cals, 36g fat, 38g carbohydrate

SERVES 6

FOR THE PASTRY

225g (8oz) plain flour, sifted

100g (3½oz) unsalted butter, diced and chilled

1 medium egg yolk

FOR THE FILLING

15g (½oz) butter

1 tbsp olive oil

4 medium red onions, sliced into fine wedges and tossed
   in 1 tbsp lemon juice

200ml tub crème fraîche

1 level tbsp freshly chopped thyme plus thyme sprigs to
   garnish

50g (2oz) freshly grated Parmesan

1 To make the pastry, put the flour and butter in a food processor and whiz until the mixture resembles breadcrumbs.

2 Put the mixture into a bowl, add a pinch of salt, the egg yolk and 7 tsp of cold water. Mix well and bring the dough together with your hands. Wrap and chill for 15 minutes.

3 To make the filling, melt the butter and oil in a pan and sauté the onions for 15 minutes. Put to one side.

4 Divide the pastry into six. Roll each piece on a floured board and use to line six greased 11cm (4¼in) loose-based tartlet tins. Prick the base and sides with a fork. Put on a lipped baking sheet, cover with clingfilm and freeze for 10 minutes.

5 Preheat the oven to 200°C (180°C fan oven) mark 6. Line the tartlet tins with greaseproof paper and baking beans and bake for 10–15 minutes. Remove the paper and beans and return to the oven for 5 minutes or until dry in the centre.

6 Increase the oven temperature to 230°C (210°C fan oven) mark 8. Put half the onions in the pastry cases. Mix the crème fraîche and thyme together, season with salt and freshly ground black pepper and spoon half over the onions. Add half the Parmesan. Top with the rest of the onion, crème fraîche and Parmesan and bake for 5–10 minutes or until golden. Serve garnished with a thyme sprig.

STICKY ORANGE POUSSINS

PREPARATION TIME: 40 minutes,
plus minimum 4 hours marinating
COOKING TIME: 1 hour
PER SERVING: 200cals, 8g fat, 18g carbohydrate

SERVES 12

450ml (¾ pint) bourbon
175g (6oz) orange marmalade
Grated zest and juice of 6 oranges
50g (2oz) butter
12 poussins – around 400g (14oz) each, or chicken
   pieces
4 oranges, roughly chopped
Mixed green salad to serve

1 Put the bourbon, marmalade, orange zest and butter in a pan and gently heat until the butter has melted. Add the orange juice and leave to cool.

2 Put the poussins, backbone uppermost, on a chopping board and cut down either side of the bone with a strong sharp pair of scissors. Open out the poussins, cover with clingfilm and use the base of a strong, heavy pan to flatten. (This process is known as spatchcock; your butcher will do it for you if you ask in advance.) If using chicken pieces, slash the skin two or three times. Put the poussins, skin-side uppermost, in two large non-stick roasting tins and season with salt and freshly ground black pepper.

3 Scatter the chopped oranges around the poussins in the roasting tin and pour the bourbon marinade over the top. Cover and chill for at least 4 hours, or even better overnight.

4 Preheat the oven to 220°C (200°C fan oven) mark 7. Pour off most of the marinade into a wide pan and set aside. Roast the poussins for 20 minutes. Baste with the juices and swap the roasting tins round in the oven halfway through.

5 Reduce the oven temperature to 190°C (170°C fan oven) mark 5 and cook for a further 40 minutes, or until the juices run clear when a thigh is pierced with a sharp knife.

6 Meanwhile, bring the reserved marinade to the boil and simmer for 10–15 minutes or until lightly syrupy. Put the poussins and oranges in a serving dish, cover and keep warm. Pour the juices from the roasting tin into the reduced marinade, bring to the boil and bubble for 5–10 minutes or until syrupy. Drizzle the sauce over the poussins and serve with a mixed green salad.

MUSTARD CHICKEN WINGS WITH THYME

PREPARATION TIME: 5 minutes,
plus 20 minutes chilling
COOKING TIME: 40 minutes
PER SERVING: 340cals, 23g fat, 4g carbohydrate

SERVES 6

12 large chicken wings
4tbsp set honey
Zest and juice of 2 unwaxed lemons
4tbsp Dijon mustard
4tbsp olive oil
Handful of fresh thyme, roughly chopped

1 Lay the chicken wings in a shallow ceramic bowl. Mix the honey, lemon zest and juice, mustard, oil and thyme together and pour over the wings. Cover, chill and marinate the chicken for at least 20 minutes.

2 Preheat the oven to 200°C (180°C fan oven) mark 6. Put the chicken wings together with the marinade in a roasting tin and season well with salt and freshly ground black pepper. Roast for 40 minutes or until the juices run clear, turning and basting halfway through the cooking time. Serve at once.

SPICED BEAN AND VEGETABLE STEW

PREPARATION TIME: 10 minutes

COOKING TIME: 40 minutes

PER SERVING: 250cals, 8g fat, 42g carbohydrate

SERVES 6

3tbsp olive oil

2 small onions, sliced

2 garlic cloves, crushed

1 level tbsp sweet paprika

1 small dried red chilli, deseeded and finely chopped

700g (1½lb) sweet potatoes, peeled and cubed

700g (1½lb) pumpkin, peeled and cut into chunks

125g (4oz) okra, trimmed

500g bottle or carton passata

400g can haricot or cannellini beans, drained

1 Heat the oil in a large heavy-based pan, add the onions and garlic and cook over a very gentle heat for 5 minutes.

2 Stir in the paprika and chilli and cook for 2 minutes, then add the sweet potatoes, pumpkin, okra, passata and 900ml (1½ pints) of water. Season generously with salt and freshly ground black pepper. Cover, bring to the boil and simmer for 20 minutes until the vegetables are tender.

3 Add the beans and cook for 3 minutes to warm through.

(Illustrated)

STICKY RIBS

PREPARATION TIME: 5 minutes,
plus minimum 4 hours marinating
COOKING TIME: 10 minutes
PER SERVING: 430cals, 24g fat, 19g carbohydrate

SERVES 4

7.5cm (3in) piece fresh root ginger, peeled and grated
6 garlic cloves, crushed
6tbsp runny honey
6tbsp light soy sauce
6tbsp dry sherry
2tsp hot chilli sauce
1.4kg (3lb) pork spare ribs, cut into individual ribs
Lime halves and coriander sprigs to garnish

1 Mix all the ingredients except the spare ribs in a medium-sized bowl. Add the spare ribs and stir to coat in the marinade. Cover and chill for at least 4 hours, or even better overnight.

2 Preheat the grill for 5–10 minutes. Reserving the marinade, cook the ribs under the grill for 4–5 minutes on each side or until the meat is well browned and comes off the bone easily. (See Cook's Tip.) Transfer to a serving dish and keep warm.

3 Pour the grill pan juices into a small pan and add the reserved marinade. Bring to the boil and bubble to reduce until sticky. Brush over the ribs. Garnish with the lime halves and coriander sprigs and serve.

TO PREPARE AHEAD Complete the recipe to the end of step 1 up to one day in advance.
TO USE Complete the recipe.
COOK'S TIP Alternatively, the spare ribs can be cooked in a roasting tin at 240°C (220°C fan oven) mark 9 for 35–40 minutes.

(Illustrated)

SEAFOOD PIE WITH LEEKS AND BLUE CHEESE

PREPARATION TIME: 40 minutes
COOKING TIME: 45 minutes
PER SERVING: 670cals, 33g fat, 48g carbohydrate

SERVES 4

700g (1½lb) floury potatoes, peeled and cut into
    5mm (¼in) thick slices
450g (1lb) cod or haddock fillet
450ml (¾ pint) milk
75g (3oz) butter
350g (12oz) trimmed leeks, well washed and sliced
Freshly grated nutmeg
3 level tbsp plain flour
125g (4oz) blue Stilton cheese
4tbsp single cream
225g (8oz) large cooked, peeled prawns

1 Cook the potatoes in a pan of boiling salted water for 5 minutes or until partially softened, then drain them thoroughly.

2 Put the fish in a shallow pan. Pour over 50ml (2fl oz) of the milk and season lightly with salt and freshly ground black pepper. Cover and poach for 5 minutes until tender. Drain, reserving the liquor. Flake the fish, discarding the skin and bones.

3 Melt 25g (1oz) of the butter in a pan and fry the leeks for 3 minutes, adding plenty of grated nutmeg. Lightly butter a 1.7 litre (3 pint) pie dish and put on a baking sheet.

4 Melt the remaining butter in a small pan. Add the flour and cook, stirring, for 1 minute. Off the heat, gradually blend in the remaining milk and the reserved fish liquor.

5 Return the pan to the heat. Cook, stirring, until the sauce has thickened. Crumble in the Stilton, then add the cream and season to taste.

6 Preheat the oven to 190°C (170°C fan oven) mark 5. Put the fish, leeks and prawns in the dish. Spoon over half the sauce, add the potatoes and pour over the remaining sauce. Cook for 45 minutes. Serve at once.

TO PREPARE AHEAD Complete the recipe to the end of step 6 up to one hour ahead, but do not cook.
TO USE Complete the recipe.

PENNE, CHEESE AND HAM BAKE

PREPARATION TIME: 15 minutes
COOKING TIME: 45 minutes
PER SERVING FOR 4: 850cals, 48g fat,
77g carbohydrate
PER SERVING FOR 6: 570cals, 32g fat,
51g carbohydrate

SERVES 4–6

50g (2oz) butter, plus a little extra for the spinach
25g (1oz) plain flour
1 level tbsp English mustard powder
450ml (¾ pint) full-fat milk
125g (4oz) Cheddar cheese, grated
142ml carton double cream
125g (4oz) cooked sliced ham, roughly chopped
Pinch of nutmeg
350g (12oz) dried penne pasta
150g (5oz) baby spinach
25g (1oz) Parmesan cheese

1 Melt the butter in a pan, stir in the flour and cook for a couple of minutes on a medium heat.
2 Add the mustard powder and milk and stir until smooth. Whisk the sauce as it comes to the boil, then simmer gently for 10 minutes. Remove from the heat, then beat in the Cheddar cheese gradually until it melts. Add the cream and ham, then season with nutmeg, salt and freshly ground black pepper.
3 Cook the pasta in boiling salted water then drain thoroughly. Meanwhile, melt a knob of butter in a large pan, add the spinach and cook for 3 minutes until wilted.
4 Preheat the oven to 200°C (180°C fan oven) mark 6. Mix together the sauce, penne and spinach and pour into a shallow ovenproof dish. Grate the Parmesan over the top and cook for 20–30 minutes or until golden.

TO PREPARE AHEAD Complete the recipe up to one day ahead but don't cook it. Cool, wrap and chill.
TO USE Cook at at 200°C (180°C fan oven) mark 6 for 35–40 minutes or until golden.

(Illustrated)

MEATBALLS WITH OLIVE AND PESTO PASTA

PREPARATION TIME: 15 minutes
COOKING TIME: 30 minutes
PER SERVING: 710cals, 42g fat, 59g carbohydrate

SERVES 4

450g (1lb) premium-quality coarse pork sausages
2tbsp olive oil
350g (12oz) red onion, sliced
225g (8oz) dried pappardelle pasta
125g (4oz) black olives
2 level tbsp freshly chopped parsley or chives (or a mix of
  both)
2 level tbsp pesto sauce
Snipped and whole chives to garnish

1 Slit the sausages from top to bottom with a sharp knife then peel off the skin. Break each sausage in half and roll each piece into a ball then flatten slightly.
2 Heat the oil in a non-stick pan and fry the meatballs for about 10 minutes until cooked through. Lift out and put to one side on a plate. Add the onion to the pan and fry until soft and golden – about 10 minutes. Add the onion to the meatballs.
3 Cook the pasta in boiling salted water according to the packet instructions. Drain and return to the pan. Stir the olives, herbs and pesto into the pasta, heat for 1 minute then add the meatballs and onions and any juices that have collected on the plate. Season with freshly ground black pepper. To avoid breaking up the meatballs, shake the pan gently over the heat rather than stirring. Garnish with the chives and serve at once.

TO PREPARE AHEAD Complete the recipe to the end of step 2. Cool quickly, cover and chill overnight.
TO USE Complete the recipe.

PORK WITH PRUNES, APPLES AND SAGE

PREPARATION TIME: 30 minutes

COOKING TIME: 2 hours 35 minutes

PER SERVING: 400cals, 21g fat, 19g carbohydrate

SERVES 8

125g (4oz) no-soak, pitted prunes, roughly chopped

3 level tbsp freshly chopped sage

2 garlic cloves, crushed

75g (3oz) butter

1.6kg (3½lb) boned leg of pork

350g (12oz) apples, such as Cox's, peeled, cored and
  roughly chopped

1 tbsp lemon juice

3 tbsp oil

350g (12oz) shallots, blanched in boiling water, peeled
  and roughly chopped

600ml (1 pint) apple juice

300ml (½ pint) chicken stock

1 Mix the prunes with 2 level tbsp of the sage, the garlic and 50g (2oz) of the butter.

2 Remove the rind from the pork and put to one side. Open the pork out like a book, season with freshly ground black pepper and spread with the prune mixture. Reshape the pork and secure with string.

3 Toss the apples in the lemon juice. Heat 2 tbsp of the oil and the remaining butter in a 2.6 litre (4½ pint) flameproof and ovenproof casserole, brown the pork and put to one side. Add the shallots and cook, stirring, for 10 minutes or until soft and golden. Add the apples and cook for 5 minutes.

4 Preheat the oven to 180°C (160°C fan oven) mark 4. Return the pork to the casserole, add the apple juice and bring to the boil. Cover, put in the oven and cook for 1½–1¾ hours.

5 Meanwhile, brush the rind with the remaining oil and coat in salt. Cut into 1cm (½in) pieces with sharp scissors. Put on a baking sheet and cook on the top shelf of the oven for 40–50 minutes or until very crisp, then drain.

6 Remove the pork from the casserole (see Cook's Tip). Skim the juices of any fat, add the stock and the remaining sage, bring to the boil and bubble for 30 minutes or until syrupy. Season and serve with the sliced pork and crispy rind.

COOK'S TIP Leave the pork to rest, covered with foil, in a warm place for 20 minutes before carving.

BRAISED RED CABBAGE

PREPARATION TIME: 25 minutes

COOKING TIME: About 3 hours

PER SERVING: 190cals, 8g fat, 29g carbohydrate

SERVES 6

1.4kg (3lb) red cabbage, stalk and outer leaves
  discarded, leaves finely shredded

450g (1lb) red onions, finely sliced

50g (2oz) butter

5cm (2in) piece fresh root ginger, peeled and grated

7 level tbsp light muscovado sugar

7 tbsp red wine vinegar

1 Preheat the oven to 150°C (130°C fan oven) mark 2. Layer the cabbage and onions in a casserole, seasoning with salt and freshly ground black pepper as you go. Melt the butter in a small pan and fry the ginger for 2–3 minutes. Off the heat, stir in the sugar and vinegar and pour over the cabbage.

2 Cover tightly and cook for 3 hours, stirring occasionally. Adjust the seasoning and serve.

CELERIAC MASH

PREPARATION TIME: 10 minutes
COOKING TIME: 30–40 minutes
PER SERVING: 250cals, 13g fat, 29g carbohydrate

SERVES 12

1.8kg (4lb) celeriac, peeled and roughly chopped
1.8kg (4lb) potatoes, peeled and roughly chopped
284ml carton double cream
300ml (½ pint) milk

1 Put the celeriac and potatoes in a pan of salted water. Bring to the boil and cook for 20–30 minutes or until the vegetables are tender. Drain and mash either with a potato masher or by whizzing quickly in a food processor (don't overmix).
2 Heat the cream with the milk and beat into the mash over a low heat. Season well with salt and freshly ground black pepper.

TO PREPARE AHEAD Peel and chop the celeriac and potatoes, put in a bowl of cold water with a slice of lemon and chill overnight.
TO USE Complete the recipe.

CABBAGE WITH CARAWAY SEEDS

PREPARATION TIME: 5 minutes
COOKING TIME: 5 minutes
PER SERVING: 60cals, 5g fat, 2g carbohydrate

SERVES 8

450g (1lb) finely shredded cabbage
½ level tsp caraway seeds
50g (2oz) butter
Lemon juice

1 Cook the cabbage in boiling salted water until just tender.
2 Meanwhile, fry the caraway seeds in a dry pan until toasted. Off the heat add the butter and leave to melt in the heat of the pan.
3 Toss the butter through the drained cabbage and serve with a squeeze of lemon juice.

GLAZED TURNIPS

PREPARATION TIME: 10 minutes
COOKING TIME: 25 minutes
PER SERVING: 100cals, 6g fat, 12g carbohydrate

SERVES 6

40g (1½oz) butter
1kg (2¼lb) turnips, peeled and cut into wedges
2 level tbsp golden caster sugar
300ml (½ pint) fresh chicken stock

1 Put the butter, turnips, sugar and stock into a large pan. Season with salt and freshly ground black pepper. Bring the stock to the boil and simmer, covered, for 20 minutes or until the turnips are tender.
2 Remove the pan lid and cook for a further 5 minutes or until the liquid is reduced and turnips are glazed, then serve.

CHILLI RED ONIONS WITH GOAT'S CHEESE

PREPARATION TIME: 10 minutes
COOKING TIME: 40–45 minutes
PER SERVING: 230cals, 18g fat, 10g carbohydrate

SERVES 6

75g (3oz) unsalted butter, softened
2 medium red chillies, deseeded and finely diced
1 level tsp crushed chillies
6 small red onions, peeled
3 x 100g Somerset goat's cheese
Balsamic vinegar to serve

1 Preheat the oven to 200°C (180°C fan oven) mark 6. Put the butter in a small bowl, beat in the diced and the crushed chillies and season well with salt and freshly ground black pepper.

2 Cut the root off one of the onions, sit it on its base, then make several deep cuts in the top to create a star shape, slicing about two-thirds of the way down the onion. Do the same with the other five onions, then divide the chilli butter equally between them, pushing it down into the cuts. Put the onions in a small roasting tin, cover with foil and bake for 40–45 minutes or until soft.

3 About 5 minutes before the onions are ready, slice each goat's cheese into two, leaving the rind intact, then put on a baking sheet and bake for 2–3 minutes. Put the onion on top of the goat's cheese and serve drizzled with balsamic vinegar.

(Illustrated)

MUSTARD ROAST POTATOES AND PARSNIPS

PREPARATION TIME: 25 minutes
FREEZING TIME: Minimum 4 hours
COOKING TIME: 1 hour 20 minutes
PER SERVING: 220cals, 5g fat, 41g carbohydrate

SERVES 8

1.5kg (3lb) small even-sized potatoes
800g (1lb 12oz) small parsnips, peeled
50g (2oz) goose fat
1–2 level tbsp black mustard seeds
1 level tbsp sea salt

1 Cut out small wedges from one side of each of the potatoes and parsnips (this will help make them extra crispy). Put them into a pan of cold salted water, bring to the boil and cook for 6 minutes. Drain well.

2 Spread the vegetables out on a baking tray and leave to cool, then freeze on the tray. When the potatoes and parsnips are solid, put them into a plastic bag and store in the freezer for up to three months (see Cook's Tip).

3 The vegetables can be cooked from frozen. Preheat the oven to 200°C (180°C fan oven) mark 6. Heat the goose fat in a roasting tin for 4 minutes until sizzling hot. Add the potatoes, toss in the fat and roast for 30 minutes. Add the parsnips and sprinkle over the mustard seeds and sea salt. Roast for a further 45 minutes, turning halfway, or until the vegetables are golden.

COOK'S TIP The secret to these being the crispiest roasties imaginable is to parboil and freeze them ahead of time.

POMEGRANATE JELLIES

PREPARATION TIME: 25 minutes,

plus overnight setting

COOKING TIME: 5–10 minutes

PER SERVING: 180cals, 13g fat, 12g carbohydrate

SERVES 6

8 large ripe pomegranates, halved and peeled

25g (1oz) – around 8 sheets – fine leaf gelatine, broken
   into pieces

Juice of ½ lemon, strained

50g (2oz) golden caster sugar

1–2tbsp sirop de grenadine

200ml tub crème fraîche

1 Put the pomegranate pulp and seeds into a food processor and pulse to break the seeds and extract the juice. Transfer to a sieve resting over a large bowl and, using the base of a ladle, press the fruit pulp to strain all the juice through – you need 750ml (1¼ pints). Alternatively, cut the pomegranates in half and extract the juice using a citrus squeezer.

2 Meanwhile, put the gelatine into a bowl with 150ml (¼ pint) of the pomegranate juice. Leave to soak for 5 minutes.

3 Put the remaining fruit juice into a pan, add the lemon juice and sugar and heat gently, stirring until the sugar has completely dissolved.

4 Add the soaked gelatine and juice to the pan along with the sirop de grenadine and stir well until the gelatine has dissolved. (The liquid should be hot enough to melt the gelatine but it must not boil.)

5 Divide the liquid jelly among six 150ml (5fl oz) glasses and leave to cool. Cover and chill overnight.

6 To serve, spoon the crème fraîche into a piping bag fitted with a 1cm (½in) plain nozzle and pipe a little on the top of each jelly.

TO PREPARE AHEAD: Complete the recipe to the end of step 5 up to five days ahead. Chill.

ZUPPE INGLESE

PREPARATION TIME: 10 minutes

COOKING TIME: 10 minutes, plus 3 hours chilling

PER SERVING: 780cals, 38g fat, 96g carbohydrate

SERVES 6

175g (6oz) golden icing sugar

25g (1oz) plain flour

4 large egg yolks

1tbsp vanilla extract

750ml (1¼ pints) full-fat milk

142ml carton whipping cream

175g (6oz) plain chocolate, chopped

3 level tsp cocoa powder

350g (12oz) Madeira cake, thinly sliced lengthways

2tbsp each brandy and rum

Grated chocolate or chocolate curls to decorate

1 Sift the icing sugar and flour into a large bowl. Make a well in the centre, add the egg yolks and vanilla extract and stir until mixed.

2 Heat the milk and cream to scalding point. Add to the egg mixture, stirring all the time. Return to the pan and cook over a medium heat, stirring, for 5–6 minutes, until it forms a thin coating consistency. Remove half the custard and put to one side.

3 Add the chocolate to the remaining custard in the pan and stir in until melted. Spoon half the chocolate custard into the bottom of a glass serving dish. Dust with 1 level tsp of the cocoa powder and cover with a third of the Madeira slices. Drizzle with 4tsp of the mixed brandy and rum.

4 Spoon over half the reserved vanilla custard and dust with 1 level tsp of the cocoa powder. Cover the vanilla custard with half the remaining cake slices, and drizzle with more of the alcohol.

5 Spoon the remaining chocolate custard on top and dust with the remaining cocoa powder. Add a final layer of cake, drizzle with the remaining alcohol and spoon over the remaining vanilla custard.

6 Cover the bowl with clingfilm and chill for 3 hours or overnight. Decorate with grated chocolate or chocolate curls before serving.

CHARDONNAY PEARS

PREPARATION TIME: 20 minutes, plus cooling
COOKING TIME: 25 minutes
PER PEAR: 200cals, 0g fat, 41g carbohydrate

**MAKES 1 X 600ML (1 PINT) JAR AND
1 X 1 LITRE (1¾ PINTS) JAR**

8 medium, firm pears, peeled, halved and cored
Juice of 1 large lemon
150g (5oz) golden granulated sugar
450ml (¾ pint) white wine, such as Chardonnay
3 fresh bay leaves
1 cinnamon stick

1. Put the pears and lemon juice in a bowl and toss to coat. Put to one side.
2. Put the sugar in a large pan, add the white wine, bay leaves and cinnamon stick and 300ml (½ pint) of water. Heat gently to dissolve the sugar.
3. Add the pears and any juice to the pan, then bring to the boil, cover with greaseproof paper and a lid and simmer for 15–20 minutes, or until tender to the centre. The pears must be cooked through or they will discolour when stored.
4. Sterilize the jars, then put the pears into the jars. Measure the liquid – there should be around 600ml (1 pint). If necessary, bring it to the boil and simmer to reduce, then leave to cool slightly.
5. Pour the syrup over the pears, making sure they are completely covered, then seal, label and store in the fridge. Use within 2 weeks.

COOK'S TIP Serve with a vanilla custard for a warming dessert.

FRUIT IN SPICED RED WINE

PREPARATION TIME: 20 minutes
COOKING TIME: 15 minutes, plus cooling
PER SERVING: 650cals, 13g fat, 102g carbohydrate

SERVES 6

1 level tbsp black peppercorns, crushed
1 level tsp each juniper berries and coriander seeds, crushed
1 cinnamon stick, broken
2 bay leaves, plus extra to decorate
75cl bottle red wine
125g (4oz) golden granulated sugar
¼ level tsp grated nutmeg
Zest and juice of 1 lemon
Zest and juice of 1 large orange
250g (9oz) each ready-to-eat dried figs, peaches and prunes
175g (6oz) pack Medjool dates, stoned
2 level tsp arrowroot
1 orange, peeled and sliced into rounds
100ml (3½fl oz) Grand Marnier
200ml tub crème fraîche

1. Put the peppercorns, juniper berries, coriander, cinnamon stick and two bay leaves on to a piece of muslin and tie into a bag.
2. Put the wine, sugar, spice bag, nutmeg, citrus zests and juices into a large pan and heat until simmering. Add the figs and cook for 5 minutes, then add the peaches and cook for a further 5 minutes. Add the prunes and dates. Remove the spice bag.
3. Mix the arrowroot with 2tbsp water to make a paste, then add it to the wine, stirring, and bring to the boil. Remove from the heat, add the slices of orange and pour into a shallow dish to cool.
4. Spoon into individual dishes and decorate with bay leaves. Gently heat the Grand Marnier in a small pan or ladle (do not boil), then ignite using a long-handled match (it will flare up) and pour, flaming, over the fruit. Serve with the crème fraîche.

SWEET PUMPKIN CAKE WITH TOFFEE SAUCE

PREPARATION TIME: 30 minutes
COOKING TIME: 1 hour 30 minutes, plus cooling
PER SERVING: 440cals, 26g fat, 49g carbohydrate

SERVES 16

FOR THE CAKE

550g (1¼ lb) pumpkin or butternut squash, cut
  into wedges
Butter to grease
250ml (9fl oz) sunflower oil
275g (10oz) light muscovado sugar
3 large eggs
225g (8oz) self-raising flour plus extra to dust
1 level tsp bicarbonate of soda
2 level tsp ground ginger
1 level tsp each ground cinnamon and nutmeg
A pinch each ground cloves and ground allspice
Ice cream to serve (optional)

FOR THE TOFFEE SAUCE

300g (11oz) light muscovado sugar
284ml carton double cream
50g (2oz) unsalted butter

1 Preheat the oven to 200°C (180°C fan oven) mark 6. Put the pumpkin on a baking sheet and roast for 40 minutes until tender.
2 Grease a 23cm (9in) Kugelhopf tin generously with butter and dust with flour.
3 Remove the pumpkin from the oven and allow to cool for 15 minutes. Reduce the oven temperature to 180°C (160°C fan oven) mark 4. Spoon out 250g (9oz) of the pumpkin flesh, put in a mini processor and whiz to a purée.
4 Put the oil and sugar in a freestanding mixer and whisk for 2 minutes, then whisk in the eggs, one at a time.
5 Add the flour, bicarbonate of soda, ginger, cinnamon, nutmeg, cloves and allspice and fold in. Add the purée and stir in gently.
6 Pour into the prepared tin. Bake for 40–45 minutes until the cake is risen, springy and shrinking from the edges. Leave to cool in the tin for 10 minutes, then use a palette knife to ease the cake away from the edges. Turn out and cool on a wire rack.
7 For the toffee sauce, put the sugar, cream and butter in a small heavy-based pan. Heat gently to dissolve the sugar, then simmer and stir for 3 minutes to thicken slightly. Pour into a jug.
8 Drizzle the toffee sauce over the cake and serve with ice cream if you like.

CRANBERRY AND RED ONION MARMALADE

PREPARATION TIME: 30 minutes
COOKING TIME: 1 hour 5 minutes
PER SERVING: 160cals, 3g fat, 29g carbohydrate

SERVES 8

2 tbsp olive oil
500g (1lb 2oz) red onions, sliced
Juice of 1 orange
1 level tbsp pickling spice
150g (5oz) dark muscovado sugar
150ml (¼ pint) ruby port
450g (1lb) cranberries

1 Heat the oil in a medium-sized pan and fry the onions gently for 5 minutes.
2 Add the orange juice, pickling spice, sugar and port. Simmer gently for 40 minutes.
3 Add the cranberries and cook for 20 minutes. Cool and chill until needed.

(Illustrated on page 258)

THE ULTIMATE CHRISTMAS PUDDING

PREPARATION TIME: 45 minutes,
plus 30 minutes standing
COOKING TIME: Up to 6 hours
PER SERVING: 410cals, 18g fat, 58g carbohydrate

**MAKES TWO 1 LITRE (1¾ PINT) PUDDINGS,
EACH SERVING 8, OR ONE 2 LITRE (3½ PINT)
PUDDING, SERVING 16**

500g bag luxury mixed dried fruit
125g (4oz) each dried, ready-to-eat figs, dates
   and pears, chopped
75g packet dried cranberries or dried sour cherries
1 sharp eating apple, cored and coarsely grated
227g can pineapple, drained and chopped
50g (2oz) whole blanched almonds, chopped
4tbsp maple syrup
4tbsp each brandy and sherry
125g (4oz) self-raising flour
½ level tsp salt
1 level tsp each ground nutmeg, ground ginger, ground
   cinnamon and mixed spice
50g (2oz) ground almonds
225g (8oz) shredded beef or vegetable suet
175g (6oz) fresh white breadcrumbs
125g (4oz) molasses sugar
4 large eggs, beaten
150ml (¼ pint) brown ale

1 Put all the dried, fresh and canned fruit and the chopped almonds into a large mixing bowl, then add the maple syrup, brandy and sherry and leave to stand for 30 minutes.

2 Sift the flour, salt and spices into a bowl, stir together and add the ground almonds, suet, breadcrumbs and sugar. In a separate bowl, beat the eggs and brown ale together.

3 Add the egg mixture to the soaking fruit with the dry ingredients and stir to combine thoroughly. Line the pudding moulds or basins with a single layer of muslin.

4 Divide the mixture between the moulds, shape into a round, tie the muslin and secure the lid. Or spoon into basins, tie up muslin and cover with a double layer of pleated foil secured with string.

5 Put in a large pan or steamer half-filled with hot water. Cover and steam for 3–4 hours for smaller puddings or 5–6 hours for a large pudding, keeping the water level topped up throughout with boiling water.

TO STORE When cool, overwrap the muslin pudding in foil. Keep in a cool, dark place for up to six months.
TO REHEAT A small pudding will need to be steamed for 1 hour, a large pudding will take around 2 hours.

THE BOOZIEST CHRISTMAS CAKE

PREPARATION TIME: 45 minutes, plus minimum 48 hours soaking

COOKING TIME: See below

PER 60G (2½OZ) SERVING: 230cals, 10g fat, 30g carbohydrate

TO FEED This cake is very boozy so it needs feeding only once. While the cake is still warm, make a couple of small holes on the surface with a skewer and spoon over 1tbsp brandy, allowing it to soak right through.

TO STORE When the cake has cooled, wrap it in greaseproof paper, then in foil, making sure the cake is completely covered. Store in an airtight tin in a cool, dark place for up to one month. The longer you keep the cake, the more boozy, moist and dense it will become.

1 Put the dried fruit, stem ginger, prunes, lemon zest and juice into a bowl and pour the brandy and ginger wine over. Cover and leave to soak for a minimum of 48 hours.

2 Grease and line the base and sides of the tin using a double thickness of baking parchment. Wrap a double thickness of brown paper around the outside and secure with kitchen string.

3 Beat the butter and sugar with a wooden spoon or the K beater of a food mixer until light and fluffy. Add the eggs a little at a time and beat until smooth (add some flour to stop it curdling).

4 Preheat the oven to 170°C (150°C fan oven) mark 3. Sift the flour and spices on to the cake mixture and, using a large metal spoon, carefully fold together with the ground almonds.

5 Put half the soaked fruit in a food processor and whiz until it forms a purée. Fold into the cake mixture with the remaining whole fruit until evenly combined.

6 Spoon the mixture into the prepared tin and smooth the surface with a large palette knife. Bake on the centre shelf of the oven for the required cooking time (see chart).

COOK'S TIP To test if the cake is cooked: ovens vary, so insert a skewer into the centre of the cake – it should come out clean. If not, continue to cook for 15 minutes, then check again and repeat as necessary. Cover the top of the cake with foil if it's browning too quickly.

(Illustrated)

	25.5cm (10in) round / 23cm (9in) square **48 SLICES**	20.5cm (8in) round / 18cm (7in) square **24 SLICES**	15cm (6in) round/ 12.5cm (5in) square **16 SLICES**
Mixed dried fruit	650g (1lb 6oz)	375g (13oz)	250g (9oz)
Stem ginger, chopped	50g (2oz)	25g (1oz)	15g (½oz)
Ready-to-eat prunes, chopped	200g (7oz)	125g (4oz)	100g (3½oz)
Grated zest and juice of lemon	1 large	Half	1tsp zest and 1tbsp juice
Brandy	250ml (9fl oz)	150ml (¼ pint)	100ml (3½fl oz)
Ginger wine	50ml (2fl oz)	2tbsp	1tbsp
Butter, softened	375g (13oz)	225g (8oz)	150g (5oz)
Dark muscovado sugar	375g (13oz)	225g (8oz)	150g (5oz)
Medium eggs, beaten	5	3	2
Self-raising flour	375g (13oz)	225g (8oz)	150g (5oz)
Mixed spice	1 level tbsp /1½ level tsp	1 level tsp	½ level tsp
Ground cinnamon	2 level tsp	1 level tsp	½ level tsp
Ground ginger	2 level tsp	1 level tsp	½ level tsp
Ground almonds	100g (3½oz)	50g (2oz)	50g (2oz)
COOKING TIME:	3–3¾ hours; cover after 1½ hours	2–2¾ hours; cover after 1 hour	2 hours

CRANBERRY AND APPLE CHUTNEY

PREPARATION TIME: 30 minutes

COOKING TIME: 1 hour 45 minutes

PER 1 LEVEL TBSP: 25cals, trace fat,
7g carbohydrate

MAKES AROUND 5 x 300G (11OZ) JARS

1 cinnamon stick

1 level tsp allspice berries, crushed

1 level tsp cumin seeds

1kg (2¼lb) cranberries

1kg (2¼lb) Granny Smith apples, peeled, cored
    and diced

450g (1lb) onions, chopped

500g pack light muscovado sugar

284ml bottle distilled malt vinegar

1 Put the cinnamon, allspice and cumin in a piece of muslin, tie with string and put in a preserving pan.

2 Add the cranberries, apples, onions, sugar and vinegar and bring to the boil. Reduce the heat and simmer very slowly, uncovered, stirring occasionally, for around 1 hour 30 minutes or until the mixture is thick and pulpy. There should be hardly any liquid left when you draw a wooden spoon through the bottom of the pan. Remove the bag of spices.

3 Sterilise the jars (see page 54), then spoon in the cooked chutney. Cover, label and store for up to three months.

(Illustrated)

PICKLED ONIONS

PREPARATION TIME: 25 minutes,
plus minimum 2 days marinating

COOKING TIME: 10 minutes,
plus 2 hours marinating

PER 25G (1OZ): 5cals, 0g fat, 1g carbohydrate

MAKES 1.8KG (4LB)

1.8kg (4lb) pickling onions

450g (1lb) salt

FOR THE SPICED VINEGAR

1.1 litres (2 pints) vinegar

2–3 mace blades

1 tbsp allspice berries

1 tbsp cloves

Cinnamon sticks

6 black peppercorns

1 bay leaf

1 First make the spiced vinegar. Put the vinegar, spices and bay leaf in a pan, bring to the boil, then allow to cool. Cover and leave to marinate for about 2 hours. Strain the vinegar through a muslin-lined sieve into a jug. Pour into bottles and seal with airtight and vinegar-proof tops.

2 Put the onions in a large bowl. Dissolve half the salt in 2.3 litres (4 pints) of water. Pour over the onions and leave for 12 hours.

3 Drain the onions, peel away the skins, then put in a clean bowl. Dissolve the remaining salt in 2.3 litres (4 pints) of water. Pour this fresh brine over the peeled onions and leave for a further 24–36 hours.

4 Drain the onions and rinse well, then pack into sterilised jars (see page 54). Pour the spiced vinegar over the onions to cover completely. Cover in the usual way and seal with vinegar-proof tops.

DECEMBER

An exciting month, as we anticipate Christmas, when the shops are crammed with exotic luxuries and we look forward to celebrating with family and friends

EVEN BEFORE DECEMBER ARRIVES, the Christmas countdown has already begun. And as the month gets rolling, all thoughts tend in the direction of the big event. By now you should have ordered your bird if you buy from a specialist, farm-based mail-order firm, and you're certain to be thinking about plans for the holiday. But that doesn't mean you can — or should — ignore the rest of the month. There are twenty-four days before the big one, and a good supply of nice things to cook on every one of them. Apples and pears continue to dominate the domestically produced fruit, and they should still be in tiptop condition after just a short period in controlled-atmosphere storage. Bake, poach, use in tarts — do anything to make the most of these seasonal treats. They won't be around much longer. Not that it matters too much, because there are plenty of imports coming in — better citrus as the days go by, Sharon fruit from Israel, good grapes, lychees, pineapples — to help us through our own dry fruit season. Use the newly arriving oranges to make delicious puddings like the Port and Orange Jellies on page 309, and citrus to make Iced Orange and Lemon Terrine with Burnt-Sugar Sauce (page 313).

Game

Experimentation with citrus is also a good way to add variety to the continuing game season. Duck with orange is a classic combination, but other fruits work well too — and not just with duck but with the other birds. The Duck with Caramelised Kumquats and Pink Grapefruit is an usual combination with a tangy sauce (page 296). Grouse ends on the 10th of the month, but the oth-

Left: Thai Beef Daube (see page 300)

INGREDIENTS
OF THE MONTH

GAME

Grouse

Hare

Partridge

Pheasant

Wild duck

Wild goose

Woodcock

FISH

Bass

Cod

Dab

Dover sole

Haddock

Hake

Halibut

Herring

Oysters

Plaice

Salmon

Scallops

Skate

Sole

Turbot

VEGETABLES

Artichokes

Beetroot

Brussels sprouts

Cabbage

Carrots

Cauliflower

Kale

Parsnips

Potatoes

Spinach

Spring greens

Turnips

FRUIT

Apples

Chestnuts

Pears

BEST BUY

Brussels sprouts

ers go into the new year. And pheasant may be at its best now, as well as being (in all likelihood) reasonable in price due to plentiful supplies. If you want to make a game pâté for the holiday season, snap up any cheap birds you may find: some are sold at bargain prices if they're heavily damaged by shot. Cut off the breasts and any usable leg meat and freeze them, or just make the pâté in advance and freeze the finished dish. If you're really energetic, two other Christmas items that freeze really well are stuffing (without the eggs) and cranberry sauces like the one on page 303. December is one of the best months for fresh cranberries, which have the edge over frozen where taste is concerned.

Vegetables

Greenery is not at its absolute best in December if you're looking for salads or summery crunch, but it still holds some pleasant surprises – especially if you're willing to think about humble items that can be turned to extraordinary effect with a little imagination. One of the most underrated veg around is curly kale, a member of the cabbage family that differs from other cabbages in not forming an inward-curved, compact head. These frilly leaves are delicious if given any normal cabbage treatment, and better still if you blanch them, slice roughly, and then cook for a few minutes in extra-virgin olive oil and garlic. But all cabbages are good this month, especially the Brussels sprouts (see box opposite), which will form the vegetal accompaniment to so many Christmas dinners. For an unusual way of serving Brussels try them with pancetta and pecan nuts (see page 304). Root veg are the other December high point, with beetroot, Jerusalem artichokes, parsnips and potatoes forming the basis for a hundred soups during the cold winter. They're much better than the foreign imports which will command increasingly high prices in the run-up to Christmas.

Fish

Christmas make us all think of turkey, but it shouldn't blind us to the virtues of all the good fish coming in from the boats around Britain's shores. This is still the heart of the shellfish season, and you could do a lot worse during the festive season than order a big box of oysters for eating on New Year's Eve or for a luxurious lunch in the laid-back days between Christmas and New Year. Scallops are equally good, and so are flat fish: if you're not married to turkey, why not have a turbot for the big meal? December is a month to think about surprises, and the local markets should have a few ideas to help you out.

BRUSSELS SPROUTS

Until you eat a really good Brussels sprout and remember why they became so popular in the first place, it's easy to be dismissive of them. But the difficulty of buying a good one is the reason many home cooks turn to expensive imports of fancier veg. A good sprout is usually on the small side, and has tightly packed leaves without any hint of brown, yellow or spotted colour. Look at the cut stem-end: if there is significant greyness in it, the sprout was harvested too long ago and should be discarded. And give it a good squeeze: it should feel as hard as a little cannonball. Sprouts in prime condition can be prepared just by trimming off 1–2mm of the stem end – no need to cut a cross in the base, which just lets more of the cooking water into the leaves. And if you want a break from plain boiled sprouts, cut them in half and stir-fry them, or leave them whole and braise them, after quick blanching, in stock and butter.

HOT SPICED NUTS

PREPARATION TIME: 5 minutes

COOKING TIME: 10 minutes

PER SERVING FOR 6: 210cals, 20g fat,
2g carbohydrate

PER SERVING FOR 8: 160cals, 15g fat,
2g carbohydrate

SERVES 6–8

2tbsp sunflower oil

1 level tsp sea salt flakes plus extra to sprinkle

2 level tsp all-purpose seasoning

200g pack shelled natural mixed nuts

Red chilli slices, fried in sunflower oil, to garnish

1 Preheat the oven to 190°C (170°C fan oven) mark 5. Pour the oil into a roasting tin, stir in the salt and all-purpose seasoning, then heat in the oven for 2 minutes. Add the nuts to the tin, shaking it to coat the nuts in the seasoned oil. Cook for 7–10 minutes, shaking the nuts once, until golden.

2 Using a slotted spoon, transfer the nuts to kitchen paper to drain. Sprinkle with salt and serve warm, garnished with chilli slices, or store in an airtight container for up to two days. Reheat in a low oven for 5 minutes.

EASY PEA SOUP

PREPARATION TIME: 2 minutes, plus defrosting

COOKING TIME: 15 minutes

PER SERVING: 260cals, 10g fat, 35g carbohydrate

SERVES 4

1 small loaf of French stick, thinly sliced

2 tbsp basil oil plus extra to drizzle

454g bag frozen peas, defrosted

600ml (1 pint) vegetable stock

1 Preheat the oven to 220°C (200°C fan oven) mark 7. Put the bread on a baking sheet, drizzle with the 2tbsp basil oil and bake for 10–15 minutes until golden.

2 Meanwhile, put the peas in a food processor, add the vegetable stock and season with salt and freshly ground black pepper. Whiz for 2–3 minutes.

3 Pour the soup into a pan, bring to the boil and simmer for 10 minutes. Spoon into warmed bowls, add the croutons, drizzle with oil and sprinkle with salt and freshly ground black pepper.

ROQUEFORT, LEEK AND WALNUT TARTS

PREPARATION TIME: 25 minutes
COOKING TIME: 30–35 minutes
PER SERVING: 490cals, 39g fat, 24g carbohydrate

SERVES 6

375g packet fresh ready-rolled puff pastry
2 medium eggs
40g (1½oz) butter
400g (14oz) trimmed leeks, thinly sliced
2 level tbsp freshly chopped chives
100g (3½oz) Roquefort cheese, sliced into six triangles
75g (3oz) walnuts, chopped

1 Preheat the oven to 200°C (180°C fan oven) mark 6.

2 Unroll the pastry and, leaving it on its plastic wrap, cut in half lengthways, then cut each half into three squares. Using the tip of a sharp knife, score a smaller square 1cm (½in) in from the edge of each to make a frame.

3 Put the squares on a greased baking tray. Beat one egg lightly and brush over each pastry case. Bake for 10 minutes or until well risen and lightly golden. Carefully lift off the top layers of each inner square and discard, then use a fork to scoop out any uncooked pastry from each centre.

4 In the meantime, melt the butter in a frying pan, add the leeks and cook for about 10 minutes or until they're soft. Beat the remaining egg and add it to the leeks with the chives. Season with salt and freshly ground black pepper. Fill the pastry cases generously with the mixture.

5 Put the slice of cheese on to each tart and top with the walnuts. Return the tarts to the oven and bake for 10–15 minutes or until golden and heated through.

COOK'S TIP Chill the pastry cases for 10 minutes before baking as this will ensure a good, even rise.

(Illustrated)

LIME AND GIN MARINATED SALMON

PREPARATION TIME: 30 minutes,
plus overnight marinating
COOKING TIME: 12 minutes,
plus 45 minutes cooling
PER CANAPÉ: 50cals, 2g fat, 4g carbohydrate

MAKES 15

2tbsp gin

Grated zest of 1 lime

1 level tbsp sea salt flakes

1 level tbsp pink peppercorns, lightly crushed

150g (5oz) raw salmon fillet, skin and bones removed

150g (5oz) Japanese rice for sushi, washed and drained

2tbsp rice vinegar

1 level tbsp golden caster sugar

15 slices pickled ginger

1 level tbsp wasabi paste

Snipped fresh chives to garnish

1 In a bowl, mix together the gin, lime zest, sea salt flakes and peppercorns. Put the salmon in the marinade, cover and chill overnight.
2 Pour 350ml (12fl oz) of water into a large pan and add the rice. Bring to the boil, then cover and simmer for 10–12 minutes. Remove from the heat and stir in the rice vinegar and the sugar. Leave until cool, then cover.
3 Using a sharp carving knife, cut the salmon into 30 very thin slices (there's no need to remove the seasonings).
4 Wet your hands and mould the rice into 15 walnut-sized balls and flatten to form discs. Top each disc with two slices of marinated salmon, a slice of pickled ginger and a little wasabi paste. Garnish with chives.

COOK'S TIP Use Japanese sushi rice for this recipe – when cooked, its high starch content gives just the right amount of stickiness.

(Illustrated)

CHEVRE EN CROUTE

PREPARATION TIME: 5 minutes
COOKING TIME: 12 minutes
PER SERVING: 110cals, 7g fat, 8g carbohydrate

SERVES 6

½ short baguette

1–2tbsp hazelnut oil

1 small garlic clove, crushed

125g (4oz) chèvre log – around 2.5cm (1in) in diameter – cut into six slices

Paprika

6 thyme sprigs

Mixed-leaf salad to serve

1 Preheat the oven to 180°C (160°C fan oven) mark 4. Cut six 1cm (½in) thick slices from the baguette. Mix the hazelnut oil with the garlic and brush both sides of the baguette slices. Put on a baking sheet and bake for about 5 minutes.
2 Put a slice of chèvre on each baguette slice and top with a sprinkling of paprika and a sprig of thyme.
3 Return the croûtes to the oven for a further 7 minutes, or until the cheese is soft and spongy. Serve warm with a mixed-leaf salad.

WILD MUSHROOM AND
POTATO PUFFS WITH PORT SAUCE

PREPARATION TIME: 1 hour,
plus 30 minutes –1 hour cooling and chilling
COOKING TIME: 1 hour
PER SERVING WITHOUT SAUCE: 700cals, 48g fat,
58g carbohydrate

SERVES 8 (SEE COOK'S TIPS)

300ml (½ pint) milk

200ml (7fl oz) double cream

2 garlic cloves, crushed

450g (1lb) floury potatoes, thinly sliced

Grated nutmeg

50g (2oz) butter

450g (1lb) wild mushrooms, rinsed, dried and roughly
    sliced

2 level tsp freshly chopped thyme

1 large egg

Flour to dust

2 x 500g packs puff pastry

Fresh thyme sprigs to garnish

Port Sauce (see below) to serve

PORT SAUCE

PREPARATION TIME: 2 minutes
COOKING TIME: 20 minutes
PER SERVING: 70cals, 4g fat, 4g carbohydrate

40g (1½oz) butter

4 shallots, blanched in boiling water, peeled and
    finely chopped

150ml (¼ pint) port or Madeira

600ml (1 pint) vegetable stock

1 Put the milk and cream in a large heavy-based pan with the garlic. Bring to the boil, then add the potatoes, bring back to the boil and simmer gently, stirring occasionally, for 15–20 minutes or until the potatoes are tender. Season well with salt, freshly ground black pepper and grated nutmeg. Cool.

2 Melt the butter in a large frying pan. As soon as it's sizzling, add the mushrooms and cook over a high heat, stirring all the time, for 5–10 minutes or until the mushrooms are cooked and the mushroom juices have completely evaporated. Season and stir in the thyme, then put to one side to cool.

3 Lightly beat the egg with a large pinch of salt. Roll out the pastry very thinly on a lightly floured surface. Cut into eight rounds, approximately 12.5cm (5in) in diameter for the tops, and eight rounds approximately 11.5cm (4½in) in diameter for the bases (see Cook's Tips). Put the smaller pastry rounds on baking sheets and brush the edges with beaten egg. Put a large spoonful of the cooled potato mixture in the centre of each round leaving a 1cm (½in) margin. Top with a spoonful of the mushroom mixture then cover with the remaining pastry rounds. Press the edges together well to seal. Chill for 30 minutes–1 hour.

4 Preheat the oven to 220°C (200°C fan oven) mark 7. Put two baking trays in the oven to heat up. Pinch the edges of the pastry into scallops and brush the top with the remaining beaten egg. If you like, use the back of a knife to decorate the tops of the puffs.

5 Put the puffs, on their baking sheets, on the preheated baking trays (see Cook's Tips). Cook for 15–20 minutes or until deep golden brown, swapping the trays around in the oven halfway through cooking. Garnish with fresh thyme sprigs and serve immediately with the Port Sauce.

COOK'S TIPS This dish could also be served as a main-course vegetarian alternative to a traditional Christmas meal. To adapt, cut the pastry into six 13.5cm (5½in) rounds for the bases and six 15cm (6in) rounds for the tops. Cook for 20–30 minutes.
● Preheating the baking trays helps to make the bases of the puffs crisper.

1 To make the sauce, put the butter in a frying pan, add the shallots and cook for 2–3 minutes.

2 Pour in the port or Madeira and reduce by half. Add the stock, bring to the boil and bubble for 10–15 minutes or until syrupy; season with salt and freshly ground black pepper. Serve with the Wild Mushroom and Potato Puffs, above.

(Illustrated)

GINGER AND HONEY-GLAZED HAM

PREPARATION TIME: 1 hour

COOKING TIME: 5 hours 45 minutes,
plus 30 minutes cooling

PER SERVING WITH GLAZE FOR 8 : 400cals,
8g fat, 39g carbohydrate

PER SERVING WITH GLAZE FOR 10: 300cals,
6g fat, 30g carbohydrate

SERVES 8–10

4.5kg–6.8kg (10–15lb) unsmoked gammon on the bone
(see Cook's Tips)

2 shallots, peeled and halved

6 cloves

3 bay leaves

2 celery sticks, cut into 5cm (2in) pieces

2 level tbsp English mustard

5cm (2in) cube fresh root ginger, peeled and thinly sliced

FOR THE GLAZE

225g (8oz) dark muscovado sugar

2tbsp runny honey

8tbsp brandy or Madeira

FOR THE CHUTNEY

4 mangoes, peeled, sliced and chopped into 5cm (2in)
chunks

1 level tsp mixed spice

4 cardamom pods, seeds removed and crushed

2 cinnamon sticks, roughly chopped

4 level tbsp raisins

1 Put the gammon in a pan with the shallots, cloves, bay leaves, celery and enough cold water to cover. Bring to the boil, cover and simmer gently for about 5 hours. Remove any scum with a slotted spoon. Lift the ham out of the pan, discard the vegetables and herbs and cool.

2 Using a sharp knife, carefully cut away the ham's thick skin to leave an even layer of fat. Score a diamond pattern in the fat. Put the ham into a roasting tin, smother evenly with the mustard and tuck the ginger into the scored fat.

3 To make the glaze, put the sugar, honey and brandy or Madeira in a pan and heat until the sugar has dissolved. Brush over the ham.

4 Preheat the oven to 200°C (180°C fan oven) mark 6. In a bowl, mix together the chutney ingredients, add any remaining glaze, then spoon around the ham.

5 Cook the ham for 30–40 minutes, basting every 10 minutes. Remove the ham from the roasting tin and put to one side. Stir the chutney and put under a grill for 5 minutes to allow the mango to caramelise. Serve with the ham.

COOK'S TIPS Cook this the day before Christmas Eve. It will keep in the fridge for up to five days.

● When buying gammon, allow about 225g (8oz), bone in, per person.

● If using smoked gammon, soak in cold water overnight. 'Green' or unsmoked gammon may be less salty if soaked in cold water.

● Tie boned gammon with string before simmering; remove the string before glazing.

● Once the gammon is cooked, it then becomes ham.

LAMB TAGINE WITH DATES

PREPARATION TIME: 5 minutes,
plus overnight chilling
COOKING TIME: 1 hour 45 minutes
PER SERVING FOR 12: 290cals, 16g fat,
8g carbohydrate
PER SERVING FOR 14: 240cals, 14g fat,
7g carbohydrate

SERVES 12–14

1.4kg (3lb) boneless lamb, leg or shoulder, cut into large
    cubes
2 level tsp each ground ginger and coriander
½ level tsp saffron strands
5tbsp olive oil
1 garlic clove, crushed
275g (10oz) baby onions or shallots, blanched in boiling
    water and peeled
1 level tbsp flour
1 level tbsp tomato purée
2 level tbsp each freshly chopped coriander and parsley
450ml (¾ pint) chicken stock
150ml (¼ pint) sherry
1 cinnamon stick
1 bay leaf
75g (3oz) stoned dates
1 level tbsp honey
Coriander to garnish
Nutty Couscous to serve (see page 307)

1 Put the lamb in a bowl with the ginger, ground coriander, saffron and 1tbsp of the oil. Season with salt and freshly ground black pepper, cover and chill overnight.

2 Heat 1tbsp of the oil in a heavy-based casserole and brown the lamb in batches, using more oil when necessary. Put the browned lamb to one side. Add the garlic to the casserole and stir over a medium heat for 1 minute.

3 Preheat the oven to 190°C (170°C fan oven) mark 5. Return the lamb to the casserole with the onions, flour, tomato purée, fresh coriander, parsley, stock, sherry, cinnamon stick and bay leaf. Season and bring to the boil. Cover, put in the oven and cook for 1 hour 15 minutes, stirring occasionally.

4 Discard the cinnamon stick and bay leaf. Add the dates and honey and put back in the oven for 15–20 minutes. Garnish with the coriander and serve with the Nutty Couscous.

DUCK WITH CARAMELISED KUMQUATS AND PINK GRAPEFRUIT

PREPARATION TIME: 30 minutes,
plus 10 minutes standing
COOKING TIME: 1 hour 15 minutes
PER SERVING: 790cals, 62g fat, 23g carbohydrate

SERVES 6

4tbsp vegetable oil
225g (8oz) onions, finely chopped
2tbsp golden syrup
100ml (3½fl oz) white wine vinegar
450ml (¾ pint) orange juice
3 garlic cloves, crushed
3 level tsp coriander seeds, crushed
1.3 litres (2¼ pints) chicken stock
175g (6oz) kumquats, thickly sliced
2 level tbsp golden caster sugar
6 duck breasts – around 1.4kg (3lb) total weight (see
   Cook's Tip)
1 large pink grapefruit, peeled, pith removed and divided
   into segments

1 Heat 3tbsp of the oil in a large frying pan, add the onions and cook over a medium heat, stirring, for 10 minutes or until soft. Add the golden syrup and cook, stirring, until the onion begins to caramelise. Remove the pan from the heat and stir in the vinegar and orange juice. Return the pan to the heat, bring to the boil and bubble for 5 minutes. Add the garlic, coriander seeds and stock. Bring to the boil and bubble uncovered for 30 minutes. Strain through a fine sieve and put back in the pan. You should have about 450ml (¾ pint) sauce. (The sauce can be frozen or kept in the fridge for up to one day.)

2 Heat the remaining oil in a small frying pan, add the kumquats and sprinkle with the sugar and fry over a high heat until golden on each side.

3 Preheat the oven to 220°C (200°C fan oven) mark 7. Score the skin of the duck finely with a sharp knife. Heat a heavy-based non-stick frying pan until very hot. Add the duck breasts, skin-side down, and cook for 5 minutes or until well browned. Turn the breasts and cook briefly for 1 minute on the flesh side. Put in a roasting tin, skin-side up, season with salt and freshly ground black pepper and cook in the oven for about 15–20 minutes. Cover and put to one side in a warm place to rest for 10 minutes.

4 To serve, slice the duck and arrange slices on individual plates or on a large serving plate. Top with the kumquats and grapefruit segments and spoon over the warm sauce.

COOK'S TIP Look out for English Gressingham duck breasts sold at independent butchers – they're meaty with a thin layer of fat. If you buy the larger French duck breasts you'll probably only need three for this recipe.

(Illustrated)

SPICED ROAST TURKEY

PREPARATION TIME: 30 minutes

COOKING TIME: 3 hours

PER SERVING WITH STUFFING FOR 8: 710cals,
39g fat, 16g carbohydrate

PER SERVING WITH STUFFING FOR 10: 590cals,
32g fat, 13g carbohydrate

SERVES 8–10

4.5kg (10lb) oven-ready turkey with giblets

Pork, Spinach and Apple Stuffing (see page 302),
    cooked and cooled

2 level tsp Cajun spice

150g (5oz) salted butter, softened

1 Loosen the skin at the neck end of the turkey, ease your fingers up between the skin and the breast and, using a small sharp knife, remove the wishbone. Remove the giblets and put to one side to make the stock (see below).

2 Season the inside of the turkey, then spoon the cold stuffing into the neck end only. Neaten, tuck the skin under and secure with skewers or cocktail sticks. Weigh to calculate the cooking time – allow 18 minutes per 450g (1lb).

3 Preheat the oven to 190°C (170°C fan oven) mark 5. Put the turkey in a roasting tin, mix the spice with the butter, smear over the turkey and season with salt and freshly ground black pepper. Cover with a tent of foil. Roast for about 3 hours, basting from time to time. If the legs have been tied together, loosen after the first hour so they cook through more evenly. Remove the foil 45 minutes before the end of the cooking time.

4 When the turkey is cooked (the juices should run clear when a skewer is inserted into the thigh), tip the turkey so the juices run into the tin, then put the turkey on a serving dish, cover and leave to rest while you make the gravy (see below).

TURKEY STOCK

PREPARATION TIME: 5 minutes

COOKING TIME: 40 minutes

PER SERVING: see gravy below

Turkey giblets

1 carrot, peeled and thickly sliced

1 onion, cut into wedges

1 stick celery, thickly sliced

8 black peppercorns

2 bay leaves

1 Put all the ingredients into a large pan with 600ml (1 pint) of cold water. Cover and bring to the boil.

2 Simmer for 30 minutes, skimming the surface from time to time, then strain the stock and chill until needed.

TURKEY GRAVY

PREPARATION TIME: 5 minutes

COOKING TIME: 20 minutes

PER SERVING FOR 8: 70cals, 2g fat,
5g carbohydrate

PER SERVING FOR 10: 60cals, 1g fat,
3g carbohydrate

SERVES 8–10

Juices from the roast turkey

4 level tbsp plain flour

300ml (½ pint) red wine or port

1.1 litres (2 pints) turkey or chicken stock (see above)

1 Strain the juices from the roasting tin into a bowl and skim off any fat, reserving 3tbsp. Return the reserved fat to the tin and whisk in the flour to make a smooth paste. Cook over a moderate heat, whisking until the flour turns a russet brown.

2 Off the heat, add the wine or port, stir until smooth, bring to the boil and bubble for 2–3 minutes. Stir in the turkey juices and the stock, then bubble for 10–15 minutes or until reduced by half (skim off any fat). Season, strain and serve.

(*Illustrated*)

TARRAGON TURKEY AND BEAN SALAD

PREPARATION TIME: 35 minutes

PER SERVING FOR 8: 1,000cals, 90g fat, 12g carbohydrate

PER SERVING FOR 10: 800cals, 72g fat, 10g carbohydrate

SERVES 8–10

4 level tbsp each fresh tarragon and flat-leafed parsley, roughly chopped

2tbsp olive oil

125ml (4fl oz) crème fraîche

600ml (1 pint) mayonnaise

Juice of 2 lemons

900g (2lb) leftover turkey, cut into bite-sized pieces (see Cook's Tip)

3 x 300g cans cannellini beans, drained and rinsed

Half quantity shallot dressing (see page 196)

175g (6oz) sunblush or 125g (4oz) sun-dried tomatoes, roughly chopped

Finely sliced spring onion ends to garnish

1 Put the herbs in a food processor and add the oil. Whiz until the herbs are chopped. Add the crème fraîche, mayonnaise and lemon juice to the processor and season with salt and freshly ground black pepper, then whiz until well combined. If you don't have a processor, chop the herbs by hand, mix with the oil, then beat in the crème fraîche, mayonnaise, lemon juice and seasoning.

2 Toss the turkey with the dressing in a large bowl and put to one side.

3 Tip the cannellini beans into a bowl, toss with the shallot dressing and season well. Arrange the cannellini beans on a serving dish. Top with the dressed turkey and tomatoes and garnish with spring onion.

COOK'S TIP If you don't have enough leftover turkey, make up the difference by cooking a few boneless chicken breasts on a baking sheet, drizzled with olive oil and seasoned with a squeeze of lemon juice, salt and freshly ground black pepper. Cook at 200°C (180°C fan oven) mark 6 for 20–30 minutes or until cooked through. Cool and cut into bite-sized pieces.

THAI BEEF DAUBE

PREPARATION TIME: 25 minutes

COOKING TIME: 2 hours 30 minutes

PER SERVING: 520cals, 33g fat, 16g carbohydrate

SERVES 6

5tbsp sunflower oil

1.1kg (2½lb) stewing beef, such as chuck steak, cut into 3cm (1¼in) cubes

550g (1¼lb) large onions, chopped

50g (2oz) piece fresh root ginger, grated

1 large red chilli, deseeded and finely chopped

2 level tsp garam masala

4 garlic cloves, crushed

400ml can coconut milk

8 lime leaves

4 lemongrass stalks, lightly crushed

25g (1oz) butter

350g (12oz) shiitake mushrooms, sliced

Lime leaves and fried chilli slices to garnish

1 Heat 3tbsp of the oil in a large flameproof casserole, brown the beef in batches over a high heat, then put to one side. Pour the remaining oil into the casserole, add the onions and cook, stirring, for 10 minutes. Add the ginger, chilli, garam masala and garlic and cook for 5 minutes.

2 Preheat the oven to 170°C (150°C fan oven) mark 3. Return the beef to the casserole with the coconut milk, 150ml (¼ pint) of water, the lime leaves and lemongrass. Bring to the boil, season with salt and freshly ground black pepper, cover and simmer for 5 minutes, then cook for 1½–2 hours or until the beef is tender. The sauce will reduce to a rich gravy, but if it becomes too intense just add a little boiling water.

3 Once the beef is cooked, heat the butter in a large frying pan, add the mushrooms and cook, stirring, for 5 minutes or until all the juices have evaporated. Season and stir into the beef.

4 Garnish with the lime leaves and chilli and serve with rice.

(Illustrated on page 284)

SMOKED FISH GRATIN

PREPARATION TIME: 10 minutes

COOKING TIME: 1 hour 20 minutes

PER SERVING FOR 6: 750cals, 42g fat,
33g carbohydrate

PER SERVING FOR 8: 560cals, 32g fat,
25g carbohydrate

SERVES 6–8

900g (2lb) smoked haddock fillet

750ml (1¼ pints) milk

125g (4oz) butter

900g (2lb) trimmed leeks, well washed and sliced

142ml carton double cream

225g (8oz) cooked, peeled prawns

125g (4oz) small dried pasta shapes, such as penne or
  farfalle

2tsp oil

50g (2oz) plain flour

125g (4oz) Cheddar cheese, grated

1 level tbsp Dijon mustard

2 level tbsp freshly chopped parsley

2 large egg whites

Fresh flat-leafed parsley sprigs and king prawns to garnish

Mixed salad to serve

1 Put the fish in a roasting tin or large frying pan. Pour over about 600ml (1 pint) of the milk. Slowly bring to the boil, cover and simmer gently for 10–12 minutes or until tender. Remove the fish from the milk and cool slightly. Strain the milk into a jug and put to one side. Flake the fish into a bowl, discarding the skin and bones.

2 Melt half the butter in a pan. Add the leeks and cook for 10 minutes or until very soft, but not brown. Season with salt and freshly ground black pepper. Stir in the cream and add to the haddock with the prawns.

3 Cook the pasta in boiling salted water for about 8 minutes or until just tender. Drain, then stir in the oil.

4 Rinse out the pasta pan then melt the remaining butter. Off the heat, stir in the flour and gradually add the reserved milk and the remaining milk. Bring to the boil, stirring. Boil for 2 minutes then, off the heat, stir in 50g (2oz) of the cheese, the mustard and parsley.

5 Preheat the oven to 200°C (180°C fan oven) mark 6. Mix the pasta with the leek and fish mixture and put in one 3.4 litre (6 pint) or two 2 litre (3½ pint) ovenproof dishes. Whisk the egg whites in a clean grease-free bowl until stiff peaks form. Gently fold into the cheese sauce, then pour over the leek and pasta mixture. Sprinkle with the remaining cheese then cook for about 40–45 minutes or until golden brown. Garnish with flat-leafed parsley and prawns and serve with salad.

SAUSAGES WRAPPED IN BACON

PREPARATION TIME: 5 minutes

COOKING TIME: 1 hour

PER SERVING: 380cals, 32g fat, 5g carbohydrate

SERVES 8

12–16 thin streaky bacon rashers

6–8 good-quality sausages, twisted in the middle and cut
  in half

1 Preheat the oven to 200°C (180°C fan oven) mark 6. Stretch the bacon rashers by running the blunt side of a kitchen knife along each one (this stops them shrinking too much when they're cooked).

2 Roll a stretched rasher around each 'mini' sausage. Put in a small roasting tin or around the turkey and cook for about 1 hour.

PORK, SPINACH AND APPLE STUFFING

PREPARATION TIME: 45 minutes,

plus 1 hour cooling

COOKING TIME: 1 hour 30 minutes

PER SERVING FOR 8: 310cals, 24g fat,

16g carbohydrate

PER SERVING FOR 10: 250cals, 19g fat,

13g carbohydrate

SERVES 8–10

2tbsp oil

150g (5oz) onion, finely chopped

225g (8oz) fresh spinach, well washed, torn into pieces if
    the leaves are large

2 sharp apples, such as Granny Smith, peeled, cored and
    cut into chunks

450g (1lb) sausagemeat

Coarsely grated zest of 1 lemon

1 level tbsp chopped thyme

100g (3½oz) fresh breadcrumbs

2 large eggs, beaten

1 Heat the oil in a frying pan, add the onion and cook for 10 minutes or until soft. Increase the heat, add the spinach and cook until wilted.

2 Add the apples and cook for 2–3 minutes, stirring, then cool. When cold, mix with the sausagemeat, lemon zest, thyme, breadcrumbs and beaten eggs, then season with salt and freshly ground black pepper. The stuffing can be frozen at this stage or made up to two days in advance and kept in the fridge.

3 Cook the stuffing in the neck of a turkey. Alternatively cook in a buttered 900g (2lb) loaf tin, covered with foil, at 180°C (160°C fan oven) mark 4 for 1½ hours or until cooked to the centre.

TRADITIONAL BREAD SAUCE

PREPARATION TIME: 10 minutes,

plus 30 minutes infusing

COOKING TIME: 10 minutes

PER SERVING FOR 8: 190cals, 13g fat,

15g carbohydrate

PER SERVING FOR 10: 150cals, 10g fat,

12g carbohydrate

SERVES 8–10

1 small onion, halved and studded with six cloves

900ml (1½ pints) full-fat milk

2 bay leaves

10 black peppercorns

2 fresh thyme sprigs

150g (5oz) fresh breadcrumbs

25g (1oz) butter

6tbsp double cream

Freshly grated nutmeg

1 Put the onion in a pan with the milk, bay leaves, peppercorns and thyme. Bring to the boil, remove from the heat and leave to infuse for at least 30 minutes.

2 Strain the milk into a clean pan, bring to the boil and stir in the breadcrumbs. Bring back to the boil, stirring, turn down the heat and simmer for 5 minutes or until the sauce has thickened. Stir in the butter and cream. Add a little nutmeg to taste and season well.

CRANBERRY AND ORANGE SAUCE

PREPARATION TIME: 2 minutes

COOKING TIME: 5 minutes

PER SERVING FOR 8: 80cals, 0g fat,
21g carbohydrate

PER SERVING FOR 10: 60cals, 0g fat,
17g carbohydrate

SERVES 8–10

450g (1lb) cranberries

125g (4oz) golden caster sugar

2 oranges, peeled, cut into segments and
   roughly chopped

1 Put the cranberries and sugar in a pan and cook for 5 minutes
or until the fruit begins to soften. Add the orange segments,
then pour into a bowl.

2 Cool, cover and chill until needed. Serve with roast turkey.

ROAST PARSNIPS WITH HONEY GLAZE

PREPARATION TIME: 10 minutes

COOKING TIME: 1 hour

PER SERVING FOR 8: 150cals, 3g fat,
32g carbohydrate

PER SERVING FOR 10: 120cals, 2g fat,
25g carbohydrate

SERVES 8–10

2tbsp oil

700g (1½lb) each parsnips and sweet potatoes, peeled
   and cut into large chunks

4tbsp runny honey

1 Preheat the oven to 200°C (180°C fan oven) mark 6. Heat the oil in a
roasting tin on the hob. Add the parsnips and sweet potatoes and shake
the tin to coat them with oil then season with salt and freshly ground
black pepper. Roast in the oven for 45 minutes, turning the parsnips
from time to time.

2 Mix in the honey and put back in the oven for a further 10–15 minutes
or until the vegetables are glazed, sticky and a deep golden brown.
Season and turn out into a serving dish. (Don't leave the vegetables in the
tin as they may stick to the bottom.)

BRUSSELS SPROUTS WITH PANCETTA

PREPARATION TIME: 5 minutes

COOKING TIME: 10 minutes

PER SERVING FOR 8: 170cals, 13g fat, 6g carbohydrate

PER SERVING FOR 10: 140cals, 10g fat, 5g carbohydrate

SERVES 8–10

100g (3½oz) pancetta or prosciutto

1.1kg (2½lb) Brussels sprouts, trimmed

75g (3oz) pecans, roughly chopped

25g (1oz) butter

1 Grill the pancetta until golden and crisp. Drain on kitchen paper and allow to cool. Meanwhile, cook the sprouts in a large pan of boiling salted water for 7–10 minutes or until tender.

2 Drain the sprouts and put back in the pan with the pecans and butter and season with salt and freshly ground black pepper, then turn into a serving dish. Break up the pancetta and sprinkle over the top.

(*Illustrated*)

PAN-FRIED SAVOY CABBAGE

PREPARATION TIME: 5 minutes

COOKING TIME: 5 minutes

PER SERVING FOR 4: 110cals, 7g fat, 10g carbohydrate

SERVES 4

25g (1oz) butter or 2tbsp groundnut oil

½ Savoy cabbage, shredded

1 level tbsp cumin seeds

Juice of ½ lemon

1 Put the butter or oil in a wok or large frying pan and heat for 1 minute. Add the cabbage and cook, tossing from time to time, for 5 minutes.

2 Add the cumin seeds and lemon juice and season well with salt and freshly ground black pepper. Toss again and continue to cook for 1–2 minutes to heat through.

ROAST POTATOES WITH ROSEMARY AND GARLIC

PREPARATION TIME: 10 minutes

COOKING TIME: 1 hour 10 minutes

PER SERVING FOR 8: 260cals, 13g fat,
34g carbohydrate

PER SERVING FOR 10: 210cals, 10g fat,
28g carbohydrate

SERVES 8–10

1.8kg (4lb) potatoes, peeled and cut into large chunks

3tbsp vegetable oil

75g (3oz) unsalted butter

6 fresh rosemary sprigs

6 garlic cloves, unpeeled

1 Put the potatoes in a pan of cold salted water, bring to the boil and cook for 5–10 minutes or until the potatoes begin to soften. Drain and put back in the pan over a low heat and shake the pan until the potatoes are dry and a little fluffy. Put to one side.

2 Preheat the oven to 200°C (180°C fan oven) mark 6. Heat the vegetable oil and butter in a roasting tin. Put the warm potatoes in the tin with the rosemary and garlic and toss to cover them evenly in the oil and butter mixture. Season well with salt and freshly ground black pepper. Cook for 1 hour or until the potatoes are brown and crisp, turning the potatoes over from time to time to ensure they're cooked evenly.

(Illustrated)

FANTAIL POTATOES

PREPARATION TIME: 15 minutes

COOKING TIME: 1 hour

PER SERVING FOR 8: 260cals, 13g fat, 34g carbohydrate

PER SERVING FOR 10: 210cals, 10g fat, 28g carbohydrate

SERVES 8–10

1.8kg (4lb) large potatoes, such as King Edwards, scrubbed

6tbsp olive oil

2 level tsp sea salt flakes

1 Preheat the oven to 220°C (200°C fan oven) mark 7. Halve any very large potatoes lengthways. Using a sharp knife, slice down each potato widthways, three-quarters of the way through, at 5mm (¼in) intervals. If you push a skewer through the base of the potato along its length it will stop you cutting all the way through.

2 Put on a baking tray, drizzle with the oil and season with the salt and freshly ground black pepper.

3 Cook for 1 hour, basting every 10 minutes until the potatoes are crisp and cooked all the way through.

NUTTY COUSCOUS

PREPARATION TIME: 10 minutes

COOKING TIME: 10 minutes

PER SERVING FOR 12: 230cals, 7g fat, 33g carbohydrate

PER SERVING FOR 14: 200cals, 6g fat, 28g carbohydrate

SERVES 12–14

450g (1lb) couscous

450ml (¾ pint) chicken stock

25g (1oz) butter

400g can chickpeas, drained and rinsed

50g (2oz) ready-to-eat apricots, chopped

125g (4oz) mixed nuts

1 Put the couscous in a bowl with 200ml (7fl oz) of the stock. Leave for 5 minutes. Break up any lumps with a fork.

2 Add the remaining stock, the butter, chickpeas, apricots and nuts and season with salt and freshly ground black pepper. Put in a steamer, or metal colander lined with a J-cloth, over a pan of water. Cover and steam for 10 minutes. Serve at once.

COOK'S TIP This goes well with the Lamb Tagine with Dates on page 295.

VANILLA AND ORANGE CUSTARD

PREPARATION TIME: 30 minutes,
plus 30 minutes infusing
COOKING TIME: 5 minutes
PER SERVING FOR 8: 170cals, 11g fat,
12g carbohydrate
PER SERVING FOR 10: 140cals, 9g fat,
10g carbohydrate

SERVES 8–10

900ml (1½ pints) full-fat milk
Zest of 1 large orange
1 vanilla pod, split lengthways
9 large egg yolks
3 level tbsp golden caster sugar
2 level tsp arrowroot

1 Put the milk in a pan with the orange zest and vanilla pod, bring slowly to the boil and put to one side for at least 30 minutes. Beat together the egg yolks, sugar and arrowroot until well combined.

2 Strain the milk on to the egg yolk mixture and combine. In a heavy-based pan, cook the mixture over a low heat, stirring until thickened. Don't boil or it will curdle. Immediately pour the custard into a bowl, cool, cover and chill. It will keep for up to two days. Serve with Christmas Pudding.

RUM BUTTER

PREPARATION TIME: 5 minutes, plus 2 hours chilling
PER SERVING FOR 8: 200cals, 13g fat,
16g carbohydrate
PER SERVING FOR 10: 160cals, 10g fat,
13g carbohydrate

SERVES 8–10

125g (4oz) unsalted butter, softened
125g (4oz) light muscovado sugar
5tbsp dark rum (see Cook's Tip)

1 Put the butter in a bowl and beat until it becomes soft and creamy. Gradually beat in the sugar, a little at a time. The mixture should become light and fluffy in texture. Beat in the rum, 1 tablespoon at a time.

2 Spoon the butter into a bowl and chill for at least 2 hours or put the butter in a freezerproof container and freeze for up to one month. To thaw, remove from the freezer 2–3 hours before serving.

COOK'S TIP Instead of dark rum, you could use brandy or Grand Marnier.

CHOCOLATE MOUSSE

PREPARATION TIME: 20 minutes,
plus minimum 4 hours chilling
PER SERVING FOR 6: 440cals, 24g fat,
38g carbohydrate
PER SERVING FOR 8: 330cals, 18g fat,
28g carbohydrate

SERVES 6–8

350g (12oz) plain chocolate, broken into pieces
6 tbsp rum, brandy or cold black coffee
6 large eggs, separated

1 Put the chocolate, rum, brandy or black coffee in a bowl over a pan of barely simmering water. Leave to melt, stirring occasionally. Remove from the heat and cool slightly for 3–4 minutes, stirring frequently.

2 Beat the egg yolks with 2 tbsp of water, then beat into the chocolate mixture until evenly blended.

3 Whisk the egg whites with the salt in a clean grease-free bowl until stiff peaks form, then fold into the chocolate mixture.

4 Pour the mixture into a 1.4–1.7 litre (2½–3 pint) soufflé dish or divide between six to eight 150 ml (¼ pint) ramekins. Chill for at least 4 hours, or overnight, until set.

PORT AND ORANGE JELLIES

PREPARATION TIME: 25 minutes,
plus 4 hours chilling and setting
COOKING TIME: 15 minutes
PER SERVING: 200cals, 0g fat, 34g carbohydrate

SERVES 8

450ml (¾ pint) ruby port
6 level tsp powdered gelatine
125g (4oz) golden granulated sugar
8 oranges, segmented
Double cream to serve

1 Splash cold water into eight 150ml (¼ pint) fluted moulds and chill.
2 Pour the port into a bowl and sprinkle over the gelatine. Put to one side.
3 Put the sugar in a large pan with 600ml (1 pint) of cold water. Heat gently to dissolve, then bring to the boil and bubble until the liquid has reduced by half (about 15 minutes).
4 Stir in the soaked gelatine until completely dissolved.
5 Put the orange segments in the flutes of the moulds so they stand up and rest against the edge of the mould. Pour in enough liquid to come halfway up the sides. Chill to set, then pour in the rest of the liquid and chill again.
6 To serve, dip each mould briefly in a bowl of hot water to loosen. Upturn on to a plate and pour the cream over.

(Illustrated)

CREOLE CHRISTMAS CAKE

PREPARATION TIME: 45 minutes,
plus 24 hours soaking
COOKING TIME: 3 hours, plus cooling
PER SERVING: 440cals, 12g fat, 78g carbohydrate

SERVES 16–20

175g (6oz) each prunes, roughly chopped, raisins and
   currants
125g (4oz) natural glacé cherries, halved
100g (3½oz) candied peel, chopped
250ml (9fl oz) dark rum
175g (6oz) unsalted butter, softened, plus extra to grease
175g (6oz) dark molasses sugar, sieved
4 medium eggs, beaten
200g (7oz) self-raising flour
3 level tbsp molasses
1 tbsp vanilla extract
40g (1½oz) stem ginger pieces, chopped

FOR THE TOPPING

450g (1lb) golden icing sugar, sifted
3 level tbsp glucose syrup
50g (2oz) unsalted butter, softened
3 tbsp dark rum
25g (1oz) dried cranberries to decorate

1 Put the prunes, raisins, currants, cherries and peel in a lidded container
   and add the rum. Cover and leave to stand for at least 24 hours or up to
   two weeks, stirring occasionally, until most of the rum is absorbed.
2 Grease and line an 18cm (7in) round deep cake tin with greaseproof
   paper. Using a slotted spoon, drain and weigh out 450g (1lb) of the
   soaked fruit. Transfer to a food processor and whiz to a thick purée.
   Preheat the oven to 150°C (130°C fan oven) mark 2.
3 Beat together the butter and sugar until creamy. Beat in the eggs, a little at a
   time, adding some of the flour if the mixture starts to curdle. Add the remaining fruit and any rum juices to the bowl along with the dried fruit purée,
   molasses, vanilla extract, stem ginger and remaining flour. Using a large
   metal spoon, gently fold the ingredients together until evenly combined.
4 Turn into the prepared tin and bake for 3 hours or until firm and a skewer
   inserted into the centre comes out clean. Leave to cool in the tin, then wrap
   in foil and store for up to two weeks or until ready to decorate.
5 To decorate the cake, put the icing sugar in a bowl and add the glucose,
   butter and rum. Beat with an electric whisk until the mixture is smooth,
   creamy and softly peaking.
6 Put the cake on a flat serving plate and swirl the icing over the top and
   sides using a palette knife. Scatter over the cranberries.

TO PREPARE AHEAD Soak the fruit as in step 1 up to two weeks ahead.
Make the cake to the end of step 4 up to one month ahead. Wrap in foil
and store in an airtight container. Decorate the cake, then store in an
airtight container in the fridge and eat within a week, or freeze.
TO FREEZE Open-freeze the iced cake until solid, then wrap in clingfilm, label
and store for up to three months. Thaw at cool room temperature overnight.

(Illustrated)

FRESH ORANGE CURD

PREPARATION TIME: 20 minutes
COOKING TIME: 20 minutes
PER 25G (1OZ) SERVING: 110cals, 6g fat,
13g carbohydrate

MAKES AROUND 2 X 250G (9OZ) JARS

Grated zest and juice of 2 large oranges
Juice of ½ lemon
225g (8oz) golden caster sugar
125g (4oz) unsalted butter
3 egg yolks, beaten

1 Put all the ingredients into a double boiler or a large heatproof bowl set
   over a pan of simmering water. Stir the mixture until the sugar has
   dissolved. Continue to heat gently, stirring frequently, for 20 minutes or
   until the curd is thick enough to coat the back of a spoon – don't allow it
   to boil or it will curdle.
2 Strain the curd through a fine sieve, then spoon into sterilised jars (see
   page 54), add lids and leave to cool. Store in the fridge and use within
   one week.

MINCEMEAT AND RICOTTA TART

PREPARATION TIME: 45 minutes,
plus 1 hour chilling and 30 minutes cooling
COOKING TIME: 1 hour 15 minutes
PER SERVING: 600cals, 29g fat, 81g carbohydrate

SERVES 8

FOR THE PASTRY

175g (6oz) plain flour plus extra to dust
125g (4oz) butter, cut into cubes
25g (1oz) ground almonds
25g (1oz) golden caster sugar
1 large egg yolk

FOR THE FILLING AND TOPPING

250g tub ricotta cheese
25g (1oz) golden icing sugar
2 large egg yolks
3tbsp double cream
700g (1½lb) good-quality mincemeat
Grated zest of 1 lemon
1tbsp brandy or lemon juice
25g (1oz) natural glacé cherries, sliced
2 level tbsp flaked almonds
Icing sugar to dust

1 To make the pastry, whiz the flour and butter in a food processor until the mixture resembles fine crumbs. Add the ground almonds, caster sugar and egg yolk with 1tbsp of cold water. Pulse until the mixture just comes together, turn out on to a floured surface, knead lightly, wrap and chill for at least 30 minutes.

2 Roll out the pastry on a lightly floured surface to a rectangle measuring 15x38cm (6x15in). Line a 10x33cm (4x13in) loose-based tin with the pastry, prick the bottom with a fork and chill for 30 minutes.

3 Preheat the oven to 190°C (170°C fan oven) mark 5. Line the pastry case with greaseproof paper and fill with baking beans. Bake for 15 minutes, remove the paper and beans and cook for a further 10–15 minutes or until the pastry is just cooked in the centre. Cool for 15 minutes and reduce the oven to 180°C (160°C fan oven) mark 4.

4 Beat the ricotta with the icing sugar, egg yolks and cream until combined. Spread over the base of the pastry and cook for 20–25 minutes or until lightly set.

5 Mix the mincemeat with the lemon zest and brandy or lemon juice and spoon over the tart. Scatter the cherries and almonds on top and cook for 20 minutes. Allow to cool a little then dust with icing sugar to serve.

COOK'S TIP As this freezes brilliantly, you can make it well in advance. Thaw overnight, then warm through in a moderate oven just before serving.

MULLED WINE

PREPARATION TIME: 10 minutes,
plus 10 minutes standing
COOKING TIME: 5 minutes
PER SERVING: 180cals, 0g fat, 22g carbohydrate

SERVES 8

125g (4oz) golden caster sugar
1 cinnamon stick
6 crushed juniper berries
Pinch of freshly grated nutmeg
1 orange, studded with cloves, then cut into thin slices
1 lemon, thinly sliced
150ml (¼ pint) orange liqueur, such as Cointreau
75cl bottle red wine

1 Put the sugar in a pan with 450ml (¾ pint) of water. Add the cinnamon stick, juniper berries, nutmeg, one orange slice and the lemon slices. Heat gently to dissolve the sugar. Bring to the boil, then turn off the heat and leave for 10 minutes to allow everything to infuse.

2 Add the liqueur and wine and heat through gently, then pour into a jug. Add the remaining orange slices and serve.

HOT GINGER CUP

PREPARATION TIME: 5 minutes

PER SERVING: 110cals, 0g fat, 7g carbohydrate

MAKES 1.8 LITRES (3¼ PINTS); SERVES 10

300ml (½ pint) Morgan's Spiced Rum

600ml (1 pint) ginger beer

600ml (1 pint) cider

300ml (½ pint) fizzy water

2 small apples, sliced into rounds

Pour the liquid ingredients into a pan and warm gently for 1–2 minutes until heated through. Add the apple and serve.

COOK'S TIP This is also good served cold – chill it by adding ice just before serving.

ICED ORANGE AND LEMON TERRINE WITH BURNT-SUGAR SAUCE

PREPARATION TIME: 10 minutes

CHILLING/FREEZING TIME: 3 hours

COOKING TIME: 8 minutes

PER SERVING: 400cals, 28g fat, 36g carbohydrate

SERVES 6

4 large egg yolks

175g (6oz) golden caster sugar

300ml (½ pint) whipping cream

Finely grated zest and juice of 1 orange

Finely grated zest of 1 lemon

Juice of ½ lemon

142ml carton single cream

Mandarin or orange segments to decorate

1 Using an electric whisk, whisk together the egg yolks and 2 level tbsp of the sugar for 5 minutes or until pale and thick.

2 Lightly whip the cream until it just holds its shape. Fold it into the egg mixture, along with the orange juice and orange and lemon zests. The mixture will become quite liquid.

3 Line a 1.1 litre (2 pint) terrine or loaf tin with clingfilm. Pour in the mixture and freeze for 3 hours or overnight.

4 To make the Burnt-Sugar Sauce, put 125g (4oz) of the caster sugar plus 125ml (4fl oz) of water and the lemon juice in a heavy-based pan. Put over a medium heat for about 3 minutes, until the sugar has dissolved. Do not stir. Increase the heat and cook for about 5 minutes, until the sugar is a light caramel colour. Add a pinch of salt and, off the heat, stir in the cream. Chill the sauce for 3 hours or overnight.

5 Briefly dip the terrine tin into hot water, then invert the terrine on to a serving plate. Remove the clingfilm and slice with a hot knife. Soften at room temperature for about 10 minutes then serve with Burnt-Sugar Sauce and decorate with a few mandarin or orange segments.

TO FREEZE Complete the Iced Orange and Lemon Terrine, pack and freeze. Make and freeze the Burnt-sugar Sauce. Store for up to one month.

TO USE Thaw the Burnt-sugar Sauce overnight in the fridge. Serve with the Terrine as in step 5.

CRANBERRY AND APPLE MINCE PIES

PREPARATION TIME FOR MINCEMEAT: 20 minutes
plus 24 hours soaking
PREPARATION TIME FOR PIES: 45 minutes,
plus 1 hour 10 minutes chilling and 15 minutes cooling
COOKING TIME: 12–15 minutes
PER PIE: 160cals, 8g fat, 22g carbohydrate

**MAKES 2.5KG (5½LB) MINCEMEAT;
400G (14OZ) FILLS 12 PIES; MAKES 48 PIES**

FOR THE MINCEMEAT

450g (1lb) Bramley apples, cored and chopped
225g (8oz) fresh cranberries
125g (4oz) candied peel, finely chopped
350g (12oz) each raisins, sultanas and currants
175g (6oz) each light and dark muscovado sugar
1 level tbsp ground mixed spice
Pinch of ground nutmeg
Grated zest and juice of 2 medium oranges
150ml (¼ pint) Calvados

FOR THE ALMOND PASTRY

225g (8oz) plain flour, sifted, plus extra to dust
Large pinch of salt
50g (2oz) ground almonds
75g (3oz) golden icing sugar
175g (6oz) unsalted butter, chilled and diced
2 medium egg yolks

FOR THE SHORTBREAD TOPPING

75g (3oz) unsalted butter, softened
27g (1oz) golden caster sugar, plus extra to sprinkle
75g (3oz) plain flour
50g (2oz) ground almonds

1 For the mincemeat, combine all the ingredients together in a large bowl. Put into five warm sterilised jars, seal and label. Leave for at least 24 hours.

2 For the pastry, put the flour, salt, ground almonds and icing sugar in a food processor and pulse for 30 seconds. Add the butter and whiz until the mixture resembles fine crumbs. Add the egg yolks and process until the mixture just comes together (if a little dry, add 1–2tsp of cold water. Knead lightly on a floured surface to bring together, then wrap and chill for 1 hour.

3 For the topping, beat the butter and sugar until light and fluffy, then mix in the flour and almonds. Bring together with your hands, then wrap and chill for 15 minutes. Line 48 patty tins with paper cases.

4 On a floured surface, roll out the pastry to a thickness of 2mm (¹⁄₁₆in) and, using a 7.5cm (3in) fluted pastry cutter, cut out rounds. Put in the paper cases, prick the bases with a fork and chill for 10 minutes. Fill each one with 1tbsp of mincemeat.

5 Preheat the oven to 190°C (170°C fan oven) mark 5. Roll the pastry trimmings to 2mm (¹⁄₁₆in) thick. Using a 4x2.5cm (1½x1in) holly cutter, cut two leaves for each pie. With the back of a knife, mark the leaves with veins and put on top of each pie, then decorate each with two cranberries picked out of the remaining mincemeat. Sprinkle with sugar and bake for 12–15 minutes or until golden. Cool for 15 minutes, then put on a wire rack to cool completely.

TO PREPARE AHEAD Complete the recipe up to 2 days ahead. Store in an airtight container. Warm the pies through at 190°C (170°C fan oven) mark 5 for 5 minutes.
TO FREEZE Complete the recipe, but don't bake. Freeze pies in their trays.
TO SERVE Cook from frozen at 190°C (170°C fan oven) mark 5 for 18–20 minutes

(Illustrated)

INDEX

ACKNOWLEDGEMENTS

Photo credits:

Marie Louise Avery
27, 32, 39, 41, 51, 53, 76, 65, 96, 112, 221, 229, 247, 263, 267, 283, 315, 204

Steve Baxter
22, 49, 114, 127, 128, 186, 191, 237, 309

Martin Brigdale
104, 109, 117, 141, 161

Linda Burgess
151

Jean Cazals
29, 208, 266, 275, 293

Laurie Evans
21, 91, 125, 171, 201, 269

Christine Hanscombe
203, 249

Food Features
p 60

Graham Kirk
47, 56, 101, 111, 115, 167, 298, 305, 306, 177

William Lingwood
123, 188, 255

David Mumms
70, 73, 133, 152, 199, 223

James Murphy
2, 5, 45, 119, 143, 145, 177, 182, 291

Sean Myers
212

Mike O'Toole
135

George Seper
85

Roger Stowell
242, 253, 281

Clive Streeter
17, 93

Martin Thompson
5, 95, 231, 232, 258, 289, 311

Philip Webb
5, 8, 13, 37, 168, 217

Tim D Winter
284, 297

Elizabeth Zeschin
15, 67, 80, 89, 103, 137, 156, 207, 215, 239, 271

Thanks to Richard Ehrlich for the chapter introductions.